People's Liberation Army Navy

COMBAT SYSTEMS TECHNOLOGY, 1949–2010

People's Liberation Army Navy

COMBAT SYSTEMS TECHNOLOGY,
1949–2010

James C. Bussert and Bruce A. Elleman

Naval Institute Press
Annapolis, Maryland

Naval Institute Press
291 Wood Road
Annapolis, MD 21402

Library of Congress Cataloging-in-Publication Data

Bussert, James C.
  People's Liberation Army Navy (PLAN) : combat systems technology,
1949–2010 / James C. Bussert and Bruce A. Elleman.
      p. cm.
  Includes bibliographical references and index.
  ISBN 978-1-59114-080-1 (hardcover : alk. paper) 1. China. Zhongguo
ren min jie fang jun. Hai jun—Weapons systems. 2. Warships—China. I.
Elleman, Bruce A., date II. Title.
  VA633.B87 2011
  359.80951—dc22
                                    2010052837

Printed in the United States of America.

19 18 17 16 15 14 13 12 11   9 8 7 6 5 4 3 2 1
First printing

Contents

Illustrations and Tables

Foreword

The United States and China are arguably the world's most important countries. Their hot-and-cold bilateral relations exhibit signs of both a strategic partnership based on common interests and a stressful association stemming from enduring differences in policies and practices. These differences have the potential to disrupt the relationship and even threaten international stability. Unsurprisingly, there are many troubling questions about China and its relations with the United States and the world. Among these is the matter of whether China and its navy are a potent adversary or potential partner of the United States, its allies and friends, and others. If seen as a threat, how should that be managed; how can that situation be altered? If viewed as a partner, how can engagement best be undertaken? As these questions suggest, I want in this foreword to put in perspective the evolution of China's navy and the implications of this phenomenon, the development of which is uniquely presented in this remarkable volume.

However, first, a few words are warranted about the evolution of Jim Bussert and Bruce Elleman's impressive book. I have, over more than two years, seen the manuscript transformed from a rudimentary draft into a volume that will serve and please many categories of readers with diverse interests. *People's Liberation Army Navy (PLAN): Combat Systems Technology, 1949–2010* is, among other things, a primer for those in the United States, East Asia, or elsewhere who want, or need, to be prepared to confront, fight, deter, engage, or cooperate with China's navy. The authors have produced an informative examination of equipment characteristics, acquisition processes, technology, and political-military, strategic, and tactical factors related to China's maritime military capacity and associated with other countries' military relations, technology transfers, and maritime cooperation with China. The book is invaluable as well for those who simply want to be informed about the second most important navy in the world. But the book is more than that.

The generalist who picks up this book will appreciate the interesting saga of the PLA Navy, or PLAN, as China's navy is called. The story, as the authors have woven it, has a warp of plainly technical threads of equipment characteristics and capabilities and ship construction programs; the woof of the tapestry are the threads of colorful domestic failures, setbacks, and accidents, intriguing international interactions, and the implications of both achieving combat capabilities and, in some important areas, failing to do so. This story starts with a navy composed of small ships, largely of Soviet origin. These unimpressive ships were armed with early, rudimentary—but still lethal—cruise missiles, employed in the 1950s and even later, in a desperate but inspired attempt to be able to cope with potential adversaries with navies far superior in technology, firepower, tactics, and combat experience. This navy then haltingly navigated through the difficult periods where it faced enormous technology gaps and lacked capable air and missile defenses and antisubmarine capability, even surprisingly getting assistance from the United States for a decade, as explained in the book. The PLAN presciently kept itself credible by relying on advancing cruise missile technologies that were increasingly difficult to defend against.

The PLAN eventually becomes a purposefully and astutely woven tapestry—a force, built at home or bought abroad, that includes capable, quiet, numerous, and diverse nuclear-powered *and* conventional submarines, many of them new and some quite modern; formidable guided-missile destroyers led in firepower by a Russian-built behemoth and frigates, with some of these surface combatants equipped with modern air defenses; modern, fast missile craft, amphibious lift, and auxiliaries; and a naval air force that, although lacking aircraft carriers so far, includes maritime interdiction and very advanced multirole tactical aircraft—much of it made or designed in Russia. Most of the frontline platforms in today's PLAN deliver advanced missiles that, by virtue of range, speed, evasiveness, and lethality, tend to offset various other disadvantages and technological shortcomings in the circumstances where China is likely to be challenged.

For the technical wonk, Chinese naval systems are described in appropriate detail and context so that the capabilities, shortcomings, and technical aspects and their places in the fabric of the PLAN are comprehensible. The policy-wonk reader may only skim the tables of shipboard electronic equipment and frequency bands but will be fully engrossed by the details of how these systems came to be in the PLAN and the international intrigues involved. For those with a historical bent, the chronology of the PLAN's origins, its rise as a brown- or green-water navy, and current modernization and transformation into a blue-water navy are presented so that one can digest it all, choosing individually how much technology to chew on. For the military buff who revels in sorting out ship classes, weapon systems and their designations and specifications, electronic suites, and the like, this book provides both a reference source and matrices of how these items fit in the PLAN. Some expert or disputatious readers will take exception to certain assertions and conclusions, but more often the fair-minded reader will feel he or she has been provided with balanced explanations of contentious issues and insightful examinations of controversies.

In that vein, the scope of effort that went into writing this book is noteworthy. It was a complex and difficult, if not nearly impossible, task—one not likely to be replicated. The authors started with a large collection of technical details; bits of accurate, questionable, or erroneous information; a mix of valid, dubious, and faulty conclusions; and an uncollated assortment of misconceptions and solid judgments—as is generally the case when researching such issues with respect to China. Chinese secrecy on military matters severely complicates access to such detailed information and the means to corroborate facts. The authors are to be congratulated for discovering, collecting, compiling, and sorting out a very large amount of information and misinformation—and putting it together while avoiding the exaggeration that often taints texts on the PLA, highlighting important aspects, correcting misconceptions, and revealing disinformation.

This effort is all the more noteworthy for both the span of time covered, six decades, and for overcoming these obstacles to getting accurate and sufficient information concerning China. The roller-coaster nature of U.S.-PRC military relations has added other complications as the two countries have bounced around between engagement, confrontation, occasional cooperation, and constant hedging—with the ever-present possibility of armed conflict, even if odds of that seem low at the present.

In that regard, *People's Liberation Army Navy (PLAN): Combat Systems Technology, 1949–2010* should be especially welcomed in the United States by those who deal with China and its important, modernizing navy, whether as analyst, researcher, bureaucrat, policy maker, China watcher, or hopeful entrepreneur. The book, naturally, should also have a rapt readership in Taiwan, which China claims as its own; in neighboring divided Korea, where China has soaring trade relations with the South and a somewhat ambiguous alliance with the North; in Japan, so widely distrusted by generations of Chinese even up to the present; and among the neighbors or near-neighbors of Southeast and South Asia who must economically deal with and militarily tolerate huge looming China—as well as Australia, which prides itself on its progressive China policy and whose former prime minister was a Mandarin-speaking

China specialist. Landlocked Mongolia, which simultaneously seeks and fears Chinese economic development, and Central Asia, where four countries join China and Russia as members of the Shanghai Cooperation Organization, all have good reasons to scrutinize China's ongoing transformation from a continental to a maritime power. This book will help inform the European debate on the transfer to China of military and dual-use technologies—curtailed after the 1989 Tiananmen events. Only marginally less interest is likely in Africa and Latin America, where China seeks natural resources and good relations but is seen by some as an ominous player in Africa and a threat to the hoary tenets of the Monroe Doctrine in the Western Hemisphere.

The point is that China's navy is now a significant factor worldwide in China's rise as a global economic and military power. That navy, its history, its technological aspects, and its capabilities and limitations should be of interest to many in the world who, we can realistically hope, will look beyond the fear of China as a potential adversary and use this book to understand China better, cooperate with China more, and avoid conflict with China more successfully. China denies aggressive or expansionist intent. However, its future strategic intentions are not set in concrete, and those who best understand China and its navy will best be able to influence or shape whether a more modern, prosperous, and stronger China will be a more dangerous or a more responsible China—or at least better perceive its incipient tendencies.

Of course, the largest factor in determining how the world views China's maritime strategic intentions will be how and where Beijing employs the PLA Navy. As a result of the recent two decades or more of enhancement of naval capabilities, as described in this book, Chinese leaders now have a broad range of capabilities and feasible courses of action from which to choose, some admirable or at least understandable and some highly imprudent but not out of the question. That menu might include the following:

- Defense of Chinese sovereignty, including both undisputed territory, the complex issue of Taiwan, and various disputed claims, primarily with Japan and Southeast Asian countries
  - > Responsible, proportionate defense of recognized Chinese territory and interests
  - > Sporadic aggressive, hegemonic maritime undertakings as in the South China Sea island-grabs of the final quarter of the last century (Paracel Islands, Mischief Reef)
  - > The routine employment or threat of the use of gunboat diplomacy in pursuit of offshore claims on land features and seabed resources

- Engagement with other navies to protect ocean commerce, including energy security

- Cooperative international efforts to meet newly prominent, nontraditional threats such as piracy, terrorism, and proliferation of weapons of mass destruction

- Participation in disaster relief operations, generally with other navies

- Extended deployments to distant operational areas—as the PLAN is now doing off the eastern coast of Africa

- Deployment of new nuclear-powered submarines, both attack boats and ballistic-missile carriers, to distant locations to protect Chinese interests or, alternatively, to threaten other countries—including the United States

- An attack on Taiwan based on perceptions of intolerable actions toward independence

  > Destruction of the Taiwanese navy and conduct of modest amphibious assaults to secure lodgments for the introduction of occupation forces

  > Operations intended (success far from assured) to prevent timely and effective intervention by U.S. Navy forces in a Taiwan scenario

It will be up to China's leaders to make wise choices on such matters as whether, how, and when to press the Taiwan issue and other territorial and seabed claims. But, for the leaders of other nations, Beijing's options and decisions will be more clearly discerned—and possibly influenced—by those abroad who have a comprehensive understanding of the navy described in this book, the navy that Beijing commands, its history, and its unique Chinese qualities: that is, a modern navy with Chinese characteristics.

The PLA Navy of today is not nearly the equal of the U.S. Navy, but it has found in significant measure, and continues to seek further, the asymmetric means to complicate, delay, or deter American intervention in a PLA attack on Taiwan. The PLAN that Bussert and Elleman describe in detail already possesses submarines with long-range, submerged-launch, supersonic, highly evasive, and very lethal antiship cruise missiles (ASCMs) that can threaten the U.S. Navy's carrier strike groups headed for waters near Taiwan, especially if the PLA devises the means consistently and reliably to detect, track, and target the carrier groups. That is the prominent extant threat to U.S. Navy intervention forces.

On the horizon, under development, is a medium-range antiship ballistic missile (ASBM), to be launched securely from well within China, that can maneuver on reentry first to avoid intercept and then to hit a carrier or other major ship. Alone or in highly complementary combination, these ASCMs and ASBMs, plus other submarine-, surface-, and air-launched missiles, are potentially major factors in decisions American leaders would have to make concerning deployment to the area of the U.S. Navy carrier strike groups.

Would a U.S. president send five carrier strike groups to an area with dozens of unlocated submarines? What if at least eight of those submarines were armed with potent ASCMs designed to defeat American defenses and ready to make sea-skimming attacks? Add salvos of ASBMs that might simultaneously reenter the atmosphere and maneuver at Mach 12, then distribute submunitions to disable defenses and damage carrier flight decks? The decision urgently to dispatch carriers in time to help a Taiwan about to fall would be all the more difficult because China at least threatens to disrupt at the outset of conflict critical U.S. communications, command and control, computer networks, intelligence, surveillance, and reconnaissance (C4ISR) and then, if there is any success with initial attacks, to bring to bear forces ready to conduct follow-up attacks on units with degraded defenses.

The chances are that the PLA, lacking recent combat experience, would not be able to coordinate successfully this complex dual campaign against Taiwan and the world's only superpower, but a strategy of counting on the enemy to stumble is not very satisfying. Moreover, we would then be engaged in a war with China—an unprecedented war between two nuclear-armed major nations, an outcome surely to be avoided.

The other side of this coin is the prospect that cross-strait tensions continue to ease. Then, looking beyond gloomy Taiwan scenarios, the future could, and should, find the U.S. Navy and PLA Navy operating together to provide, as suggested above, protection of ocean commerce. Partnership is needed in

- enhancing energy security by deterring or defending against disruption of the flow of oil and natural gas across the Indian and Pacific Oceans, and
- making safe the sea-lanes that carry the products and commodities vital to the economies of China and so many countries of the world.

There is, as is being demonstrated by the rotating PLAN task force off Somalia now, the need for PLAN cooperation with other navies to curb piracy. There is a crying need for USN-PLAN cooperation in providing humanitarian assistance and disaster relief. The international teams that take on the tasks of aiding the victims of future tsunamis, earthquakes, hurricanes or typhoons, cyclones, and potential man-made massive destruction wrought by terrorists or irresponsible combatant nations should, wherever appropriate, include the PLA Navy. It should be joining with the U.S. Navy and other partners—even the Republic of China (ROC) Navy and certainly the Japanese Maritime Self-Defense Force (JMSDF) and the Republic of Korea (ROK) Navy—to provide assistance and relief in regional disasters. Not only is aid provided to the needy, but also trust and confidence are developed among the nations involved. We can, thereby, greatly increase the odds that all these forces from other nations will, ten years from now, be *operating with* a modest PLA Navy aircraft carrier chasing pirates or saving lives rather than *shooting at* that carrier in a conflict over Taiwan.

The modern and capable PLA Navy, described in the concluding chapter of this book, need not be seen as competitor or potential adversary but rather as a welcome partner to the steadily shrinking navies around the globe that strive with limited resources to make the world a safer and better place. That rosy outlook is, of course, neither a foregone conclusion nor an easy objective, but it is certainly a goal that warrants extraordinary effort and imagination. Read the book and judge whether we want to, or must, live with the PLA Navy as an adversary or should strive for the admittedly optimistic outcome I have suggested.

In sum, to the authors' credit, from all these diverse factors, elements, complications, and problems, Jim Bussert and Bruce Elleman have assembled a satisfying narrative and an up-to-date, as well as historical, reference volume—a book that tells the story of the PLA Navy, evaluates its capabilities, displays its composition, explains its technology, reveals the reasoning behind its development and modernization, clears up many misconceptions about it, and, in doing all this, adds significantly to the library of serious literature on the Chinese military broadly and the Chinese navy specifically—knowledge that is of great value regardless of the direction that U.S.-China relations take in coming years.

—ERIC A. McVADON
Rear Admiral, USN (Ret.)
Former Defense and Naval Attaché at the U.S. Embassy in Beijing
Consultant on East Asia Security Affairs
Senior Adviser and Director Emeritus, Asia-Pacific Studies,
Institute for Foreign Policy Analysis

Great Falls, Virginia
March 2010

Acronyms and Abbreviations

AWACS	airborne warning and control system
AXT	auxiliary training ship
CCP	Chinese Communist Party
CDS	combat direction system
C4I	command, control, communications, computers, and intelligence
CG	guided-missile cruiser
CIC	combat information center
CIWS	close-in weapon system
CMS	China Marine Surveillance
CNET	Chinese naval escort taskforce
CNO	chief of naval operations
CODOG	combined diesel or gas turbine
CPU	central processing unit
CRT	cathode-ray tube
CSEE	Compagnie de Signaux et d'Entreprises Electriques
CSI	combat system integration
CSSC	China State Shipbuilding Corporation
C3	command, control, and communications
C2	command and control
DC	direct current
D/C	depth charge
DD	destroyer
DDG	guided-missile destroyer
DER	destroyer escort, radar picket
D/F	direction finder
DFH	Dong Fang Hong (satellite)

DGPS	Differential Global Positioning System
DSRV	deep submergence rescue vehicle
ECM	electronic countermeasure
EEZ	exclusive economic zone
EHF	extremely high frequency
ELF	extremely low frequency
ELINT	electronic intelligence
EMI	electromagnetic interference
E-O	electro-optic
ESM	electronic warfare support measures
EW	electronic warfare
FAC	fast attack craft
FC	fire control
FCS	fire control system
FDDI	Fiber Distributed Data Interface
FF	frigate
FFG	guided-missile frigate
FLEC	Fisheries Law Enforcement Command
FLIR	forward-looking infrared
F22P	export frigate (Pakistan)
GHz	gigahertz
GLD	General Logistics Department
GLONASS	global navigation satellite system
GPS	Global Positioning System
HF	high frequency
HMAS	Her Majesty's Australian Ship
HM&E	hull, mechanical, and engineering
HP	high pressure
HQ	headquarters
HUD	head-up display
Hz	hertz
ICBM	intercontinental ballistic missile
IEC	International Electrotechnical Commission
IEEE	Institute of Electrical and Electronics Engineers
IFF	identification, friend or foe
IJN	Imperial Japanese Navy
IMO	International Maritime Organization

INS	inertial navigation system
IPS	information-processing system
IR	infrared
IRBM	intermediate-range ballistic missile
JMSDF	Japanese Maritime Self-Defense Force
Ka	Kamov (Soviet helicopter manufacturer)
KHz	kilohertz
km	kilometer
KPA	Korean People's Army
kts	knots
Ku	14,000 kilohertz (air tracking)
KYD	one thousand yards
LAN	local area network
LCAC	landing craft, air cushion
LCI	landing craft, infantry
LCM	landing craft, medium
LCS	littoral combat ship
LCU	landing craft, utility
LF	low frequency
LORAN	long-range navigation
LPD	landing platform, dock
LR	long range
LSD	landing ship, dock
LSIL	landing ship, infantry, large
LSM	landing ship, mechanized
LST	landing ship, tank
m	meter
MBDF	Maritime Border Defense Force
MEO	middle earth orbit
MF	medium frequency
MHz	megahertz
MIRV	multiple independently targeted reentry vehicle
ML	minelayer
mm	millimeter
MPA	maritime patrol aircraft
MRBM	medium-range ballistic missile
MSA	Maritime Safety Administration

MSC	minesweeper, coastal
MSC	Military Sealift Command
MSO	minesweeper, ocean
NATO	North Atlantic Treaty Organization
NCO	noncommissioned officer
NTDS	naval tactical data system
OTH	over-the-horizon
OTH-B	over-the-horizon, backscatter
OTH-SW	over-the-horizon, surface wave
OTH-T	over-the-horizon, targeting
PAP	People's Armed Police
PAR	phased array radar
PB	patrol boat
PC	patrol craft
PCI	peripheral component interconnect
PGM	missile patrol boat
PLA	People's Liberation Army
PLAAF	People's Liberation Army Air Force
PLAN	People's Liberation Army Navy
PLANAF	People's Liberation Army Navy Air Force
PRC	People's Republic of China
PRF	pulse repetition frequency
PTG	missile patrol craft
PTH	patrol torpedo, hydrofoil
RAN	Royal Australian Navy
R & D	research and development
RBN	radio beacon navigation
RBOC	Rapid-Blooming Off-Board Chaff
RCS	radar cross section
ROC	Republic of China
ROK	Republic of Korea
RPM	rounds per minute
RWR	radar warning receiver
SAM	surface-to-air missile
SAR	search and rescue
SATCOMM	satellite communications
SATNAV	satellite navigation

SCO	Shanghai Cooperation Organization
SCS	South China Sea
SHF	superhigh frequency
SIGINT	signals intelligence
SLBM	submarine-launched ballistic missile
SLF	superlow frequency
SLOC	sea line of communication
SOA	State Oceanic Administration
SR	ship demagnetizing
SRBOC	Super Rapid-Blooming Off-Board Chaff
SS	diesel submarine
SSB	ballistic-missile diesel submarine
SSBN	ballistic-missile nuclear submarine
SSG	guided-missile diesel submarine
SSGN	guided-missile nuclear submarine
SSM	surface-to-surface missile
SSN	nuclear-powered submarine
STANAG	NATO Standardization Agreement
SUEC	Shanghai United Electric Company
SVTT	surface vessel torpedo tube
TADIL-A	NATO data link 11
TAVITAC	Traitement Automatique et Visualisation Tactique
TBO	time between overhaul
3-D	three-dimensional
25T	export frigate
UHF	ultrahigh frequency
ULF	ultralow frequency
USS	United States ship
VAC	volts, alternating current
VADM	vice admiral
VDS	variable-depth sonar
VHF	veryhigh frequency
VLF	verylow frequency
VLS	vertical launch system
V/STOL	vertical or short takeoff and landing
VTS	vessel traffic service
WHEC	high-endurance cutter

People's Liberation Army Navy

COMBAT SYSTEMS TECHNOLOGY,
1949–2010

—— 1 ——

Systems Integration and China's Naval Technology Growth, 1949–89

There are reference books on all warships of the world or all weapon systems in the world, but no text describing only the People's Liberation Army Navy (PLAN) combat systems. This book will trace the evolution from the founding of the PLAN in 1949 up to today's increasingly modern combat systems, both foreign and Chinese developed equipment. A book examining the PLAN's combat systems technology is timely and important since, in the post–Cold War era, Western military experts frequently point to China as the next major rival for U.S. naval dominance in the Pacific. Although the present volume is not intended as another text on strategy and Chinese policies, the history of how the Chinese go about changing ship type and combat system priority hints at their intentions. The funding of shipyard construction, ship armaments, and base locations is where government support results in the physical fleet.

This book will begin with the PLA's first ships and equipment, which were primarily Soviet-supplied. In the ensuing sixty years, most have been replaced by newer vessels, but some vessels from the 1950s and 1960s still remain active or in reserve status. In order to describe fully the earlier systems, the first two chapters will focus on the period up to 1989. The Tiananmen Square boycott cut off Western sources, which negatively impacted the PLAN's importation of naval systems from that point on. Later chapters include the newest PLAN high technology, both indigenous and imported.

This text contains many tables of various combat systems from World War II vintage to the most modern, and frequency bands are significant information when describing these systems. Unfortunately there are many frequency band tables that vary from nation to nation, product vendors, and international organizations, but two primary bands that overlap are illustrated in Table 1. There is the letters A-M band of frequencies, commonly termed "electronic-warfare" (EW) band frequencies, and the Institute of Electrical and Electronics Engineers (IEEE)/American National Standards

Institute (ANSI) Standard 527, called "RADAR BAND," from extremely low frequency (ELF) to extremely high frequency (EHF).

This results in a given frequency having a different designation for different systems. To work around the frequency band confusion, Table 1 was created showing both standards and their common frequencies. Combat system designations are added to indicate applications of the system bands to systems in this book. Source references to "short" or "medium" waves cross to high frequency (HF) and medium frequency (MF), but "long" and "ultra-short" waves are a maze of different national interpretations and will be avoided.

Stories of dramatic technical advances in the military capabilities of the People's Republic of China (PRC) seem to crop up regularly in the Western press, including an endless list of startling "revelations" about China's military developments that are usually exaggerated or perhaps disinformation. Past experience suggests that most such reports should be discounted; the more dramatic the story, the less likely it is to prove true. Notwithstanding some of the more outrageous claims from 1949 to 1989, the PLAN has made some very real progress in its capabilities. During ten years of this period, from 1979 to 1989, the United States actively cooperated with China in assisting China's naval military programs, which were aimed mainly against the USSR. Although U.S. military sales halted quickly after 1989, the collapse of the USSR in 1991 opened up a whole new market in Soviet-era naval equipment. During the past twenty years, the PLAN has made rapid progress by combining foreign military purchases with its own indigenously produced equipment.

The Soviet Technology Legacy

Although China had developed a naval force prior to World War II, most of its ships were either scuttled or captured by Japan during the war. In 1949 the Chinese Communist Party (CCP) inherited a large number of navy ships—mainly of Japanese and American origin—from the retreating Nationalist forces. Most of the PLA Navy's new vessels, however, were provided by the Soviet Union during the 1950s and 1960s, either as actual equipment or in the form of plans, tools, and production facilities.

The 1989 inventory of PRC naval electronics indicates that through the 1980s, very little basic equipment had changed since the 1950s. During the nine years from 1957 to 1966, for example, the USSR provided four navigation radars that had maximum ranges from 16 to 64 miles. During the 1980s, Soviet navigation radars—including "Neptune" and similar I-band radars—were installed on nearly a thousand of the two thousand PRC naval vessels and the Soviet "Snoop Plate"[1] was the standard submarine-type surface search

Table 1. Composite Combat System Frequency Bands Application

EW BAND	FREQUENCY	RADAR BAND	APPLICATION
A	3 Hz–30 Hz	ELF	
A	30 Hz–300 Hz	SLF	
A	300 Hz–3000 Hz	ULF	
A	3 KHz–30 KHz	VLF	Surface sonar
A	30 KHz–300 KHz	LF	Minesweep sonar
A	300 KHz–MHz	MF	
A	3 MHz–30 MHz	HF	
A	0 Hz–250 MHz 30 MHz–300 MHz	VHF	LR radar
B	250 MHz–500 MHz 300 MHz–1,000 MHz	UHF	Data link
C	500 MHz–1,000 MHz		
D	1,000 MHz–2,000 MHz	L	
E	2 GHz–3 GHz		Air search
F	3 GHz–4 GHz 2 GHz–4 GHz	S	AA fire control
G	4 GHz–6 GHz		
H	5 GHz–8 GHz 4 GHz–8 GHz	C	Surface search Navigation
I	8 GHz–10 GHz 8 GHz–12 GHz 12 GHz–18 GHz	X Ku	Fire control
J	10 GHz–20 GHz 18 GHz–27 GHz 3 GHz–30 GHz 27 GHz–40 GHz	K SHF Ka	Sat comms
K	20 GHz–40 GHz		
L	40 GHz–60 GHz 40 GHz–75 GHz	V	
M	60 GHz –100 GHz 75 GHz–110 GHz 30 GHz–300 GHz	W EHF	

radar.[2] The Soviet NEL 3-7 series fathometers over time gradually increased in size from 130 to 400 kilograms, with a commensurate increase in power. The depth scales increased with NEL-M1 (five hundred to six thousand fathoms) for larger ships and deeper waters, showing Chinese improvements and more demanding needs of larger vessels.[3]

In many other areas the Soviet-era technology remained predominant in the PLAN through the 1980s. For example, for almost forty years the PLA Navy's shipboard electronic warfare support measure (ESM) capability was limited to simple 1940s-vintage Soviet identification, friend or foe (IFF) antennas, direction finder (D/F) loops, and multiband receivers. For antisubmarine warfare (ASW), PRC vessels were provided with elderly twenty-five kilohertz World War II–era sonars, based on Allied Lend-Lease equipment. The Luda-class destroyers (DD) added an Eye Shield long-range search radar atop the foremast and a Bean Sticks search radar forward of the after stack; some frigates also added the Eye Shield, which was based on the Soviet Slim Net design. In 1984 a new-construction Luda-class ship was seen with a planar-array radar on the aft lattice mast similar to the Hughes SPS-49, designated Rice Screen, and four new antiair-warfare (AAW) gun mounts.[4]

The Soviet technology transfers of the 1950s and early 1960s included many radar systems (see Table 2). The table establishes a baseline of PLAN radar technology, and will put the newer systems described in later chapters into perspective regarding increased operational capabilities. It is noteworthy that several of these 1950-vintage Soviet radars, such as the Knife Rest, are still used on new construction vessels. Some deficiencies were corrected through indigenous designs. During the 1970s, for example, the PRC constructed a prototype Hola-class missile patrol boat, with a unique 12-foot surface search dome aft, later known as Round Ball, which is an I-band gun radar. Over time a slotted wave-guide radar began to replace the Skin Head radar, which had been the only surface search radar on hundreds of patrol craft (PCs) and torpedo attack craft for decades.

The PRC has also made notable advances in the design and production of ship surface-to-air missiles (SAM). Ten PRC-designed HQ-2 SAMs were demonstrated at Dacheng County Militia Training Base in 1984, and the Jiangdong SAM frigate finally had a PRC-made phased-array search radar and associated missile. The large-scale naval AAW exercise by the East Sea Fleet in September 1984 was evidence of progress in the AAW field. The CSS-NX-4 missile displayed in the 1984 Anniversary Parade is another good example; the trucks towing the missiles were manned by sailors, and the PRC completed its first submerged missile tests from a modified Golf-class ballistic missile submarine (SSB) in 1982.

Table 2. USSR Radars on Early PLAN Units

NAME	TYPE	BAND	YEAR	PLATFORM
Skin Head	Surface search	H, I	1948	Hainan, Osa, Shanghai
Knife Rest	Early warning	VHF	1953	Luda
Slim Net	LR air/surface	E, F	1953	Riga
Neptune	Navigation	H, I	1953	Jianghu
Fire Iron	Gun fire control	H	1947	*Anshan* (Russian class name was Gordy; Chinese lead ship was *Anshan*)
Cross Bird	Air search	A	1947	*Anshan*
Post I amp	Target acquisition	X	1953	Jianghu
Top Bow	Track radar	H, I	1952	Jianghu, Luda
Gyuis	Air warning	X	1945	Riga
High Sieve	Air/surface	E/F	1947	*Anshan*

In addition to acquiring from the USSR the basic naval equipment that the PLAN needed to conduct maritime operations, a whole range of supporting technologies were needed to make them effective. Fire control (FC) radars were one of the most essential components for directing naval fire, and many PRC fire control systems were obsolescent. For example, the older *Anshan*-class (Soviet Gordy-class) destroyers were sent to China with 1947 Fire Iron H-band radars. Other than the Wasp Head director, the only other optical naval FC was the 1947 vintage Four Eyes optical director for the 130-millimeter Gordy main batteries.

Even during periods of so-called Sino-Soviet friendship, the USSR withheld modern and even standard FC equipment on Chinese exports, with the goal of keeping the Chinese navy weaker than their Soviet counterparts, which increased after the 1960s split. For example, the Soviets removed Strut Curve and Drum Tilt fire control radars from the Osa-class missile attack craft sent to the PRC in the early 1960s and also withheld the 1952-vintage Owl Screech and Hawk Screech gun fire control radars. Photographs from the 1980s reveal that the PRC Osas still had only the Square Tie radar. Many Chinese warships still had the Wasp Head optical main directors without the associated Sun Visor FC radar, normally found on all Soviet units. Because of this Russian policy of removing fire control radars on vessels exported to China, these fire control systems changed very little through the mid-1980s.

While some of China's more modern patrol boats were well equipped—Magnavox satellite navigation receivers have been observed on small Hainan attack boats—the Shanghai-class patrol boats were more typical, with no sign of IFF or FC for 37-millimeter and 25-millimeter weapons. In conjunction with the Styx antiship missile (ASM), however, the Square Tie did provide modest standoff surface-to-surface missile (SSM) firepower for some of the PRC patrol vessels. Still, a severe lack of naval sensors limited the usefulness of many of China's patrol craft.

Over time indigenous advances were made possible by China's increasingly large and resourceful shipbuilding and electronics industries. Starting from only a very small industrial base, the Chinese gradually were able to narrow the gap with the West in terms of basic shipbuilding techniques. With these advances, China's naval technology foundation also grew exponentially, which began to provide China with reverse-engineered naval equipment that it had formerly lacked. Therefore, Chinese naval shipyards and production plants played an important role in allowing the PLAN to modernize.

Chinese Naval Shipyards

Although much of the PLAN's early naval equipment came from the USSR, China had long been a seagoing nation, with some shipyards dating back hundreds of years; Shanghai's Jiangnan and Hudong shipyards date from 1865 and 1928, respectively. When the Communists came to power in 1949, some of China's best ports had recently been occupied by European colonialists who left behind their shipyards and railroad infrastructure, such as Germany and Japan at Qingdao, the British at Shanghai and Weihaiwei, and the Russians and Japanese at Dalian. For example, the Dalian shipyards were built in 1894 with help from Russia, were under Japanese control from 1895 to 1898, Russia from 1898 to 1905, and retaken by Japan in 1905 and held until 1945, when it was seized by the USSR, and then finally turned over to China in 1955. In 1953 the USSR assisted China in establishing the first new military shipyard in Bohai at Huludao, which would construct the most modern submarines. With Dalian's return in 1955, China's shipbuilding capabilities grew quickly. As summarized in Table 3, there were well over a hundred other shipyards of all sizes throughout the country that could build small and medium warships, but the foreign-built shipyards mainly built the larger, more complex warships. After the Sino-Soviet split, China established the Sixth Ministry for Shipbuilding in 1963 to help coordinate its ship-building programs.[5]

By 1989 there were about 110 shipyards in the PRC, but China's most capable shipyards were located in the north at Dalian, in the east at Zhonghua near Shanghai, and in the south near Guangzhou, which built many of the Luda destroyers. Submarine construction of numerous 030 Whiskey and 033 Romeo submarines was accomplished at Jiangnan (Shanghai) and Whampoa (Guangzhou). After the Sino-Soviet split, the Huludao shipyard constructed China's nuclear submarines. Meanwhile, smaller patrol craft such as "Shanghai" PCs were produced by the hundreds at numerous shipyards.

Table 3. PRC Warship Construction Shipyards, 1950–89

CITY	SHIPYARD	1990 BUILDS	PAST CONSTRUCTION
Shanghai	Hudong	Jianghu, Jiangwei, Huangfun, Dadong, Yunnan, Yuanwang	Hudong, Riga, 033, Fulin, Haiku, Chengdu, Dajiang, Dazhi, Fuzhou, Yuanwang, Jiangdong, Huchuan
Shanghai	Jiangnan	Luhu, Hainan, Jianghu, Xiangyanghong	033, 030, Kronstadt, Shantou, Huangfeng PTG, Jiangnan, P-6
Shanghai	Zhonghua	Jianghu, Yukan, Yuting, Yudeng	Luda, Kansha, Yenka, Yenlai, Yanqian, Zhonghua
Shanghai	Qiuxin	Houxin, Haiqing	Jiangdong, Haibing, Yanha
Shanghai	Shanghai E.	Shanghai II	Shanghai I
Guangzhou	Guangzhou	Jiangwei, Qiongsha, Yuling	Luda, Dalang, Jiangnan, Riga, T-43, 033, Huangfen, Hegu
Guangzhou	Huangpu	Houjian	Jianghu I, Huang
Guangzhou	Whampoa	gunboats	030, 033, gunboats, Qiongsha AP
Wuhan	Wuchang	Wuhan C	030, 033, T 43, Wuhan A, DSRV, Dadie
Dalian	Dalian	Beleijan	Luda, Golf, Fuqing, Gromovoy, Shantou
Huludao	Bohai	Ming upgrade	033
Shantou	Shantou	LCMs	Jiangnan, Yuliang
Wuhu	Wuhu	Dalang II	Huchuan, Dongxiu, Houka, Gromov

Photo 1. The newest air defense Type 051C DDG under construction in Dalian Shipyard. Note the Russian SA-N-6 VLS fore and aft, but the associated Flap Lid radar aft is retracted. Source: Kanwa

Shanghai alone had ten major shipyards that built many medium and large warships and auxiliaries.

Using 1984 as an example, these shipyards altogether jointly built only ten ships displacing more than 10,000 tons; but since the largest PLA Navy vessels at that time displaced less than 5,000 tons, this imposed no restriction on the building of warships. The two main naval shipyard centers were Shanghai and Guangzhou, with six shipyards in each location. A variety of ships were built at these yards, from submarines to large space event vessels. The early achievements of the PLA Navy, the nuclear-powered Han-class torpedo attack submarine (SSN) and Xia-class ballistic-missile submarine (SSBN), come from the high-technology Huludao shipyard, one of five near the Liaodong Peninsula in Manchuria. Dalian Shipyard was known for producing the Golf-class SSB, the first Luda-class DDs, and the large Fuqing-class oilers, while the Dagu yard has built experimental hovercraft such as the Jingsha.

Over the years Chinese shipyards have undergone several major reorganizations and consolidations. In 1982 the China State Shipbuilding Corporation (CSSC) was formed; it included twenty-five shipyards, fifty-seven manufacturing plants, and thirty-six research-and-development (R & D) institutes.[6]

This has not only benefited their ability to construct ships for the PLAN but also to build large vessels for Chinese commercial exports. Chinese shipyards are constantly expanding and increasing dry dock and crane capacities, as well as hiring skilled workers and engineers. Their success is based directly on China's naval technology industries.

China's Naval Technology Foundation

Following the 1960 Sino-Soviet split, China had to develop its own industries to support the PLAN. For building ships, these industries included diesel engines, naval electronics, computer hardware and software, and radios. For the aircraft that supported seagoing vessels, these industries included aircraft engines, avionics, and more modern wing designs. Over time China's indigenous capabilities have increased to the point where it can supply the PLAN with almost all of its basic equipment needs, with advanced technology still coming from abroad, as needed.

One of the most important components in any naval ship is its propulsion. Until Chinese production plants were opened in the early 1970s, most marine power plants were imported from Poland and Yugoslavia. Later the PRC's primary marine diesel engine construction plants were collocated with the large shipyard complexes in Shanghai and Guangzhou and produced seventeen different diesels with horsepower ratings up to 12,000. Diesel power plants remained the PLAN's primary propulsion type until the post-1990 new guided-missile destroyers (DDGs).

Despite many years of aircraft turbine engine experience, the Chinese seemed reluctant to rely upon them for marine use until the Luhu-class DDG in 1991. There was experimentation with turbine power on a Jianghu-class frigate in the 1970s, but the ship was soon reconverted back to diesel. In 1984 a Chinese delegation visited General Electric's U.S. facilities, possibly shopping for the LM-2500 gas turbine. The 1989 Tiananmen boycott interfered with the transfer of this technology except for five LM-2500s for the Luhu DDGs, which were completed in 1991. A third Luhu hull 114 was canceled due to a lack of two LM-2500 plants for it.

Development of PLA Navy electronics depended both on importing foreign technology and improving domestically produced systems. The first modern electronics manufacturing plant was the Beijing Wire Communication Plant No. 738, which was built by the Soviets in 1957 and produced China's first domestic computer in 1962. But as late as in 1984, there were only twelve computer plants or research centers in the PRC. The Shanghai Radio Plant No. 13 produced the PRC's most powerful computer, capable of a million operations per second, but China still relied on imported equipment made by IBM, Gould, Honeywell, and Data General. There were seven major telecommunications factories in Shanghai, three in Beijing and Hangzhou, and two in Guangzhou. The Zibo No. 5 Radio Plant made survey sonars, and ship radars were produced by the Shanghai Marine Meter Plant.

In 1974 Jiangnan Shipyard launched the 10,000-ton freighter *Fengqing*. This was the first ship with all Chinese-made equipment. Until then the PRC maritime industry had relied totally or partially on foreign designs.

The capability of China's aircraft industry to produce high-performance aircraft to support the PLAN was another challenge. Most aircraft still being flown in 1981 by the People's Liberation Army Navy Air Force (PLANAF) were of 1950s Soviet vintage. Though many appeared identical with Soviet models, there had been some improvements made by the Chinese. For example, the Soviet MiG-19 Turmansky RD-9B engine required maintenance twice as often as the Chinese WP-6 version, produced in Shenyang. While the F-6 was twenty-eight years old, Pakistani pilots firmly believed the PRC F-6 could outperform Mirage III fighters in combat. Table 4 shows jet engine time between overhaul (TBO) reliability of Chinese versus Soviet and French fighters.

Table 4. Jet Engine Reliability

AIRCRAFT	ENGINE	ENGINE HOURS	AIRFRAME HOURS
Soviet MiG-19	RD-9B	65	400
PRC F-6	WP-6	100	800
Mirage III	Atar-9B	600	1,800

After sixty engines were completed, production ceased on the F-8 and the B-6 (Tu-16) because of engine problems.[7] Soviet MiG-21F production began in 1957, and models given to the PRC had minimal avionics. For example, early 1980s F-8s had Odd Rod IFF and Sirena radar warning receivers (RWRs), which were not produced until after 1960, but the F-4 and F-6 aircraft lacked crucial radar warning receivers to alert pilots of radar lock-on.

Reports of a new PRC-designed twin-jet Mach-2 supersonic fighter leaked out in the late 1960s. PRC fighters have "J" (Jian) prefix and export models are "F" (Fighter). It was initially called the FANTAN-A; later it was renamed F-9 Shenyang, then F-6-bis, and finally designated Qian-5, or "attack plane five." The Nanchang factory design was an enlarged MiG-19 with external ordnance hardpoints, and an internal bomb bay, but this bulky ground-support plane was hardly supersonic during operations. China encountered problems trying to develop a copy of the swing-wing MiG-23 similar to those in China's nuclear submarine and missile development programs.

Technology Problems with Nuclear Submarines and Missiles

The USSR assisted China in building a G-class ballistic-missile submarine (SSB) in the 1950s, but balked at transferring nuclear technology for SSBN or submarine-launched ballistic missiles (SLBMs). Soviet reluctance to sell this high-tech equipment forced China to develop nuclear submarines on its own. China also developed a surface-launched SLBM for its submarines by modifying the People's Liberation Army (PLA) Frog missiles, which is the NATO designation for "Free Rocket Over Ground."[8]

Without significant Soviet assistance, the first twenty-two-kiloton PRC nuclear explosion took place on 16 October 1964. After five more tests, the nuclear program culminated in a 3.3-megaton fusion explosion on 17 June 1967.[9] The fission-to-fusion jump in three years proved to many that the PRC had the ability to acquire and build its own technology in selected priority programs in its nuclear-submarine program. A Han SSN was modified to the Xia-class SSBN. With a force of more than a hundred 030- and 033-class diesel submarines, the PRC had still produced only two nuclear-propulsion submarines by the mid-1980s. A February 1980 report stated that PRC SSN and SSBN hulls were on operational trials, but China's one Xia SSBN, with six tubes for twelve CSS-N-3 SLBMs, was not active until 1987. Most China experts feel the Xia never made an operational patrol and was not a viable strategic asset. The first respectable SSBN would not be realized until the 094 SSBN decades later.

Other than the Styx missiles and naval SSM, the only other PLA tactical missile was the early Frog-1 and Frog-2 unguided 7-to-20-mile-range weapons that first appeared in 1957 Moscow parades. The CSS-1 medium-range ballistic missile (MRBM) was road transportable, had a 600-mile range, and was deployed in 1966. The CSS-1 force of forty to ninety units was replaced by the intermediate-range ballistic missile (IRBM) CSS-2. The CSS-2 became operational in 1972 with a 1,500-mile range; sixty to eighty-five units were deployed. Two limited-range CSS-3 ICBMs, with a 4,000-mile range, became operational in 1975, followed by the CSS-4, with an 8,000-mile range, of which four were tested in 1979. Some analysts thought that the CSS-4's successful 6,200-to-7,000-mile South Pacific test flights in May 1980 were aimed not at the United States, but at making the "risks of an attack against the PRC too high for the Soviets to contemplate seriously."[10]

The DF-21 CSS-5 IRBM was based upon the JL-1 solid fuel design as a land-mobile IRBM. The DF-31 solid-fuel land-mobile intercontinental ballistic missile (ICBM), which began development in 1986, would be the basis for the future next generation SLBM JL-2.[11]

Most of these missiles were launched from the PRC's space complex at Shuangcheng, Manchuria. Although not as highly developed as U.S. missiles, their lethality should not be discounted. One retired Taiwanese Air Force colonel, Ding-Jong Tyan, even warned in 2002: "Such ground-to-ground missiles combined with air-to-ground and underwater-to-ground ballistic missiles can even threaten the U.S.'s Honolulu, or to fleets of aircraft carriers deployed in Southeast Pacific Ocean, and this can deter the U.S. military from directly intervening in the cross-straits war."[12] To a large degree, China's advances in these fields were aided by its purchases from the West.

China's Technology Purchases from the West during the 1980s

Following President Richard Nixon's visit to China in the early 1970s, and President Jimmy Carter's decision to recognize the PRC in the late 1970s, U.S. military sales to China increased. Although the West was eager to sell aircraft and avionics to the PRC in the 1980s, it had little initial success, except for helicopters (see Table 5). Even with the Sino-Soviet split, however, the PRC imported helicopters from Russia and the West for search and rescue (SAR) and ASW. These included 1965-vintage Mi-8 helicopters, and also civil AN-24, AN-26, and AN-30 transport aircraft. French Aérospatiale Frelon and Dauphin helicopter sales to the PLAN have been especially successful. Several American and German helicopters, such as the Bell 212, the Boeing CH-47, and the German Bo-105, were also sold to China, but were used by the PLA. Rather than be dependent upon outside sources for large jet transports, such as the 707, however, the PRC built a Y-10 near Shanghai that "was a reverse-engineered design based on the Boeing 707."[13]

Sixty-five British aerospace companies exhibited and marketed in Shanghai during March-April 1980, which typified the aggressive sales campaigns being conducted by various Western governments inside China. January 1986 saw the first Chinese International Defence Industries Expo, which had forty-five U.S. and thirty-one French booths.[14] The Asian Defence Technology Exposition (Asiandex) featured Chinese military exports in November 1986.[15] Because of PRC budget limitations, however, large-scale purchases were unlikely and technology transfer or license production rights were sought by the PRC to stimulate arms purchases. North Atlantic Treaty

Table 5. Foreign Helicopters for PLAN Service, 1960–83

HELICOPTER	NATION	DESIGNATION	MISSION/STATUS
Mi-4	USSR	Z-5	SAR/inactive
Mi-8	USSR		Transport /inactive
SA-321 Super Frelon	France	Z-8 F	Transport SAR /20 active on board large ships
AS-365N Dauphin	France	Z-9 C	ASW/36 active on board older DDs, frigates
AS-342	France		Utility/inactive
AS-350N	France	Z-11	SAR/inactive
Ka-25/27	USSR		ASW/trials
Ka-28	USSR		ASW (16), SAR (3)/active on board new DDGs and frigates

Organization (NATO) navies, such as the Italian in 1979 and the French and the British in 1980, began visiting mainland China.

Air defense (AD) remained a serious PLA weakness during the 1980s even though it had 15,000 antiaircraft (AA) guns, 4,500 HQ-2 SAM sites, and 1,500 AD and early warning radars. Its only operational SAM was the obsolete CSA-1 and associated Ginsling FC radars (Soviet SA-2 and Fan Song-A). Although these were copies of Soviet models, some appeared to be modified and improved designs.

A June 1980 U.S. government sale of Westinghouse Electric's AN/TPS-43 three-dimensional tactical air defense radar may have aided later PLAN radar designs, just as Crotale SAMs in a $350 million French antitank sale ended up on later PLAN updates. As for early warning systems, there was reportedly only one phased-array missile warning radar in western China, unless others were concealed from satellite surveillance. U.S.-installed sensors inside China were to provide warning of Soviet missile tests or preparations to fire SS-20 or other missiles at China.

In May 1980 Secretary of Defense Harold Brown told PRC vice premier Geng Biao that the United States was prepared to sell China military items, including radars and communications equipment. Specific export applications, which were approved, included tactical air defense radar sets, transport helicopters and planes, jet engine test devices, tropospheric communications, early warning radar antennas, and passive countermeasures.

In August 1981 PRC officials visited Washington to discuss increased arms purchases. A June 1981 congressional study stated that PRC wanted antitank, antiship, and antiaircraft missiles, ASW equipment, diesel marine engines, and aircraft, but the 1981 PRC defense budget reduced defense spending.[16] The Chinese bargained hard for license production rights and technology transfer from the United States and through the late 1980s were largely successful in its efforts. However, after 1989 many of these military sales were canceled.

Conclusions

Until 1989 the relative status of the PLAN could be easily judged by its per capita expenditures. In 1985, for example, the PLAN spent only $560 per sailor per year on shipboard electronics, in sharp contrast to the Soviet expenditure of $4,000 per sailor per year or the still higher U.S. investment of $5,700. This discrepancy perhaps explains why PRC warships went to sea without air search or fire control radars and why innovative domestic designs seemed to remain in prototype stages for years. Even with these severe limitations, however, the Chinese were able to build adequate equipment, and their combat aircraft performed particularly well in the Third World market.

As for naval exports, naval ships were the PRC's most numerous military export, with thirteen or more client nations. Patrol boats and other smaller vessels were the most common Chinese export, except for twenty diesel submarines and four frigates, as shown in Table 6. This upward trend in Chinese military exports began in the early 1980s, and largely corresponded with China's post–Deng Xiaoping "Open Door" reforms, which included widespread bureaucratic and industrial restructuring. U.S. technological assistance to China also made a huge difference, although following the Tiananmen Square boycott the United States put strict limits on what kinds of equipment China could purchase.

In 1980 there was still an estimated ten-to-fifteen-year lag in PRC naval platforms, weapons, and electronic technology. Beginning in the 1980s, the Chinese navy began to close this gap. This gap narrowed even more in the 1990s, after the 1991 collapse of the USSR suddenly opened the door for purchasing Soviet-era military and naval equipment. China's economic growth became a major determinant to the growth of the PLAN, since China had more foreign reserves to buy equipment. For example, from 1980–84 to

Table 6. PRC Naval Exports, 1955–85

CUSTOMER	SHANGHAI	HAINAN	KOMAR, OSA	FAST ATTACK	SS	FRIGATE
Albania	6		4	32		
Bangladesh	12	4	5	10		
Burma	7					
Cameroon	4					
Congo	2					
Egypt	4	28	6		6	4
Guinea	6					
N. Korea	14	6		8	7	
N. Vietnam	8					
Pakistan	12	4	8	4		4
Romania	21			24		
Sierra Leone	3					
Tanzania	7			2		

1995–97, annual exports increased more than seven times, with some annual growth rates as high as 14.6 percent.[17] Throughout the 1990s, yearly growth rates regularly hit 7 percent, and in the early part of the twenty-first century have hit 9 percent per year. In 2008 the Chinese government said it would spend $61 billion on defense, up 17 percent from 2007.[18]

China's foreign currency accounts allowed it to buy enormous quantities of foreign-made naval equipment. In early April 2001, Zheng Ming, director of PLAN's Armament and Technology Department, stressed that the "PLA must speed up the modernization of its naval forces so that China can transform from a large oceanic country into a strong ocean power at an early date."[19] However, China's decision to purchase much of its most modern naval equipment from a wide variety of countries and foreign manufacturers has led to serious systems integration concerns. Once foreign equipment has been purchased, either legally or in secret, it can be difficult and time consuming to get it to work properly. Encountering problems with integrating new technology is not unusual. On occasion China has even failed to acquire the entire foreign weapon system, usually due to illegal procurement from a third party.

In view of recent technological developments within the PRC, and their possible effect on future relations with the West, the PLAN's evolving capabilities are well worth assessing. This book will examine in greater detail this period in the PLAN's history, so as to analyze the current capabilities of the PLAN, some of the most important military trends, and potential pitfalls, including most importantly the PLAN's integration of foreign and domestic technology into a seamless whole. Later chapters will include integration problems such as imported Shkval high-speed torpedoes, unlicensed copies of the Aegis system, and the naval S-300 air defense system, among many others.

2

Earlier Chinese Destroyers

The PLAN surface navy backbone has always been its destroyer force, summarized in Table 7. This chapter will begin with a discussion of the Soviet *Anshan*-class destroyer and the Chinese-designed follow-on destroyers. The Type 051 Luda has been upgraded constantly since its development during the late 1960s, the launch of the first hull in 1971, and the launch of the last hull in 1993. Follow-on Type 052– and Type 052A–class destroyers are also described in this chapter. The wide range of upgrades and increased capabilities continues even in 2010.

Table 7. PLAN Destroyer Types

TYPE	DESTROYER	HULL NUMBERS
07	*Anshan*	DD 101–104
051	Luda	DD 107, 108, 131–34, 160–64
051DT	Luda I MOD	DD 106, 109, 110, 165
051	Luda II	DD 105
051G	Luda III	DD 166
052	Luhu	DDG 112, 113
052A	Luhai	DDG 167
052B	Luyang I	DDG 168, 169
052C	Luyang II	DDG 170, 171
051C	Luzhou	DDG 115, 116

This chapter will provide a more thorough understanding of how the Luda destroyer was created and changed over time. Even more important, the equipment changes in the Luda are essential for understanding the progressive development of China's modern, indigenously produced naval forces. This development helped to establish the growth trends that the PLAN is still pursuing.

The Luda III, in particular, was the test bed for combat systems that later appeared on the modern, larger-size Luhu, Luhai, and Luyang destroyers, which weigh in at 5,700 and 6,600 tons.

Anshan-Class Destroyers

The USSR built forty-eight Type 7 destroyers during World War II, of which seven were in the Pacific Fleet after the war. These ships were laid down beginning in 1936, and the first was commissioned in 1941. The sleek hull and capped funnel reflected Italian design assistance, but these ships sat in port in World War II and did not even participate in the Soviet Union's August 1945 naval invasions of Korea, Sakhalin, and the Kuril Islands.

During the 1950s four were towed from Komsomolsk to Vladivostok for fitting out. One problem with these 2,200-ton ships was vibration that appeared in the geared turbines when they operated at high speeds. The 130-millimeter open mounts, 76.2- and 37-millimeter AA guns, and Big Eyes stereo-optic range finder would be primary weapons not only on these vessels, but also on initial Chinese-built warships.

In 1954 the Soviet Union sold China the *Rekordny* Type 7, renamed the *Anshan* (DD 101) by China. In 1955 three more followed: the *Reshitelny-2*, *Retivy*, and *Rezkyi*, renamed the *Changchun* (*Chang Chun*) (DD 102), *Jilin* (*Chi Lin*) (DD 103), and *Fushun* (DD 104).[1] The *Anshan*-class destroyers were the PLAN's only large, surface fighting ships until the Ludas were built beginning in the late 1960s. This does not include the British cruiser *Chongqing*, which was salvaged during the early 1950s and renamed the *Beijing (Peking)*. This ship was never completely refurbished and was more of a symbol than a useful vessel.[2]

Two Chinese major ports, Dalian and Lüshun, are neighbors, and are so closely related that China formed a Port Arthur–Dalian garrison, referring to them jointly as "Luda" (short for Lüshun and Dalian). Beginning in 1969 China had the *Anshan*-class ship's boilers replaced and upgraded the combat systems at the Luda shipyard. In particular, Chinese twin 37-millimeter

AA guns replaced single mounts and Styx SSN-1 tubes replaced the midships 21-inch torpedo tubes. The 95-kilometer-range HY-2 surface-to-surface missile (SSM), designated SY-1A Seersucker[3] by the PLAN, had either an active homing radar, a passive IR homing head, or a television-equipped target seeker, depending on the exact model.[4] The Square Tie Fire Control radars fed the SSM and the Post Lamp optic director for the main battery, and Soviet IFF and Cross Bird radars were also added.

Even though greatly improved, these old ships were limited to the Bohai Gulf operation area, while the newly constructed Ludas became China's first real Pacific Ocean–capable destroyers. Two of the Gordys were decommissioned in 1985, and the final two around ten years later, although the *Jilin* is still a PLAN museum ship in Qingdao.[5]

Type 051 Luda-Class Destroyers

Following the 1960 Sino-Soviet split, the first eight indigenously built Luda keels were laid between 1967 and 1971, with nine more vessels launched since 1980. Although China does not publicize accidents, it is known that Luda hull 160 from the South Sea Fleet was destroyed by an internal explosion near Zhanjiang in March 1978.[6] From 1970 to 1974, the Luda shipyard took these units down to the main deck, replaced boilers, added some electronics, and modernized the weapons. Most significant was the replacement of the torpedo tubes with two twin CSS-N-1 Styx SSM missile launchers, including an FC radar. New electronics included a Russian Square Tie, and a Post Lamp FC radar was installed on top of the Soviet optic gun director. The initial Luda DDs carried 6 SSM launchers and 20 guns ranging from 130 millimeters to 25 millimeters, but had no jamming, chaff, or decoy launchers to counter enemy SSMs.

China's seventeen Luda-class destroyers (DD 105 and 107 were decommissioned in 2007 and DD 161 in 2008) were the PRC's primary open-ocean surface combatants until the new Luhu DDG 112/113 construction in 1993. Although surface-to-surface missiles and various mixes of radar sensors had been fitted on the vessels over the years, these 3,700-ton ships typified the anomaly of offensive ordnance lacking any combat direction system (CDS) for weapon control. Pre-1990 upgrades included a three-coordinate G-band Sea Eagle radar on DD 110, 108, and 132 and a twin 57-millimeter AA and a Rice Lamp FC radar on the latter two. A Wok Wan gun FC director radar was added on five other Ludas.

Photo 2. The Luda-class destroyer 134 alongside the pier in Dalian, undergoing antenna upgrades on the foremast. Source: Kanwa

Gaps in active/passive electronic countermeasures and antiair warfare remained serious deficiencies for a blue-water destroyer. In the 1980s China undertook two abortive attempts to add combat direction system capability and modern Western systems to its Ludas. The most ambitious foreign technology project was a December 1982 contract with the British to upgrade the combat capabilities of fourteen Luda-class DDs. The system's 100 million pound sterling ($375 million) price tag proved to be too great, however, and the PRC canceled the deal in 1983.[7] Another upgrade model for the Luda class involving the United States was proposed in 1986, but it was canceled after the Tiananmen Square boycott in 1989.[8] In 1987 China installed the Luda II upgrade to the *Jinan* (DD 105), including a helicopter deck and hangar aft, two triple cell C-801 SSMs, and possibly a new sonar. Coincidentally, the Luda III 051G upgrade to the *Zhuhai* (DD 166) occurred in 1991, the same year that the first new-generation Luhu-class DDG was commissioned. DD 165, DD 109, and DD 110 also were upgraded in 1991, and are mistakenly considered Luda III ships by many. For example, only the *Zhanjiang* (DD 165) replaced old semiautomatic 130-millimeter Russian gun mounts with new twin French Creusot-Loire fully automatic loading 100-millimeter guns. The *Kaifeng* (DD 109) installed three Type 76A 37-millimeter gun mounts, two Type 61 25-millimeter gun mounts, triple ASW torpedo tubes, and a French Crotale SAM launcher aft (DD 165 and 110 received HQ-7 Chinese copies).

Through the 1980s none of the Luda destroyers had any integrated weapon and sensor capability, and therefore no combat information center (CIC) in the bridge area. Beginning in 1990 this limitation was rectified in the Luda III class upgrade. The 1991 Luda III upgrade was a trial platform for systems that would later appear in the new gas turbine Luhu/Luhai-class guided missile destroyers. It featured a Thomson-CSF (now called Thales) Traitement Automatique et Visualisation Tactique (TAVITAC) combat direction system that made the Luda III the first Chinese vessel with a multithreat picture CDS display. The Luda III includes French communications and electronics to handle advanced weaponry, but the vessel seems lacking in means to pass data to fleet headquarters ashore using satellite communications or ultrahigh frequency (UHF) data links, although HN-900 links were added later on some Ludas. The SATCOMM was a British SHF band SNTI-240 antenna with associated terminal.

Even so, if the Luda III is intended to combat other Asian navies, it is sufficiently equipped to handle local threats and to assert Chinese territorial claims in places like the disputed South China Sea. Weak antiship and ASW capability on earlier Ludas has been improved with China's C-801 Strike Eagle missiles (similar to French Exocets) and CY-1 (a copy of the U.S. antisubmarine rocket [ASROC]) installations.

References to 051DT or 051Z upgrades or 051G on other than DD 166 are not reflected in a Russian book on the PLAN.[9] Although many Ludas have received upgrades since that time, a few still do not have a long-range (LR) search radar or a gun fire control radar. Three earlier Chinese vessel types—Chengdu, Huchuan, and Shanghai—featured enlarged bridges to house upgraded systems, but the bridge structure on Luda III appears to be unchanged. Luda-class combat systems are summarized in Table 8.

The Luda's Gun and Missile Systems

The Luda's Soviet twin 130-millimeter gun mounts remained except for two Luda III ships that were equipped with the French Creusot-Loire Compact gun and Luda IIIs' new Chinese twin 100-millimeter/56-caliber guns with automatic reloaders. Antiaircraft weapons had long been a serious limitation of ships of the Luda class equipped with old Russian twin 37-millimeter guns. In 1987 two Ludas were upgraded to water-cooled Russian 57-millimeter/70-caliber guns and modern Rice Screen three-dimensional air search radars. Luda IIIs were the first with the new Italian Breda 40-millimeter/70-caliber antiaircraft guns. China procured a French modular Crotale launcher with eight surface-to-air missiles to provide a vital antiaircraft-warfare need, which were only installed as HQ-7 on DD 166 and 109 in 1991 and DD 110 and 165 in 2002–3. The Luda III may not have had enough space to install the indigenous HQ-61 SAM twin launcher with below-deck reloads. China's elderly Silkworm surface-to-surface missiles were based on the 1970s-vintage Chinese copy of the Russian Styx P-5 as the SY-1 designated CSS-N-1. These SSMs on basic Luda models were limited by the scan seeker and the inability to fly close to the water, which made them easier to counter. Luda updates replaced this with the SY-1 Chinese version.[10]

Table 8. Luda Combat Systems

RADAR	TYPE	BAND	RANGE	DESIGNATION
Bean Sticks	LR search	P	40 km	Type 17
Square Tie	SSM target	X	73 km	Type 331
Fin Curve	Navigation	I	25 km	Type 756
Eye Shield	Air/surface search	G, H	80 km	Type 354
Rice Lamp	AA fire control	H/I	70 km	Type 347G
Sun Visor	Wok Wan director	X	72 km	Type 343
ECM	**TYPE**	**BAND**	**RANGE**	**DETAIL**
High Pole	Transponder	C	Horizon	One sensor
Square Head	Interrogator	C	Horizon	Three sensors
Jug Pair	Jammer	2–18 GHz	Horizon	RW-23-1
MISSILE	**TYPE**	**CELLS**	**RANGE**	**SPEED**
C-201 (HY-2)	Antiship	8 (2 launchers)	42 km	Mach 0.9
Yu-7	ASW torpedo	6 (2 launchers)	6 km	43 kts
GUN	**BARREL**	**ROUNDS/MINUTE**	**RANGE**	**NOTE**
130mm/58	Twin	14	27 km	Elevate 80
37 mm/60	Twin	160	9 km	Elevate 80
25mm/60	Twin	800	2.7 km	Elevate 85

The Luda's Radar and Electronic Support

The Luda has recently incorporated many Western systems into its combat suite. The Thomson-CSF Castor II and Sea Tiger radars are associated with the Vega II fire control system. The solid-state, digital Castor II tracking radar uses Doppler filtering to acquire small, low-flying air targets in a jamming environment with an associated optical tracker as an alternative mode of operation. This I/J band monopulse radar operates in either fully or semiautomatic modes.

The DBRV-15 Sea Tiger radar replaced the Eye Shield surface search radar, which was based on a thirty-year-old Soviet design. The Sea Tiger surveillance radar is capable of detecting and designating air, surface, and sea-skimming missile targets. The unit features two pulse operating modes and two types of frequency agility to allow antijamming operation. This S-band, sixty-kilowatt radar provides digital data to the Vega fire control system.

The navigation radar is either a Decca 1290 or the Chinese copy of Decca 707, called Fin Curve. The Luda's long-range early warning radars are either the Bean Sticks or the new Pea Sticks, which has a larger, four-bay, eight-dipole type of antenna. Either of these large, bedspring-shaped yagi antennas feeds the same radar display and transmitter/receiver units belowdecks.

The Luda's RW-23–1 (Jug Pair) electronic support measure domes are a Chinese variant of the Soviet Watch Dog electronic support measures provided in the 1970s. The vessel's IFF system, consisting of a High Pole-A and three Square Heads, are of the same Soviet vintage.

China has not claimed a Western electronic warfare capability for Luda III, although several U.S., British, Italian, and French electronic countermeasure systems have been marketed in Chinese naval military shows. For example, a number of Jianghu III export frigates have Elettronica ELT-838 jammer and Newton electronic countermeasure units; some of these ELT-series electronic countermeasure and electronic support measure systems could also be installed on the Luda III. Several earlier Ludas were reported to have portable chaff decoy launchers, and improved fixed decoy launchers are likely.

The Luda's Antisubmarine Warfare Capability

The basic Luda sonars were the Pegas 2M search and Tamir-2 attack sonars. The Luda III *Zhuhai* (DD 166) has a hull- or bow-mounted French medium-frequency (MF) DUBV-23 sonar, or another medium-frequency bow sonar and a DUBV-43 medium-frequency variable-depth sonar (VDS) mounted aft.[11] These were designated SJD-8/9 and ESS-1 when copied by China.[12] Antisubmarine warfare weapons on Luda III still include the old Soviet

BMB-2 aft depth charge projectors, FQF-2500 A/S forward projectors, and triple-tube antisubmarine-warfare torpedo launchers amidships. The torpedo tubes are Italian Whitehead models, with Yu-7 copies of U.S. MK 46 Mod 1 antisubmarine torpedoes that were sold to China in the 1980s.

A Chinese copy of the U.S. ASROC was on display for export at the 1986 Asiandex naval exhibit, but China never admitted it was installed on any ships.[13] A Russian source reveals that the CY-1 was operational on Luda III vessels.[14] The extended-range missile with a lightweight torpedo payload loaded in the vessel's aft surface-to-surface missile launcher was a major leap for Chinese antisubmarine weapon capability. The first photograph of a Luda in a Shanghai dry dock with a large bow sonar dome appeared in 1987.

Navigation Aids on the Luda

Little information exists on the technology of navigation equipment on Luda destroyers, but nearly all of the Ludas had copies of Soviet systems such as the NEL-series fathometers with a maximum depth scale of 500 meters (1,650 feet).

Older Soviet ship speed pitlogs included the LR-5, containing a mercury sensor with 500-volt, 50-hertz output; or the LG-4, with a bellows sensor and 300-volt, 400-hertz pulse. The Soviet 1950-vintage navigation radars were 1,600–3,200 megahertz and had a maximum range of 24 to 50 kilometers.[15] Soviet automatic course plotters from radar data, designated Briz-E, were based on U.S. DigiPlot units. Table 8 summarizes the combat systems in the basic 1971–90 Luda and does not include Luda III.

Ludas have Western Decca RM-1290 or Soviet Fin Curve navigation radars. The Fin Curve is a Type 756 navigation radar when manufactured by the 4th Shanghai Radio Factory. Type 756 has X-band and S-band slotted waveguide antennas that connect to two radar consoles via a switching unit. Eight models of Russian navigation radars use the 9,400-to-9,460 megahertz band and three have a second 3,030-to-3,090 megahertz band.[16] With the amount of Thomson-CSF equipment on the Luda III, modern, solid-state French navigation systems also are a distinct possibility.[17] As for logistical requirements, the Luda has two refuel high line stations and a king post for dry supply transfer.

Type 052 DDG 112 and 113 Luhu

In the 1990s, China launched three large guided missile destroyer programs that would range in size from 4,600 tons to more than 6,000 tons. The first of these was the Luhu class. The PRC is commissioning increasingly versatile large destroyers adaptable for multirole missions in more distant waters. These vessels are capable of antisubmarine operations or regional air defense commonly attributed to blue-water fleets, and they feature advanced indigenous and imported weapons technologies. Combat systems on the Luda III, Luhu, and Luhai classes are summarized in Table 10.

Two Luhu DDGs are based out of the North Sea Fleet headquarters at Qingdao. DDG 112 was built at Jiangnan Shipyard in 1991, and DDG 113 in Shanghai in 1993. Nearly all imported systems of Luda III are in the Luhu vessels. Naval references all list the French TAVITAC as the CDS on Luhu-class ships, but a photo taken in a Luhu combat information center (CIC) shows the Italian Selenia Elsag IPN-10 CDS console. Italy has never acknowledged exporting this complex system to China. These vessels incorporate a variety of new combat systems that include advanced Western technologies, and China imported two-thirds of the combat systems on these ships from France and Italy. The Luhu and Luhai share ships' active and passive electronic countermeasures (ECM) equipment. These are a copy of the Soviet Bell Tap warning receiver (Chinese BM-8610), the Jug Pair electronic warfare support measures (ESM) domes (Chinese RW-23), and the High Pole IFF. Chaff launchers include the Type 945PJ and a domestic 26-barrel version. The Luhu bridge and masts feature several electronic warfare radomes identified as Signaal RAPIDS and Scimitar jammers. Some domes may be Chinese RWD-8 intercept receivers that were also installed on modern frigates. Topside Luhu-class communications include two HN-900 ultrahigh-frequency (UHF)/very high frequency (VHF) data links, similar to the naval tactical data system (NTDS), on the foremast and two large SHF satellite communications (SATCOMM) radomes aft of the bridge. There are two 3.5-meter VHF whip antennas on top of the bridge and two 10-meter whips on the engineer stack. One six-wire bundle of LF/MF antennas are suspended from the main mast aft to the pedestal of the huge Hai Ying antenna and a second six-wire bundle goes forward to the stack. On top of the helicopter hanger, there are two 3-meter UHF/VHF helicopter control whips and a pair of 10-meter and 14-meter low-frequency (LF)/high-frequency (HF) whip antennas.

The Luhu features a huge air search radar that dominates its aft helicopter hanger. This domestic Hai Ying radar's capabilities can be inferred from its Chinese name, which translates to "God's Eye." The L-band radar has a two-hundred-mile range and was developed by the Marine Institute in Nanjing. The huge antenna with the robust lattice support mast seems top-heavy for the Luhu, even though it is not mounted at mast height. Topside weight or poor performance may be reasons for this radar not being used on later new-construction DDG classes.

A pair of twin-barrel, 37-millimeter antiaircraft guns each have an associated Type 347G Rice Lamp fire control radar based on an Italian Selenia RTN design. The shipboard surface-to-surface missiles and 100-millimeter guns are linked to the Type 347 fire control radar. The Russian 100-millimeter FC radar has a range of 75 kilometers.[18] The forward Crotale (Chinese HQ-7) 8-cell surface-to-air missile launcher has a 16-round missile reload box behind it and a Thomson-CSF Castor II fire control radar mounted on top of the bridge. The fire control radars have two GDG-775 electro-optic (E-O) backup directors with laser, infrared (IR), and television combination sensors. These ships utilize the same surface search (Chinese ESR-1) and navigation (Decca 1290) radars as the Luda III. Both Luhu-class vessels DDG 112 and 113 featured imported GE LM-2500 main propulsion gas turbine engines, although some references initially believed 113 had Ukrainian turbines.

Table 9. C-801 Variants According to Platform

MODEL	DESIGNATION	RANGE (KM)	PLATFORM
SY-2	CSS-N-X4	42	Luda
SY-2	FL-2	50	Jianghu
YJ-7	C-701	15	Z-8, Z-9C
YJ-8	C-801	42	Jianghu III, Han, Wuhan
YJ-81	C-801A	80	Jiangwei, Luda III, Luhu
YJ-82	C-801Q	80	Song platforms not in other entries
YJ-8K	C-801K	50	JH-7, Q-5, H-5

The C-801 Strike Eagle is very similar to the French Exocet missile with its radar homing, 165-kilogram warhead, and sea-skimmer flight profile. The variants of the C-801 SSM among platforms would be fragmented if discussed in different sections. Table 9 summarizes the C-801 variants for different platforms.[19] The Luhu ships initially had YJ-8 C-801 SSMs with a range of eighty kilometers, but during 2003 and 2004 refits were converted to improved two-hundred-kilometer-range YJ-83 C-803 missiles. The Luhu has the most impressive antisubmarine warfare suite of any PLAN warship class. In particular, its French hull-mounted DUBV-23 and VDS were a quantum improvement to the dated Soviet sonar copies on previous Luda destroyers. The *Harbin* (DDG 112) has either an American DE 1160 VDS[20] or a French DUBV-43.[21] The forward-mounted antisubmarine-warfare launchers are the ubiquitous 12-barrel FQF-2500 mortars, based on a 1960 Soviet model. Italian triple-tube antisubmarine-warfare torpedo launchers carry either Italian A-244 or Yu-7 Chinese copies of U.S. MK 46 torpedoes. The Luhu carries the venerable Z-9A, a licensed copy of the French SA-365N Dauphin helicopter.

Equipped with an advanced sonar suite and an aft helicopter hangar, the ship appears to be designed for primarily ASW operations. It represented a new level of sophistication for the PLAN.

Type 052A DDG 167 Luhai

The 6,000-ton Luhai Project 052 new-construction DDG 167 was probably built in the Dalian New Shipyard, which is a very large and modern shipyard. Besides the expected marine diesel workshops and varied repair capabilities, the new shipyard includes the Dalian Ship Design and Research Institute. China claims that Luhai is the first PLAN warship with stealth features. The hull and structures are angled to avoid direct radar paths and has radar-absorbent material, designated SM07, which is effective against the 2-to-18 gigahertz frequency band.[22] This covers the spectrum from the E-band LR air search radars to G-band surface search, and includes I-band fire control radars.

In contrast to the hull and VDS sonars and the two ASW weapons on Luhu, the larger Luhai has only hull sonars and torpedo tubes. The Luhai has a standard ASW suite because antisurface warfare (ASuW) is the main mission, as it is for most PLAN surface warships. The doubling of SSM launchers emphasizes that Luhai's primary mission is ASuW and the four-cell launchers have the newest C-803 Mach 1.6 YJ-83 missiles.

The main gun battery on these ships is a new twin 100-millimeter mount that is superior to old Soviet 130-millimeter mounts found on previous warships. The 100-millimeters are old Soviet barrels, but French quick-loading systems are in the mount. During a 2005 refit, new stealthy 100-millimeter mounts were installed and the HQ-7 SAM was updated to HQ-7A improved performance, including a hatch that opens to a below-deck reload magazine. The Chinese LY-60 surface-to-air missile could be carried in some launcher cells. These are unlicensed copies of Alenia Aspide missiles, which China bought from Italy. Each destroyer class has eight 37-millimeter antiaircraft guns, but while Luhu has them mounted fore and aft for good AA coverage, the Luhai employs both mounts aft on the helicopter hangar. The Luhai has

Table 10. Luda III, Luhu, and Luhai Combat Systems

LUDA III

RADAR	TYPE	BAND	SYSTEM	NOTE
Sea Tiger	Air/surface	S	Vega FC input	Type 363
Castor II	Gun FC	I/J	Vega FC input	Type 345
Type 345	SAM FC	I/J	HQ-7 FC	MR-35
GUN/MISSILE	BARREL	TYPE	RANGE	RELOAD
100 mm/56 gun	Twin	Dual purpose	22 km	Auto
FQF-2500	8	ASW mortar	2.5 km	Manual
CY-1	1–4	ASROC	8 km	Manual
HQ-7	8	SAM	13 km	Topside box magazine

LUHU

RADAR	TYPE	BAND	RANGE	NOTE
Hai Ying	LR search	L	360 km	Type 318
SONAR	DOME	FREQUENCY	RANGE	TYPE
DUBV-23	Bow	4.9–5.4 KHz	8–12 km	SJD-8/9
DUBV-43	VDS	4.9–5.4 KHz	20 km	ESS-1
ESR-1	Low level	S	12 km	Type 362
BM-8610	Passive/jam	2–18 GHz	Horizon	Type 862

LUHAI

RADAR	TYPE	BAND	RANGE	NOTE
Sea Gull	FC Radar	I	70 km (est.)	100 mm, SSM
Rice Screen	3-D air	G	180 km	Type 381
MISSILES	CELLS	TYPE	RANGE	NOTE
HQ-7	8	SAM	13 km	Below-deck auto reload

a flight deck and hangars for two ASW helicopters. In 1998 China bought five ASW-version and three SAR-version Ka-28 helicopters from Russia to be deployed on the Luhai vessels, and these could be backfitted to one or more of the Luhu ships as well. If true, this provides another significant upgrade to Luhu's ASW capabilities. The Luhai has a three-dimensional Rice Screen air search radar, also referred to as Sea Eagle, on top of its aft upper level that had been seen on three earlier modernized Luda II and III ships.

The new destroyers' command and control (C2) draws from several sources. Integration problems with the French TAVITAC combat control system and various French- and Russian-style equipment was probably minimized on these vessels because the architecture was previously integrated and debugged on the Luda III test bed. Chinese combat systems employ a common display console approach such as the U.S. OJ-452 or newer UYQ-70 for various systems that portends display sharing and common bus architecture. The Chinese 2JK consoles have system codes, similar to the 2KJ-8 for fire control, 2KJ-5 for sonar, and 2KJ-3 for radar, which again indicates open-architecture mission displays.

The U.S. embargo halted further LM-2500 imports, on which China had counted. An alternate source was the huge Nikolayev plant in Ukraine that provided GT-25000M main propulsion for all major Soviet warships. The combined design and production team of Mashproekt and Zarya sold four gas turbine engines to China in July 1997. Luhai was the first PLAN warship with combined diesel and gas turbine propulsion (CODOG), and two of the Ukrainian gas turbines supplemented the Shaanxi copy of 12V 1163 TB83 diesels on Luhai.[23] The Ukrainian manufacturer Mashproekt has a license agreement for GT-25000 gas turbines with Xi'an Aero-Engine Corporation and the Harbin marine boiler and turbine works, which is the second-largest marine generator plant in China. Because of its central location in Manchuria, and also because of the railway construction carried out by both Russia and Japan, it is conveniently sited just up the railroad line from Dalian Shipyard.

Both classes of vessels have two MTU 12V TB83 diesels designed by Siemens AG of Germany. Similar units have been used on new Chinese domestic and export frigates as well as modern German-built MEKO frigates and other Australian and Spanish ships. The China State Shipbuilding Corporation advertises licensed production of marine generator sets, diesels, and switchboards. Because of the shipyard's proximity to the Siemens AG office in Guangzhou, which has been working on the massive Three Gorges Dam project since the 1980s, Siemens diesels on new-construction warships are likely to be built in Chinese plants.[24] The Shaanxi diesel engine works has a license agreement for model 1163 high-speed diesel engines with MTU Friedrichshafen GmbH, Germany, to be used on Luhu, Luhai, and Luyang destroyers.[25]

The PLAN's Contemporary Technology Challenges

China's first high-technology destroyer combat system upgrades were performed on the Luda III. These were used as test platforms for the new-construction Luhu and Luhai classes ten years later.

China's SAM technology is changing quickly and several of the upgraded DDGs have the Crotale SAM system by Thomson-CSF. The system maintenance and operation needs include not only the launcher, loader, magazine, and missiles, but also associated Sea Tiger search and Castor missile guidance radars, an infrared localizer, and a television tracker. Chinese-built LN-60 missiles are unlicensed copies of Italian Aspide air-to-air missiles. The HQ-7 system designation indicates possible independence from France for the SAM systems. An Italian IPN-10 CDS, which was never openly sold to China, was observed in Luhu's CIC. Although the type of CDS and country of origin is unknown on later ships, it is probable that there is no vendor training, production rights, or logistical support.

Hull, mechanical, and engineering (HM&E) are areas of concern on large surface warships. Electrical source data for the Luda are not mentioned in reference sources, but Soviet Kotlin data would probably be similar. The Kotlin needed 1,200 kilowatts of power from two 400-kilowatt turbogenerators and two 200-kilowatt diesel generators; by comparison, the later Sovremennyy-class destroyers required 4,900 kilowatts.[26] The Luda II and III equipment upgrades were power eaters; so additional diesel and/or turbogenerators must have been added to meet the additional kilowatt needs. Because the Luhu, Luhai, and newer DDGs use marine generators built in Chinese factories in Dalian, Shenyang, or Shanghai, these should be comparatively easy to support and repair. The single Luhai DDG is based in the South Sea Fleet's headquarters in Zhanjiang, with many operational advantages for the ship and crew. It is logical to base complex new ships near their home shipyards for repair, support, parts, and expertise, as the Ludas were.

The four-month cruise in 1997 of the 230-man crew from the *Harbin* (DDG 112), the 280-man crew of the *Zhuhai* (DD 166), and the 280-man *Nancang* auxiliary oiler (AO 953), during which the ships visited Hawaii and San Diego, was a major success for the PRC. On 15 May 2002, two PLAN ships, the *Qingdao* (DDG 113) and the *Taicang*, an oiler, departed on a 33,000-mile round-the-world voyage that took them to ten countries, including the United States and Russia, and through the Panama and Suez canals.[27] Although the PLAN was established in 1949, its first foreign cruise did not take place until 1985, when the destroyer *Hefei* and the supply ship *Fencang* visited Pakistan, Sri Lanka, and Bangladesh. The PLAN training ship *Zheng He* made a port call at Pearl Harbor in 1989.

In 2004 two new 23,000-ton auxiliary oilers (AOs) were built, and the *Weishanhu* (AO 887) immediately participated in long cruises. In 2005 Luhai DDG 167 and AO 887 exercised with Pakistani and Indian navies; in July 2007 AO 887 and the 052B DDG 168 began an eighty-seven-day cruise to

Saint Petersburg, Russia, and three other NATO nations. In September 2007 DDG 112 and AO 887 cruised from the North Sea Fleet to visit Australia and New Zealand and carry out joint exercises with both countries' navies. The first PLAN naval participation in an international operation occurred in early 2009 when China sent three ships, followed by relief groups, to fight pirates off the coast of Somalia. Since 1985 the PLAN has sent thirty-three fleets with more than forty warships to more than thirty countries on five continents.

Conclusions

While the Luda I, Luda II, Luda III, Luhu, and Luhai destroyers may not be as advanced as the latest ships found in other countries, they formed a solid backbone for a rapidly modernizing Chinese navy. Even though these ships are indigenously constructed, and are evolutionary in upgrades, there are doubts if the crews can maintain, repair, and properly operate the complex systems at sea. The recent operations off Somalia are a sign of improvement.

Most important, these earlier destroyer models served as test beds for experimenting with new destroyer designs. These incrementally more complex ships must be given credit for allowing the Chinese to produce a whole new series of modern Luyang-class destroyers, which will be described in the next chapter.

—3—

New-Generation Destroyers

Chinese combat systems on the impressive imported Sovremennyy-class destroyers, which China purchased over the last decade, will be discussed first in this chapter. After examining the two new 052B DDG 168 and 169 Luyang I destroyers, this chapter will then discuss the Aegis-class Luyang II warships 052C DDG 170 and 171, and lastly the area defense 051C DDG 115 and 116 Luzhou destroyers.

The PLAN CDS are among the most important elements in these foreign purchases. After evaluating the CDS on indigenously produced warships, this chapter will discuss the pluses and minuses of China's decision to buy military equipment from abroad, versus producing it domestically.

Russian Sovremennyy-Class Destroyers

The most impressive large guided-missile destroyers (DDGs) operated by the PLAN are the four Russian Project 956 Sovremennyys, which enabled new operations and responsibilities beyond traditional coastal roles. The ships' sensors, missiles, and combat systems are of Russian origin. However, China is faced now with the challenge of operating, integrating, and maintaining these advanced systems to create a credible threat to foreign navies in Far Eastern or possibly more distant waters. Since much of China's emerging blue-water fleet still is comprised of older ships, these new and more advanced Russian ships will present fresh operational and support challenges.

In December 1996, after three years of negotiation, China signed a deal with Russia to purchase two 956E Sovremennyy destroyers. They were completed in Saint Petersburg's Severnaya Verf (Northern Shipyard), with the first ship renamed and given hull number 136 when it was turned over to a Chinese crew in Russia in February 1999. The first Chinese crew arrived at the shipyard in May 1999 for six months of training, and in January 2000 a mixed Sino-Russian crew manned the ship for its long journey from Saint

Petersburg to Dinghai, China. The second ship, renamed the *Fuzhou* (DDG 137), arrived in China during late 2000. The second ship's crew did not travel to the shipyard until October 2000, and the ship was turned over in November 2000. It transited to the PLAN East Sea Fleet in December 2000 with forty Russian crewmen and advisers aboard. This means that the second ship's crew was trained mainly in China, and not in Russia like the first crew.

However, China is still largely dependent on Russian advisers for training and operations. Maintenance and repair of foreign equipment can be particularly difficult, and China's Sovremennyys rely on Russian technicians for maintenance. China was forced to return two Russian-made Type 2D-42 diesel generators to the Elektrosila plant in Russia for repairs.

The Sovremennyys largely remain in the Russian support cocoon at the isolated port of Dinghai, on Zhoushan Island, rather than at a large city fleet base. Russia repeatedly urges China to have overhauls conducted by its Zvezdochka Factory, which has facilities and documentation for 956E and EM as well as Kilo submarines. China repeatedly refuses and is trying to establish 956 maintenance capability at Bohai Shipyard, and Russia has so far trained thirty-five technical staff.[1] Every piece of equipment was totally new to the PLAN except for the Palm Frond navigation radar, the RBU-1000 ASW launcher, the Kite Screech and FC radars, the SA-N-7 Shtil SAM, and the Ka-28 ASW helicopter. The KA-28 Helix ASW helicopter was sold to China a few years earlier and so was familiar to the Chinese, although Z-9 Chinese-produced copies of the Dauphin helicopter had served as their previous ship helicopters. The modern Kilo submarines have a similar Soviet technical support enclave at the nearby harbor of Xiangshan, while Kilo submarine crews are trained and supported there.

Both of these Russian support complexes are near the East Sea Fleet headquarters at Ningbo. Keeping certain ships and submarines isolated in Dinghai and Xiangshan could degrade fleet integration and coordinated operations. Without technical support from their Russian advisers, however, it is unclear whether the Chinese could keep these ships and submarines in good operational order.

The large multimode LF MGK-335EM bow sonar and the MG-7 high-frequency attack sonar are a whole new level of sonar technology for the PLAN. Ka-25 helos are equipped with secure data link in addition to Taifun and Burau communication HF, VHF, and UHF radios and Pritsep SATCOMM. Sovremennyys are the only PLAN ships with the new K-130 130-millimeter/70 (MR-184) dual gun mounts, but, again, Russia degraded the auto loader from 65 rounds per minute (RPM) to 35 RPM for export to China. The lead two 956E had fore and aft 130-millimeter twin gun mounts, but the two 956EMs modified to Chinese design changes had the aft 130-millimeter main battery removed. China replaced the aft 130-millimeter gun on the 956EM with two Kashtan CIWS after a shipyard fire, but that reduced gun fire support and surface-warfare rounds on target by half. Since all new PLAN-designed DDGs and frigates since the Jianghu have no aft gun, it is in line with the way China has designed all modern warships. Sovremennyy had the Russian Sapfir-U CDS for ASW and other weapon and sensor mission plotting.

The first three Sovremennyys were equipped with the 120-kilometer-range, ramjet-powered Mach 2.4 ASM Russian designation Moskit SS-N-22 (Sunburn), which is a formidable weapon. Sovremennyys had Light Bulb data links, Bell Strike video link to midlevel guidance aircraft, and Band Stand radar track data link to the SS-N-22 SSM. The first twenty-four out of a reported purchase of forty-eight 3M80E Moskit missiles were received by China by mid-2000 and were first test-launched from PLAN 956 in September 2001.[2] These are nuclear capable, but Russia claims it did not provide nuclear warheads on the missiles; however, it is possible that China might have added its own nuclear warheads. Evidently China has also reverse engineered SS-N-22 into its C-301, which have four ramjets for a speed of Mach 2.5 and a range of 130 kilometers. No Western navy has developed hypersonic ramjet SSMs because those speeds greatly decrease range, as a trade-off. The versatile Band Stand, Russian Mineral-ME with active/passive tracking radar was added to the SS-N-22 SSM on PLAN Sovremennyy-class ships purchased from Russia. The SAN-7 Shtil SAM and six Front Dome tracking radars provided increased long-range air defense capability. The 250-kilometer-range active and 450-kilometer-range passive radars were linked to the 30-kilometer-range S-band target designator/data link system.[3]

These more advanced missiles pose a new threat in any Taiwanese area naval operations, including against U.S. Navy aircraft carriers, unlike in the 1996 crisis when the PLAN did not have ships or missiles with these capabilities. Some reports indicate that both ships transited the Taiwan Strait just prior to an election in November 2000, but only the DDG 136 had been delivered by then. The second DDG may have actually been an earlier Luhu or Luhai in escort.

In January 2002 China signed a $1.4 billion contract for two more advanced Project 956 DDGs. The lead Sovremennyy of these two suffered a fire that killed one firefighter and injured another during late April 2005.[4] The ship was 70 percent finished, but the damage caused a delay in completion. With the added time, the Kashtan-M close-in weapon system (CIWS) mounts, with two 30-millimeter Gatling guns and eight SA-N-11 air defense missiles and IR detection sensor, replaced the AK-630.[5] The third Sovremennyy, number 138, was delivered in December 2005.

The fourth ship, DDG 139, replaced the SS-N-22 with the more powerful SS-N-27 Sizzler 3M54E.[6] Table 11 summarizes the new systems on 956E ships that had never been provided to the PLAN before.

Table 11. Sovremennyy New Combat Systems to PLAN

SENSORS	FUNCTION	FREQUENCY	RANGE	NOTE
Front Dome	SAM control	H & I bands	30 km	Copy on 052
Fregat-MA	3-D air search	S-band	300 km	Copy on 054A
Platina-C MG-7	Search sonar; attack sonar	1.5–10.9 KHz HF	15 km	Copy on 054A
Pritsep	SATCOMM	4–6 GHz		
Bell Strike	SSM video	1–4 GHz	100 km	
Band Stand	Track SSM data	I-band	250 km	Copy on 054A
Light Bulb	Link	I-band	200 km	
Start-2 EW	Jam/passive	X & Ku bands	26 km	Counter MPA
WEAPON	FUNCTION	ROUNDS	RANGE	NOTE
130 mm/70	Main battery	35 RPM	22 km	New 130 mm
Kashtan CIWS	30 mm (2 guns) SA-N-11 (8)	700 RPM 48 reloads	4 km 8 km	DDG 138, 139
SA-N-7 Shtil	SAM	48 reloads	30 km	
SS-N-22	SSM 3M80E	48 reloads	120 km	DDG 136, 137, 138
SS-N-27	SSM 3M10	48 reloads	200 km	DDG 139

The Band Stand over-the-horizon (OTH) detection capabilities coupled with supersonic surface-to-surface missiles (SSMs) are the greatest threat to other major navies. The arrival of additional Russian Sovremennyy guided-missile destroyers, which have supersonic SSMs and antiaircraft-warfare, antisubmarine-warfare, and electronic-warfare capabilities, have complemented Chinese efforts to build a fleet of offensive platforms to form a carrier battle group.

Russia has sold China a wide range of missiles, including the P-270 (3M80 missile) and P-100 (3M82 missile), variously called SS-N-22, Moskit, and Sunburn. There are large differences in speed and range between these SSMs, however, and it would be difficult for their adversary to know which is being carried. Destroyers and submarines could fire a barrage of antiship weapons that spot aircraft carriers or escort ships and then drop back down to run along the water's surface before accelerating to supersonic speeds for the kill. The U.S. Navy Aegis weapon system may be challenged to provide effective defense against such formidable OTH low-level supersonic antiship weapons.

Type 052B DDG 168 and 169 Luyang I

Two new type 052B DDGs, 168 and 169, completed at Jiangnan Shipyard in Shanghai in May and September 2002, are the first ships in the modern Luyang series. With the launching of three new classes of warships in a single year, DDG 168 and 169 were overlooked, especially when compared to the more flashy Type 054 FFG and Aegis-capable DDG 170 and 171. The high-profile development of the Aegis-like Luyang II destroyers denied the Luyang I vessels DDG 168 and 169 the attention that their impressive combat system "firsts" deserved, which introduced a new level of sophistication in PLAN shipbuilding programs.

Photo 3. The 052B Luyang I DDG 169 in Jiangnan Shipyard, Shanghai. DDG 169 was the first indigenous ship with the Band Stand fire control data link. Source: Kanwa

The 052B destroyers are unique, since, although several earlier Chinese warships had C-802 SSMs, the 052B DDG 168 and 169 were the first Chinese-designed and indigenously constructed ship with the OTH Band Stand SSM data link and Top Plate three-dimensional air/surface search radar. In 2001 Russia exported the first four Band Stand radar/data link systems to Jiangnan Shipyard in Shanghai for the new 052B DDGs. The large Russian Band Stand links to OTH surface to SSM with an I-band active radar of 250-kilometer range and a multiband passive radar of 450-kilometer range.[7] The Band Stand Mineral-3 can detect up to two hundred contacts and designate nine as targets for SS-N-9 or SS-N-22 SSMs. The Top Plate radar has a maximum AAW detection range of 230 kilometers and can detect antiship SSMs at a range of 50 kilometers.[8] The ZJK-5 command and control (C2) may use an Ethernet local area network (LAN) architecture and the aviation 1553B data bus, giving a new level of systems interoperability.[9] The DDG 168 shared the Luhai hull and engineering plant, but it was the first Chinese-built warship with the medium-range Russian SAM SAN-12 and associated four Front Door fire control links. The SAN-12 helped to correct for the serious lack of AAW defense on prior PLAN warships, including the Luhu and Luhai classes.

The pair of 30-millimeter 7-barrel CIWS gun systems looks like the American GAU-8/A Gatling gun Goalkeeper mounts, but the Netherlands claims it did not export this CIWS model to China, so it is more likely an indigenously produced Type 730 CIWS model. It appears that China has replaced the I-band Goalkeeper search and I/K band track antennas. The two 3-tube ASW torpedo launchers and two 12-barrel ASW rocket launchers were the ASW weapons in the Luhai class. The first 052B had CSS-N-8 C-802 YJ-81 SSMs with 120-kilometer range. The second 052B was upgraded to C-803 YJ-83 SSMs with 200-kilometer range and Mach 1.6 speed. A Luda upgrade first installed the rectangular C-802 SSM launchers in 1999, which carried over to the second 052B DDG. The 052B and 052C have two 18-barrel 122-millimeter rocket launchers on the forecastle, similar to the Russian BM-21MLRS, but designated Type 90 by PLAN.

The 052B DDGs 168 and 169 were a remarkable advance for China and the PLAN, and showed that China understood what its most serious naval limitations were and how to correct them. This almost completely overlooked DDG design nearly equals most of the imported Sovremennyy's capabilities, except for the OTH SSN-12 SSM. For example, all of the new-construction DDGs have Racal RM 1290 navigation radars.

Type 052C DDG 170 and 171 Luyang II

The PLAN also introduced two domestically designed and built Project 052C DDGs with Aegis-like phased-array panels, vertical launch systems (VLSs), long-range missiles, and considerable C2. This combination of capabilities was not on any previous Chinese-built DDGs. Luyang combat systems are summarized in Table 12.

The 6,600-ton DDG 170 and 171 were launched in April and October 2003 at Jiangnan Shipyard. They included a Type 348 four-panel phased-array radar (PAR) that looked strikingly similar to the U.S. SPY-1, a long-range ASM claimed by China to have SS-N-22 Moskit (Sunburn) capabilities, and a Chinese-designed HQ-9 VLS for surface-to-air missiles forward. Luyang II type ships should be integrated with other PLAN warships, but vital Russian support for the Russian electronics and SS-N-22 weapon systems were initially limited to Dinghai.

A comparison of Sky Watch, the first Soviet Aegis-type radar, and the U.S. Navy's Aegis is inevitable, and Soviet problems indicate it might be very difficult to get the Chinese system to work properly. In 1988 Sky Watch appeared on only two full-deck Soviet aircraft carriers.[10] Each of the four square-plate PAR antennas was about 5 meters in diameter and the frequency was estimated as F-band, about 850 megahertz. It seems the Soviets had considerable trouble on exercises with the *Gorshkov*'s phased-array radar, because it was replaced by mechanical scanning Top Sail/Top Pair radars on the next Soviet carrier, the *Tblisi*. During sea operations it evidently failed to detect and engage incoming ship or aircraft targets.

The Aegis technology was on the USS *Norton Sound* (AVM 1) in 1974 for nine years of development testing prior to the first installation on the USS *Ticonderoga* (CG 47) more than twenty-five years ago. Since 1983 more than fifty DDG 51 Aegis warships have been built. Integration with various indigenous ship guns and missiles and other sensors, as well as other ships' data management and weapons, is a challenge. Developing the software for signal processing and tracking a hundred air, surface, and submarine targets could take even longer for China. The Ukraine had provided a C-band PAR for evaluation, and in 1998 the Chinese Research Institute in Nanjing developed a prototype Type 346 PAR. The final Type 348 PAR on 052C is S-band, like Aegis, with a reported range of 450 kilometers.[11] In November 2005 four Chinese contractors were charged in Los Angeles with stealing military technology, including Aegis battle management data.[12] Even if China obtained access to foreign technology, until coordinated engagement capability matures, these two Luyang II ships may be limited to 1940s-era radar tasks of detecting and tracking air and surface targets for just their own ship's weapons, not for a truly joint battlespace.

The concept for the naval tactical data system (NTDS) was outlined in a chief of naval operations (CNO) study in 1955.[13] Three ships were the test beds for prototype NTDS in 1961 and operated together for years of

Table 12. Luyang Combat Systems

MINERAL ME (BAND STAND)	BAND	RANGE (KM)	TRACK	HULL
Active radar	I	250	30	052B/C
Passive radar	I, G, E, F, D	450	50	052B/C
Data link	I	30	20	052B/C

RADAR	BAND	RANGE (KM)		HULL
Type 348 Aegis	S	450		052C
Top Plate air search	E	230/50 ASM		052B/C
Type 364/SR-64 Seagull	H	100		052B/C
Front Dome SAN-7 FC	H/I	SAM link		052B
Type 344 (MR-34)	I	100 mm/SSM		All DDGs
EFR-1 track radar	I	8 (CIWS on 730)		052B/C
OFC-3 track	E-O, Laser	5–6 (E-O on 730)		052B/C
HN-900	Data link	UHF		052B/C

MISSILES	CELLS	RANGE (KM)	SPEED	HULL
C-802A	4	160	Turbojet	052B
C-803 (YJ-83)	4	200	Mach 1.6	052C
C-301	4 ramjets	130	Mach 2.5	052C
HQ-9 VLS	8 cells/module	100	Mach 1	052C
Type 90 rocket launcher	18 barrel	5–10	Mach 1	052B/C

100 MM/75 GUNS	ROUNDS/MINUTE	RANGE (KM)		HULL
Surface war	20	17		052B
Antiair war	90	9		052B

TYPE 730 GOALKEEPER	ROUNDS/MINUTE	RANGE (KM)		HULL
Aircraft	4,600–5,800	3		052B/C
Missile	4,600–5,800	1–2		052B/C

development trials. Link 11, also called TADIL-A, was an HF and UHF digitally encrypted data bus. Later a wide band Link 16 UHF, with ten times the speed, was added with antijam frequency-hopping features. Soviet NTDS-like integrated communication links first appeared on the Kara and Kresta II classes. The Bell Crown data link, which was replaced by the newer Bell Thumb in 1993, is called the Soviet Link 11. The Light Bulb SSM data link antenna serves the Link 16 joint tactical communication role, which would be replaced by newer AT-2M for Link 16 traffic. The USSR also incorporated the expected surface ship-to-aircraft and missile guidance data links on the Luyang I and II combat systems.

The Chinese Aegis DDGs have their own Ka-25 helicopters, which should have distant reconnaissance or targeting capabilities and possibly can even carry missiles, although the Aegis concept is to pass target data to a consort shooter that would launch its weapons. Long-range shore-based fighter aircraft, such as the People's Liberation Army Air Force (PLAAF) Su-30MKK with its M400 OTH multispectral reconnaissance pod, could pass target data back or could even be vectored to attack with its own long-range 3M80 Moskit missiles by the control ship. The early Su-27SK had an analog voice-encoding link, but the newer Su-30MKK has a TKS-22 data link. China is reportedly negotiating with Russia to equip future PLAN Su-30 MK2 aircraft to include the next-generation TSIMSS-1 digital data link.[14] To be effective, the DDG 170 would need the appropriate Sukhoi-variant link.

A key element required for an integrated Aegis capability is a shipboard LAN and common display consoles shared by sensors and a computer/control station. The U.S. Navy has had several generations of workstations on its Aegis ships. Chinese combat system architecture is less visible, and open literature sources do not directly describe it. A photograph of a working space on the Luhu showed several identical consoles being manned by technicians, and this was not seen on earlier stovepipe sensor and weapon equipment. The consoles do not look like any units seen on Soviet or French products, and they may have been designed and produced by Chinese firms. Possible vendors are the Jiangsu Automation Research Institute, which is known to make rugged naval computers and displays, or Huanwei Technology, which makes Ethernet switches, routers, and fiber-optic data links.

The 052C are reportedly the initial PLAN ships with the second-generation JY10G multimission information-processing system (IPS). It uses land, ship, and air radar inputs to integrate with other sensor sources and weapon systems. As on the U.S. Aegis ships, such systems can retain many of the original hardware cabinets, but the unique display console might be replaced with a standard shared console including open-architecture LAN access. China's choice of a LAN could be a Russian GOST standard or a Digibus LAN used on French TAVITAC CDS on board recent PLAN ships. The Chinese Beijing Readsoft Corporation copied the MIL-STD 1553, under the designation GJB289A. It was initially used on PLANAF J-10A Chinese avionics and PLA systems, and was adapted to 052C weapon equipments, which supports interoperability of forces. Display console software operating systems would likely be standard commercial versions such as Windows, or VX works that are in production in China.

The new-construction DDG 170 and 171 Aegis ships will probably have long-term software headaches, but eventually these ships will provide a new level of command and control. Of course, final marks can really only be determined in actual combat with enemy forces, so an exact assessment of the new Chinese platforms might remain elusive for some time to come. But in many respects these indigenously produced destroyers appear to compare favorably with the four imported Sovremennyy destroyers that China purchased from Russia.

Photo 4. The 052C DDG 170, with its unique Aegis-type radar array, moored at its forward base at Yalong Bay near Yulin, Hainan. Source: Kanwa

Taking full advantage of Aegis requires effective data links. China's newest frigates, updated Ludas, Luyang DDGs, and Houbei catamarans have the Chinese tactical data link system designated as HN-900.[15] The HN-900 probably includes some of the previously noted foreign data link technologies. Luyang DDGs have the Russian Light Bulb data link, right above the DDG 170 helicopter hangar, and Band Stand provides coordinated operations with Russian Navy and Chinese data links. The old Soviet 1950 vintage A-band Knife Rest early warning yagi antenna is also aft. This antenna was not on 052B or Luhu, but was on Luhai, 1990-vintage Luda upgrades, and Jiangwei frigates. A third element required for an integrated PAR capability is a shipboard LAN and common display consoles shared by sensors and computer/control stations. Soviet ships had first-generation force command consoles and subordinate individual ship warfare area consoles. These were used on large Soviet cruisers such as the Slava and Kirov classes, prior to the appearance of Sky Watch.

The usual PLAN antisubmarine-warfare suite would be Italian triple ASW torpedo tubes and 12-barrel Type 75 mortars. Most likely, a French DUBV-23 bow-mounted sonar dome is under the raked bow, which will be discussed more fully in a later chapter. The automatic 100-millimeter gun mount on the bow is evolved from the French Creusot-Loire.

The PLAN DDG 170 and 171 also feature six Chinese HQ-9 VLS launcher modules forward of the bridge and two aft by the helicopter hangar. The U.S. Navy installed its first MK 41 VLS on the *Ticonderoga*-class Aegis cruiser CG 52 in 1989. The first Russian VLS trials were with SAN-6 missiles on the fourth Kara-class cruiser in 1977. At first glance the Chinese VLS launcher looks like the Russian VLS, but there are major differences. The SAN-6 VLS systems featured round modules with eight cells each. The Chinese VLS modules each have two fewer cells than the original Soviet VLS, and the Russian VLS has only one hatch, as eight cells with blowout patches rotate under it to launch. The Chinese VLS has a hinged hatch above each cell and launches each missile with no rotation needed. China uses a cold launch, like the Russians, eliminating the complex smoke and flame ducts used on the American MK 41 VLS. However, there is no large Russian SAN-6 Top Dome FC radar near the VLS launchers as on the Soviet ships. The Aegis PAR radar could provide search capabilities, and a small antenna near the VLS could provide X-band acquisition and control links. The smaller guidance and tracking G/H band antennas are located as stand-alone links fore and aft. There are also several radomes fore and aft for SATCOMM or other non-VLS link functions. A very large radome atop the bridge mast is the SR 64 H-band long-range air search, surface search, and targeting radar.[16]

DDG 170 has six round tube-shaped SSM launchers of slightly larger diameter than earlier C-803 SSMs. This is the first ship with a long-range 160-kilometer version of the C-802A (YJ-82) or C-803 (YJ-83) supersonic

SSM, which has a range of 200 kilometers, but the air-launched range is over 250 kilometers through the use of a "subsonic high level cruise phase."[17] Both of the 052C DDGs have been based since 2006 at Yalong Bay in southern Hainan near the Yulin submarine base.[18]

Type 051C DDG 115 and 116 Luzhou

The two large, 6,000-ton air defense DDG hulls 115 and 116 were built at Dalian Shipyard in 2006. The type number of Chinese ship-class designs are sequential by hull class; thus, the 052B and C and 051 were all laid down in 2002, and the 052B and C were commissioned in 2004. The 051C Luzhou DDG 115 began PLAN service in late 2006, and hull 116, named the *Shijiazhuang*, was launched in early 2006.[19] Both are based in the North Sea Fleet, which had no Luyang DDGs, which indicates a perceived increased AAW threat from northern nations.

During the lengthy construction process, the Chinese retained an angular high radar cross section (RCS) design and a steam propulsion plant, instead of utilizing the modern CODOG found on other new DDGs. Still, the Luzhou 051C represents a notable area defense advancement with its two Russian SAN-6 VLS modules forward and four aft. China had purchased two advanced S-300-derived Russian area defense 30N6E1 phased-array Flap Lid antenna for 051C. The antenna is located just forward of the aft VLS cells, analogous to the position of the Russian Top Dome Volna on their SA-N-6 cruisers. These are the only VLS launchers and associated radar provided by Russia to the PLAN for any ship.

Chinese HN-900 and Russian Mineral ME3 data link command and communications provide the North Sea Fleet with the capability to conduct joint Chinese-Russian naval operations. Other systems on Luzhou, such as 100-millimeter-gun and Type 730 CIWS, are the same ones already installed on Luhai or Luyang vessels. The 051Cs carry only eight C-803 SSMs, compared to sixteen on all Luyang DDGs, emphasizing the AAW priority. The short one-or-two ship production runs are a trademark of the five post-Luda DD designs, which reflects either the rapid progress in China's warship building industry or shortfalls in mission capabilities with the Luyang versions, not fit for serial production. The Luzhous are based out of Lüshun and Qingdao.

Overview of PLAN CDS

China has made strides in its ability to produce an indigenous CDS. In 1985 the Naval Vessels Academy at Dalian established the Combat Software

Research Center, which had as one of its main missions developing surface ship combat system software.[20] Over the next twenty years, the serialized development builds have been installed on dozens of types of combat vessels. The PLAN claims that these software command systems have doubled combat efficiency over the manual command systems. The first PLAN weapon control system revealed in naval shows was the Type 88 digital computer, and the first known installation was on the 542-ton Houjian fast attack craft (FAC) 770 in 1991. The Type 88 was primarily buttons and toggle switch technology with four plug-in cards on the lower chassis. It interfaced with guns, radars, electro-optic sensors, the PL-9 SAM, and the electronic-warfare system. The Houjian had no sonar or ASW weapons on board. The first modern Western combat direction system installed on a PLAN warship was a French TAVITAC on the DD 105 Luda II in 1987, followed by DD 109. The Luhu-class DDG 112 and 113 had Chinese copies in 1994 (see Table 13).

The core of the Luda II upgrade was the Traitement Automatique et Visualisation Tactique (TAVITAC) combat direction system by France's Thomson-CSF. This larger-ship version of TAVITAC includes four operator consoles and a tactical action officer summary console. Each console has a planned position indicator display and a radar-synthetic generator with video compression features. Screens can be square or round and monochrome or color. Inputs are via keyboards, trackballs, and video control panels and each console can track from sixteen to thirty-two targets automatically.

TAVITAC has a federated architecture with two Cisma Sintra 15M05 computers that perform computations in a local area network (LAN) configuration. The two computers are linked together by a one-megabit/second digibus. If Chinese computers need to tie in with the French hardware, indigenous models are available with high-speed direct data channels and twisted-pair duplex long-line transmission networks that interface with Chinese ISBC-900 series bus connectors.[21]

Although France and China both employ fifty-hertz systems, the French export systems, such as Vega and Crotale, on the Luda are sixty hertz, according to specifications.[22] This would require some sixty-hertz-to-fifty-hertz conversion in the combat direction system. Although a relatively simple conversion, equipment differences like this can easily undermine system interoperability.

Tied in closely to TAVITAC is the Vega II digital fire control system, built around the Thomson-CSF digital computer with radar enhancements. Vega can track one air and two surface targets simultaneously while scanning for other contacts. The search console receives radar tracks and performs target designation. The gun fire control console has command of small antiair and 100-millimeter main battery guns, and it features two joysticks and firing lights. The long-range weapon console, which controls torpedoes and surface-to-surface C-801 missiles, employs status panels. Non-NATO data link type W usually is a part of the Vega II, but it is not certain if the Chinese installation includes this data link to shore commands.

The teaming of TAVITAC and Vega is called Thomsea by Thomson-CSF. Integral Vega systems include dual vertical consoles with a sixteen-inch display, a horizontal display console with a twenty-two-inch screen, a Castor II fire control radar, and the Sea Tiger surface search radar. The additional footprint of all of the French consoles requires a large combat information area on the Luda. TAVITAC and Vega II (including Sea Tiger and Castor II radars) add at least eleven consoles, transmitters, and receivers with an approximate footprint of seventy square feet to a new combat direction system area.[23]

Table 13. PLAN Combat Direction Systems

YEAR	CLASS	HULL	CDS DESIGNATION
1986	Jianghu III	FFG 536	JKJ-3
1987	Luda II	DDG 105	IPN-10 (Italy)
1991	Houjian	PTG 770, 771	Type 88
1991	Luda III	DDG 109	TAVITAC (French)
1994	Jianghu I	FF 165, 166	ZKJ-3 STS-1629 (British)
1998	Luhu	DDG 112, 113	IPN-10
1999	Jiangwei I	FFG 537	CSS-3
1999	Jiangwei II	FFG 537	ZKJ-3
2003	Luhai	DDG 167	ZKJ-4B TAVITAC copy
2004	Jiangkai	FFG 525	2KS4B TAVITAC copy
2005	052B	DDG 168, 169	ZJK-5
2006	052C	DDG 170, 171	H/ZBJ1.2
2006	051C	DDG 115	Sapfir-U

Most references list the French TAVITAC CDS on the Luhu-class *Harbin* (DDG 112) in 1997, but photos taken in the ship's CIC during its visit to San Diego in March of that year showed an Italian IPN-10 CDS in place.[24] Although reference books list various "ZKJ-#" CDS listings on several ships, it is uncertain if they are variations of Type 88, TAVITAC, IPN-10, or other Chinese or Russian design. One French Air-Defense.net Web page referred to the Type 54 frigate as "Ma'Anshan" and stated that the CDS designated "ZKS4B/6" is a copy of its TAVITAC system.[25] Earlier ZKJ systems should have lower series numbers, but the 1986 Jianghu system was ZKJ-4, and a Luda system later was ZKJ-2, which is unexpected. The 052C CDS is designated H/ZBJ1.2. Since the 051C has so many advanced weapons and sensors, the associated ASW CDS as on 956 EM is logical, which is designated Sapfir-U display.

Modern-DDG-Related Issues

The recent Chinese-built ships include more complex networks of sensors, fire control, weapons, and communications, as well as HM&E. These Chinese DDGs are a mix of locally designed and manufactured systems, foreign imports with production rights, illegally copied import equipment, and unauthorized "gifts" from friendly Third World nations with no local production capability at all. The latter two represent the most serious training and maintenance problems.

Unfortunately for the PLAN, some of the foreign-bought equipment is in the highest mission-critical areas. For example, many of the DDGs being built have a rapid-fire Type 730 Gatling gun close-in weapon system that looks like the Dutch Goalkeeper system, except for its radar. This key weapon, responsible for downing incoming cruise missiles, is probably lacking documentation and training because it might have been obtained illegally. Meanwhile, almost all modern Chinese-built DDGs have the French DUBV-type sonars. Since France has sold only two such systems to China, the additional systems must be produced under license in Chinese factories, so the PLAN should have in-country sources of parts and repair assistance.

The 6,600-ton Project 052C guided-missile destroyers feature Aegis-type phased-array panels, vertical launch systems, long-range missiles, and improved command and control. The smallest U.S. Navy Aegis ship is the 8,400-ton *Arleigh Burke*–class DDG 51, while the Russian Sky Watch system was only employed on two Soviet 30,000-ton aircraft carriers. China built only two 052C ships, however, and the next 051C ship had a different air defense radar. The PLAN experimental ship hull 891 has been testing a new

VLS that has rectangular hatches similar to the MK 41. This appeared on the 054A frigate in 2007 but was not on the next-generation Luzhou DDG built in Dalian.[26]

Long-range maritime patrol aircraft (MPA) variants of Tu-154 or Y8 converted An-12 are excellent reconnaissance assets with direct links to the Aegis control ship. Russian naval MPA used R-837 and R-807 for long-range communications, and the R-802 was the UHF command radio, all of which are on PLAN ships. China has limited ocean reconnaissance satellite capability but is known to intercept and utilize data from other nation's satellites, including the United States. Other non-Aegis warships can be good OTH data sources as long as they have Band Stand and the appropriate data links. They could even be shooters if targets are within their missile range. Naturally, the Sovremennyy, the Luhu, and the Luhai would be the best choice to conduct these types of missions, but frigates, Luda destroyers, or Houbei catamarans could also be configured for these tasks.

Conclusions

In recent years, China has sought to purchase superior naval platforms from Russia even while working on its own indigenous Aegis-class destroyer. To design, as China has done, the Luyang class ships with prototype Aegis radar, combat direction links, and a VLS launcher is very ambitious. However, making this technology work together is no easy matter. The fact that the USSR gave up on its Aegis system after years of frustrating problems on two of its own main warship classes shows how difficult it can be.

The addition of more Russian-made Sovremennyys, especially if they are equipped with Moskit (Sunburn), or the even more dangerous Sizzler missiles, would further complicate matters should the PRC elect to use them to support a military encounter. These ships have been the tip of the PLAN spear in naval confrontations with Japan. Meanwhile, the mere existence of indigenously made PLAN warships with long-range PAR, communications to other naval assets, and OTH SSMs complicates planning by other naval powers for a Taiwan intervention scenario or another conflict over disputed Pacific Ocean or South China Sea waters.

China's decision to equip new-construction surface ships with imported systems appears to have been accomplished smoothly and with relatively few problems. For example, to date no DDGs have been lost or have had serious accidents. They have also been based far from their shipyards and have made successful distant blue-water cruises, including the Gulf of Aden antipiracy operation.

—— 4 ——

Chinese Frigates

Chinese frigates are numerous, and older versions are being replaced increasingly by modern designs. They are an important part of China's methodical fleet modernization effort, which is producing a blue-water navy featuring some ships that are nearly the equal of Western counterparts. Not only does China have a large frigate force, but because of its especially lucrative export market for frigates, many technological advances that Chinese shipbuilding companies were able to make were first installed on the frigates rather than on destroyers. The newest frigate has both VLS and OTH sensors and weapons superior to most destroyers.

This chapter will discuss the Chengdu, Jiangnan, Jiangdong, Jianghu I–IV, Jiangwei, and new Jiangkai frigates. It will also evaluate China's robust export market for frigates. Largely due to this international trade, Chinese companies have made rapid strides, though sometimes through the illegal adoption of foreign technology, in producing their own versions of many foreign naval components, including computers, communications, and other electronics.

Through 2009 China has built more than sixty frigates, although nearly twenty have been decommissioned, and they have evolved enormously from backward 1950s' Soviet-vintage frigate types to vessels that have won export competitions against Western designs. Newer hull designs feature upgrades in electronics and weapons, with related combat capability enhancements. PLAN frigate types and status are summarized in Table 14.

Type 01 Chengdu-Class Frigates

China's first frigates were four Soviet Riga-class designs, renamed Chengdu and assembled in China from parts provided by the Soviet Union. These 300-foot vessels were designated Type 01 and had the standard Soviet fire control director, navigation, air search radar, and IFF sensors. The minimal electronic

Table 14. PLAN Frigate Types

TYPE	FRIGATE	HULLS	STATUS
01	Chengdu	507–510	Discarded 1980s
065	Jiangnan	230–234	Discarded 1980s
053K	Jiangdong	531, 532	Discarded 1990
053	Jianghu 1–5	Active 45	Discarded 15
053	Jianghu I	509–519	Discarded 4
053H	Jianghu II	Various hull numbers	Discarded 3
053HT	Jianghu III	535–537	Active
053HT(H)	Jianghu IV	544	Active
053HT	Jianghu V	558–560	Active
053H2	Jiangwei I	539–542	Active 4
053H3	Jiangwei II	543+	Active 10
054	Jiangkai	525, 526	New construction 2
054A	Jiangkai II	527–532+	Continuing new construction program

load is indicated by the electric auxiliary power plant, which provides only 450 kilowatts for the ship.[1]

Later, China obtained some Soviet HY-2 SS-N-2 Styx SSM and produced them domestically as the CSS-N-2, which were added to the Chengdu's armament. In 1972 China removed the midships torpedo tubes and added four CSS-N-2 SSMs. Table 15 summarizes combat systems on early PLAN frigate types from Jiangnan to Jianghu I.

Type 065 Jiangnan-Class Frigates

In 1965 China improved the basic Riga design, building five frigates of the Type 065 Jiangnan class in which the steam turbines were replaced by twin S.E.M.T. Pielstick 12 PA6 diesel engines. These license-produced French diesels became standard on all later Chinese frigates.

China's lack of electronics production was apparent on these frigates, which were not provided with detection or tracking radars. Sensors on board consisted of an ex-Soviet Pegas-2 sonar, navigation radar, and an optical fire control director. China added twin 5-barrel RBU-1200 antisubmarine warfare mortars forward, designated Type 86, and retained the previous BMB-2 depth charge throwers and stern racks.[2]

The Riga provided a baseline for subsequent indigenous Jiangnan frigate designs. The second generation of Chinese Jianghu Type 053 frigates featured five variants that were each 338 feet long and included the same basic hull design, along with S.E.M.T. Pielstick diesels.

Type 053K FFG 531 and 532 Jiangdong-Class Frigates

The Jiangdong hull 531 built in 1972 at Jiangnan Shipyard was a test vessel for an indigenous surface-to-air missile that was an attempt to fill the serious AAW gap in the Chinese navy. The second unit, 532, was launched in 1974. The HQ-61 missile and associated Fog Lamp fire control radar and Rice Screen three-dimensional air search radar on both ships were not certified for thirteen years, until 1985.[3]

Table 15. Early Frigate Combat Systems

JIANGNAN TYPE 065			
RADAR	PURPOSE	BAND	RANGE
Eye Shield	Air search	E/F	80 km
Twin Eye	Optical FC director	100-mm FC	Horizon
Pegas-2 sonar	ASW search	24 KHz	1.7 km
SRP-5	Direction finder	186–750 KHz	
Type 651	IFF	C-band	

JIANGDONG TYPE 053K			
RADAR	PURPOSE	BAND	RANGE
Fog Lamp	SAM FC track	H/I	70 km
RM-1290 (Racal)	Navigation	C	32 km
SAM RF-61	SAM launcher	Mach 3	10 km

JIANGHU TYPE I 053H			
NAME	SYSTEM	TYPE	RANGE
DM-3 range finder	100-mm director	3-m stereo-optic	Horizon
RBOC	Chaff/decoy	6-barrel	13 km
Type 343	AA FC radar	I-band	80 km

The complex SAM and radars required that the electric plant output be increased to 1,720 kilowatts, by adding one more 400-kilowatt generator than found in other Jianghu ships. In contrast, the U.S. 1964 FF 1052 *Knox*-class frigates had 3,000-kilowatt diesel generators for auxiliary power. The design can be considered unsuccessful, since both vessels were decommissioned around 1994.

Type 053H Jianghu-Class Frigates

The other vessel begun in 1975 was the first Jianghu 053H series of Type I and Type II vessels. All vessels in this series have four CSS-N-1 C-201 SSM launchers, IFF, a keel sonar, a Type 756 navigation radar, a Square Tie tracking radar, and an MX-902 air search radar. Type I had an optic range finder for a single-barrel 100 millimeter and Type II had a twin-barrel 100 millimeter and a Wasp Head director. All but seven ships of this class had two Type 86 ASW mortars; the others had four launchers. Only a few of these ships have Jug Pair ESM domes on the mast.

The Jianghu series of thirty-five frigates, which were built from 1975 until 1986, bridged a critical transition period for the PLAN. Naval experts differ on estimated sonar types and locations, although most say a keel mount for all 053H vessels. Correlating visible anchor and bow configurations to sonar technology provides one possible answer to this riddle. The first fourteen Jianghu frigates built at Jiangnan Shipyard had port/starboard anchor locations, which would indicate keel-mounted HF searchlight sonars. The following eleven Jianghus built at Hudong Shipyard after 1983 had one anchor

Photo 5. The Jianghu I frigate 514 in Shanghai. These mid-1970s-vintage frigates are being replaced by the more capable modern 054A-type frigates. Source: Kanwa

in the sharper-raked bow stem and the other farther aft on the port bow, which could indicate a bow sonar dome. These observations suggest that China acquired an HF or MF indigenous scanning sonar in 1983 that forced the redesigned bow on Jianghu and the Jiangwei frigates. The prior "search-light" sonars ping a one-directional sound beam, while scanning sonars have a 360-degree beam and visual display.

The Jianghu Type I and Type II also differ in gun armament. The Type I had single 100-millimeter manual-loading main batteries with an optical FC and twelve 37-millimeter antiaircraft guns. The Type II had twin-barrel 100-millimeter automatic loading mounts with Type 343 Sun Visor FC radar and carried four fewer 37-millimeter guns to help offset the extra weight.[4] Later some Type Is were updated to twin 100-millimeter guns.

In the early 1970s one Jianghu had an experimental turbine installed for a few years that evidently was a failure, because the ship was converted back to diesel, and no more frigate turbine plants have been seen. All Jianghu models had an auxiliary electric diesel output of 1,320 kilowatts. Reports that critical auxiliary systems, such as roll stabilizers, gun automatic loaders, or air-conditioning, were not normally operated, suggests that these ships needed a higher electrical power capability.[5]

The Jianghu IIIs were the first PLAN warships with air-conditioning and replaced old C-201 with more capable C-801 SSMs. Some references consider all Jianghu III and IV vessels as upgraded Jianghu I or II ships. These are Western designations made up by naval authors and are not used by the PLAN. For example, while hull 537 is definitely Type III, Jianghu hull 544 is the only Jianghu Type IV, similar to Luhai designation such as 051 or 052A. The first Chinese-built frigate with a helicopter capability was Jianghu Type IV hull 544. This Chinese frigate is based on the four-helicopter-equipped Type IIIs built for Thailand (see "Chinese Frigate Exports" later in this chapter). The helicopter hangar and flight deck required the removal of the aft 100-millimeter gun mount and a pair of HY-2 SSM launchers. The forward 100-millimeter weapon is one of two imported French Creusot-Loire compact dual-purpose automatic guns that fire ninety rounds per minute (RPM) with its associated Naja laser E-O director. The Model 17C long-range air search radar located amidships was previously used on some Luda destroyers.[6] The Thailand Jianghu Type IIIs had four German MTU-8V397 diesel generators, with 1,600 kilowatts of electric power, correcting a Jianghu problem.

Type 053H2 Jiangwei-Class Frigates

The appearance of the third-generation—or upgraded second-generation—Jiangwei, designated 053H2G by some Western analysts, with increased size and capability, shows the blue-water future for the PLAN frigates. The four vessels, hulls 539 to 542, were first launched in 1991 and the last completed sea trials in 1994. This is the first PLAN frigate with a new CDS, designated ZKJ-3C. This is probably the same CDS as the export CCS-3 mentioned in reference books, having data link architecture rather than point-to-point analog, like the Type 88. Combat direction systems on this and all later frigates are given in Table 16.

The most intriguing equipment on these Jiangwei frigates was the 6-cylinder cell launcher forward of the bridge. Initially it was estimated that the new CY-1 ASW rocket-propelled torpedo was loaded in the forward launcher cells, but in 1995 it was verified that the 6 cells contained CSAN-2 (RF-61) surface-to-air missiles.[7] Ironically it was revealed in 2007 that the CY-1 was actually being carried by these ships as well, but in the aft SSM launcher. Jiangwei 522, built in 1998, did not include the forward SAM launcher and the manned Wok Wan gun director.[8]

In 1997 an upgraded Jiangwei hull 597, which had an improved HQ-7 SAM and a stabilized Sun Visor FC director, intended for export to Pakistan was designated Jiangwei II. It was not exported, and ten were delivered to the PLAN. Four hulls are in the East Sea Fleet, and six Jiangwei variants are in the South Sea Fleet.

An upgraded version of the Jiangwei was marketed at the IDEX-93 exposition under the designation of F 22, with systems not on prior PLAN frigates. Designations of new systems in F 22 included a new Chinese CCS-3 CDS and SO7H MF bow sonar, imported NJ81–3 noise jammer and RWD-8 radar warning receiver, a Russian SR-60 air/surface surveillance radar, and Western RM-1290 helicopter guidance radar and Link V tactical data link. The weapons suite included French Crotale surface-to-air missiles, triple ASW torpedo tubes, and a Westland Lynx helicopter. These systems indicate the advanced electronic warfare and C2 capability of this class.[9]

Type 054 FFG 525 and 526 Jiangkai-Class Frigates

From September until November 2003, new Type 054 Jiangkai guided-missile frigate (FFG) design hulls 525 and 526 were launched at Shanghai and Guangzhou. The usual PLAN practice of building only a few hulls was continued when China bought only eight Swedish Kamewa screws for four

Table 16. Modern Frigate Combat Systems

JIANGHU II 053H, JIANGHU III 053HT

NAME	SYSTEM	DESCRIPTION	RANGE
Type 756	Navigation radar	X-band, S-band	50 km
Type 76 gun	37 mm (8 guns)	160 RPM	8 km
Wasp Head	Gun director	Optic range finder	Horizon

JIANGHU IV 053HT(H)

NAME	SYSTEM	DESCRIPTION	CALIBER
Type 946	Decoy launcher	15 rounds	100 mm
Zh-9	ASW helicopter	SA-361 copy	N/A

JIANGWEI 053H2

NAME	SYSTEM	BAND	RANGE
Rice Lamp	Type 347 gun FC	I-band, J-band	75 km
Naja	E-O, laser FC	J-band	30 km (fighter)
HQ-61	SAM	6 cells	10 km

JIANGKAI TYPE 054

NAME	SYSTEM	PERFORMANCE	RANGE
YJ-83	SSM	Mach 1.6	200 km
CDS 2KS4B	TAVITAC	N/A	TAVITAC copy
AK-630 CIWS	6-barrel Gatling	5,000 RPM	4–5 km
HQ-7A	SAM	8 cells	13 km

JIANGKAI TYPE 054A

NAME	SYSTEM	BAND	RANGE
Fregat M2-EM	3-D radar	E-band	250/40 km
MGK-335	MF bow sonar	1.5–10.9 KHz	15 km (956 copy)
HQ-9	Vertical launcher	32 cells	50 km
Type 730 CIWS	7-barrel Gatling	4,600–5,800 RPM	6 km

ships. The two Jiangkai FFGs are not similar in appearance to any preceding PLAN frigate series. The 054 compares favorably with the French *La Fayette* or the German/Spanish/Dutch Class 124 FFG. The radical, stealthy appearance of the Type 054 Jiangkai frigate indicates that, from a ship-design viewpoint, the Jiangkai is a continuation of a major PLAN streamlining program, initiated in the Luyang series DDGs. The ships are 20 meters longer and around 2,000 tons heavier than the Jiangweis, and the topside angles and slope would make 054's radar detection ranges shorter than earlier frigates. The Jiangkai's weapon suite, which includes the 100-millimeter forward gun, an HQ-7 copy of the Crotale SAM with Type 345 radar, the AK-630 CIWS, and ASW weapons are not new to this class (see Table 16). The general electronics are Chinese designs used on earlier frigates, except for a large cruise missile defense Sea Gull SR-64 radome aft, which is also on Aegis 052C.[10] Hull 525 had YJ-82 SS-N-8 SSMs with a range of 120 kilometers, but the second ship, 526, had the improved Mach 1.6 YJ-83 with a 200-kilometer range. The helicopter deck is large enough to handle the newest Russian Ka-28 helicopter, hinting that its main mission is ASW. The Chinese copy of the French TAVITAC CDS is designated 2KS4B.[11]

All of these modern combat systems require twice as much electric power as the previous Jianghu and Jiangwei frigates. The four Pielstick/MAN diesel generators produced by Shaanxi are rated at 750 kilowatts each, for 3,000 kilowatts total. The Chinese S.E.M.T. Pielstick 16 PAC STC diesels, built under license by Hudong Shipyard, have apparently broken down many times in lead hull 525's sea trials.[12] So, beyond the initial strikingly modern appearance, the first two Jiangkai seemed to be a work in progress, which was confirmed with the next two hulls launched in 2004.

Type 054A Jiangkai II–Class Frigates

Hulls 527 and 528, launched a year later from the same two shipyards and using the four remaining Swedish screws, reflected the greatly upgraded Jiangkai II 054A design. The upgrades included adding the VLS HQ-16 with four VLS modules that look like the U.S. Navy's MK 41 VLS. The HQ-16 has a fifty-kilometer range, compared to a thirteen-kilometer range on the 054 Crotale. The 054A also has an MR90 SAM tracking radar, a three-dimensional Top Pair radar, and a Mineral ME Band Stand over-the-horizon, targeting (OTH-T) radome above the bridge. The VLS and associated MR90 radar had been observed on the Wuhu-B experimental weapon ship 891. The Type 630 CIWS was replaced by the Type 730, based heavily on the Dutch Goalkeeper CIWS.

Photo 6. The latest 054A Jiangkai II berthed in Shanghai. Note the copies of the Russian Top Plate three-dimensional radar and the Band Stand missile-guidance data link radome. Source: Jim Bussert

Upon closer examination of photos, Russian trade officials reported that four major 054A systems were illegal Chinese copies of systems provided on the Sovremennyys.[13] The illegally copied systems included the Mineral ME tracking radar, the Fregate M2EM 3-D radar, the MR90 SAM tracking radar, and the modern MGK-335 MF hull sonar. It would seem likely that the Chinese had non-Russian assistance to reverse engineer such sophisticated systems in only four or five years. This has had a negative impact on future Russian sales of complex weapon systems to China. The 054A Jiangkai II will probably have a long production run similar to the Jianghu series, also built in two shipyards, making it one of the most important PLAN-designed warships. It has replaced Luyang DDGs in the Somalia antipiracy deployments.

Although Western frigate designs are superior in many respects to those produced by China, the Chinese shipbuilders have produced a number of capable frigates. Certainly they are adequate for most Southeast Asian nations to combat potential Asian foes. These vessels are even winning some foreign sales competitions because of the combination of good value and a low price, which offsets some shoddy workmanship. Promoting rapid design changes may explain China's policy of investing large sums to build more than forty frigates. Funding, industrial assets, skilled manpower, and long-term government support indicate that a high priority is placed on developing a respectable frigate force. The combat systems, appearance, and performance specifications of the 054A compare favorably with the French *La Fayette*–class frigates.

Table 17. PRC Modern Warship Construction Yards, 1990–2009

CITY	SHIPYARD	NEW BUILDS	PAST CONSTRUCTION
Shanghai	Hudong[a]	Jiangwei II FFG, Jiangkai FFG, Yunshu LSM, Fuchi AO, Dayun AF	Jiangwei I FFG, Jianghu III–V FF, supply, AGM
Shanghai	Zhonghua[a]	Yuting II LST, Yuting LST, Yunshu LSM, Yantai AE	Amphibious craft, Luda DD, AE,
Shanghai	Jiangnan[b]	Luyang I and II DDG, Song SS, Houbei 022	Luhu DDG, Jianghu II and IV FF
Shanghai	Qiuxin[b]	Houbei 022, Huoqiu MSO, Wosao MSO	Luhu DDG, ASW, MSO, Sichuan, AGM, Shichang AXT, Houxin PTG,
Shanghai CSSC	Changxing Island Waigaoqiao	Future very large warships; aircraft carrier probable	
Guangzhou	Huangpu	Jiangwei II FFG, 054, Fuchi AO, Houbei 022, Jiangkai II FFG	Luda DD, Haixun PB, Houjian PTG
Huludao	Bohai	093 SSN Shang, 094 SSBN Jin	Han SSN, Xia SSBN
Wuhan	Wuchang	Song SS, Yuan SS, Ming SS, Yuting II LST	Ming SS, Yuting II LST
Wuhan	Qingshan	Yushai LCU, Yunshu LSM	Wuhu-B AGE, AS, Wuhan-A
Dalian	Dalian	Luzhou, Varyag, Houbei 022, 071 LPD, Yuting II LST	Luhai DDG, Fuqing AO, Wolei ML, Luda
Qingdao	Qingdao	Yunshu LSM, Yubei LCU	ASW, amphibious craft, escorts
Wuhu	Wuhu	Yunshu LSM	Yuhai LCU

[a] The Hudong and Zhonghua shipyards merged in April 2001.
[b] The Jiangnan and Qiuxin shipyards merged in August 2000.

Because of Western imports, illegal reverse engineering, and license deals, Chinese computers and electronic systems for frigates are not as far behind as is commonly thought. The shipbuilding bureau has evolved through several major reorganizations from the Sixth Ministry of Machine Building in 1960 to the China State Shipbuilding Corporation (CSSC) in 1980. It operates a shipbuilding research center with more than a thousand engineers working just on ship-design issues. In 1998 the CSSC was split into two separate groups, one for large northern vessels and the other for small southern vessels. There are modern CSSC shipyards in five main ports, but most of the frigates are built in the Hudong and Zhonghua shipyards in Shanghai (see Table 17). In 2008 China surpassed Japan as the second-largest shipbuilding nation in the world.[14]

Chinese Frigate Exports

It is usually difficult to evaluate the quality and performance of one nation's combat system or ship designs as compared to other nations. In the case of the PLAN's new construction frigates, foreign sales provide useful insight on China's combat systems quality. There are a large number of customers for Chinese frigates, including Egypt, Bangladesh, Thailand, Pakistan, and Sri Lanka (see Table 18). Most have procured the hulls and basic systems from China, while replacing major combat systems with Western ones. China's successful frigate exports include two Jianghu Type I vessels bought by Egypt in 1984–85 and one by Bangladesh in 1989. The Egyptian ships had twin 57-millimeter/70-caliber water-cooled dual-purpose mounts in place of the 100-millimeter guns and had an enclosed fire control station aft of the SSM launchers. The bridge optical fire control also had a unique round housing.

Four Jianghu Type III ships, hull numbers 455 to 458, were bought by Thailand in 1988 and 1989. The first two had twin 100-millimeter guns mounted aft, and the second two had a helicopter flight deck aft. Although some journals state that Jianghu hulls 457 and 458 were Type II, the full O-1 level from the bridge to the stern deck shows they were Type III hulls. Squared SSM launchers that house eight new C-801 missiles instead of four old HY-2 missiles and roll-fin stabilizers were new additions that provided a more stable firing platform for the C-801 missiles. The C-801s are modern Chinese-built SSMs that appear very similar to the French Exocet, and Thailand reportedly paid $40 million for at least fifty C-801 missiles.[15] China installed a Type ZKJ-3 automated CDS, and sensor upgrades included a Rice Lamp FC radar aft and four new ESM domes. Upon arrival in Thailand, German communication and Italian ECM systems were installed. In 1999

Thailand replaced the Chinese ZKJ-3 CDS with an Elettronica Newton consortium mini COSYS (from "combat system") on two of the frigates, indicating an unsatisfactory performance by the Chinese system. The COSYS includes its own radars, computers, and gun in the package. The two 100-millimeter automatic-loading gun mounts, each dual barreled, were carried over from the Type II.

Many of the combat systems are the same on the Chinese and Thai versions, but some export differences exist. A major increase in capability is provided by the HQ-61 surface-to-air missile amidships, the U.S. SH-2 Seasprite helicopter, the improved SJD-5A MF bow sonar, and the Racal Decca 1290 ARPA navigation radar. The ECM suite was vastly upgraded with a Type 981 jammer, two MK-36 Super Rapid-Blooming Off-Board Chaff (SRBOC) launchers, and a Type 923 ESM. German MTU TB83 diesels replaced the S.E.M.T. Pielstick diesels and German radios were used, permitting standardized maintenance with other Thai ships.[16] After arrival in Thailand, improvements were made to the damage control systems, such as installing larger-diameter firemain pipes, and poor quality welding was redone. These frigates could be useful in coastal or South China Sea island disputes, but they were not at home on the open ocean because of a lack of draft and length.[17]

Table 18. PRC Naval Exports, 1985–2005

CUSTOMER	SSM BOATS	053H	033	25T	PB	PC	F22P	AOR	LCU
Bangladesh		1							3
Benin						2			
Egypt		2	4						
Iran	10								
Myanmar	6					10			
Pakistan							4[a]	1[a]	
Sri Lanka						3[a]			3
Tanzania	2								2
Thailand		4		2[a]	2[a]				
Tunisia	3								
Yemen	3								

[a]Western combat systems installed on Chinese hulls.

In 1989 slightly longer variants of the Jiangwei, the 2,590-ton Type 25T hull numbers 421 and 422, were ordered by Thailand; these were delivered in 1994 and 1995.[18] In order to get the 1989 contract to sell the new Type 25T frigates, China had to agree to include Western combat systems on their hull. This is significant, as it provides evidence that Chinese combat system technology lagged behind that of the West. The Chinese included many modern Western systems and a flight deck and hangar support for the Harbin Z-9A helicopter. U.S. weapons included a 5-inch/54 main battery, a Harpoon SSM, a Sea Sparrow SAM, and MK 32 ASW torpedo tubes that were added in Bangkok. The propulsion was combined diesel or gas turbine (CODOG) with two General Electric LM-2500 turbines and two TB83 diesels.

American combat systems upgrades included many U.S. sensors, such as the SLQ-32 EW, Raytheon SPS-64 navigation radars, and SPS-49 air search radars, MK 92 FC, and the Raytheon DE-1160C sonar. European systems installed were Signaal LW08 air search radar, STIR FC for guns and missiles, and Beta intercept and jamming from Elettronica Newton. The only PLAN systems delivered were the SJD-7 sonar, the 37-millimeter AA gun, the optical weapon director, and the decoy launcher. These ships, delivered in 1995, were rated far superior by Thailand to the prior four 053HT. Obviously Thailand or other potential customers would prefer a Western frigate over a Chinese one, but other factors exist besides the low price. For instance, Thailand can service the C-801 SSMs in-country, but Harpoons, as just one example, must be returned to the United States for maintenance. Thai naval authorities stated that the Chinese frigates were one-quarter the price of the German MEKO class and about 90 percent as effective. The Thai versions of the Jiangwei 25T look like the F 22.

Pakistan ordered four F 22 export frigates in 2005. China built and delivered the first two in 2009 and 2010. Pakistan delivered its first home-built unit in 2010, and a second is due in 2013. These are upgraded Jiangwei-class vessels, and Pakistan is also insisting on many Western combat systems. Pakistan had installed American navigation radars, the MK 36 SRBOC launcher, and the 20-millimeter Phalanx CIWS on a Fuqing-class replenishment ship built in Dalian Shipyard.

In 1994 Myanmar also purchased two modified Jianghu frigates. Two 1,300-ton patrol vessels delivered from Qiuxin Shipyard in 2005 were equipped with Western guns and search and FC radars, along with the COSYS combat direction system, but with Russian propulsion.

The Chinese military electronics industry has developed a variety of indigenous designs to meet most Third World frigate coastal warfare needs. Blue-water or extended cruises required systems beyond China's domestic production. Emphasis on selected weapons or sensors left gaps in common HM&E needs such as firefighting, adequate power sources, and even basic crew comforts such as laundry facilities. The new 054A frigates show improvement, but hard lessons are still being learned in the extended three-month Somali deployments.

Conclusions

By combining an inexpensive Chinese hull with modern Western systems, developing nations can obtain an economical modern frigate. Despite the Western arms embargo imposed since the Tiananmen Square boycott, many European systems are being bought, and probably more Russian hardware lies in the future for Chinese frigates. China's reverse engineering of the newest Russian technology on the Jiangkai II FFGs may possibly threaten these future Russian imports to China.

Without a doubt, the increased availability of many complex French naval weapons and electronics, as well as other Western systems, greatly improved the capabilities of several classes of Chinese export frigates over the past decade. As noted in the previous chapter, this method of mixing Chinese and foreign technology has aided China in producing a number of new-generation destroyers and frigates.

For surface ships, however, the demands placed upon them during peacetime are much less rigorous than in battle. By contrast, for submerged submarines the challenges during peace and war are more nearly the same. As chapter 5 will show, the same high success and safety rate for China's surface ships may soon be achieved within the PLAN submarine force.

———5———

PLAN Submarines

P
LAN submarines have transformed from the old Soviet imports to quiet, high-technology, and respectable indigenously designed diesel submarines (SSs) and modern nuclear-powered submarines (SSNs). A dramatic increase in Chinese diesel boat technology negates the comfortable stereotype of noisy old Soviet-style submarine copies clanking around China's coast. China's Han nuclear-powered attack submarines were noisy, but the new Yuan diesel SS, Shang SSN, and Jin SSBN are quieter. Russian Kilo boats equipped with the Club-S antiship and antisubmarine missiles must be respected in light of their capabilities and operational tactics.[1]

The first PLAN submarine base construction began at Qingdao in 1952, and until 1970 Chinese submarines were located mainly in the North Sea Fleet and East Sea Fleet. By the late 1980s the eighty-five submarines of the Romeo (Type 033) class were equally distributed among all three fleets. China has operated forty to fifty submarines for more than thirty years, but these vessels were not a viable factor in Far Eastern naval affairs until recently. This changed when a Han attack submarine was engaged by aircraft from the aircraft carrier USS *Kitty Hawk* in the Yellow Sea on 27–29 October 1994, again in November 2004 when a Han SSN transited through Japanese-claimed waters south of Okinawa, and most recently on 26 October 2006 when a Song-class submarine approached within a few miles of the *Kitty Hawk* undetected.

A reliance on purchases of older vessels has been supplemented by the indigenous production of modern diesel-electric submarines along with recent acquisitions of ten new Kilo-class Russian boats. The same shift that we have observed previously with regard to destroyers toward advanced domestic manufacture is also evident for Chinese nuclear attack and ballistic-missile submarines. The new boats give China's submarine fleet an extended reach and increased tactical capabilities. This chapter will examine the transition from diesel Whiskeys to Kilos, and the new indigenous SSN and SSBN (see Table 19). Finally, it will conclude by talking about support for submarines, including Chinese submarine bases, and also current technology challenges.

Table 19. PLAN Submarine Types

TYPE	CLASS	PROPULSION	ACTIVE
03	Whiskey	SS	None
031	Golf	SSB	Reserve
033	Romeo	SS	6
035	Ming	SS	17
039	Song	SS/SSG	14
041	Yuan	SS	2
091	Han	SSN	3
092	Xia	SSBN	1
877/636	Kilo	SS	12
093	Shang	SSN	3
094	Jin	SSBN	2

Early Soviet Submarines

The history of PLAN submarines begins with several old World War II submarines provided by the USSR in 1955. Four S-class submarines (S 51–53 and S 57) were given to China in 1955, although other references differ.[2] The S class was 1,070 tons submerged, with one 100-millimeter gun forward and one 45 millimeter aft, and had China's first submarine sonar, the Mars-12 passive sonar. The Okun, Schchuka, and Ryejd radio transmitters and Dozor and Myetel receivers from the Soviet Union would also appear on later PLAN submarines. The S-class submarines had six 533-millimeter torpedo tubes and six reloads apiece. Two sixty-two-cell type 46U batteries allowed seventy-two hours maximum submerged time. Although various authorities state that four M-class submarines were given to China, only hull number M 29 could be confirmed.[3] The M-class submarines were much smaller than the S class, at 353 tons submerged, and had only two torpedo tubes with no reloads, no sonar, and only rudimentary communications. Until China's first postwar Whiskey submarines came off the production lines, these M and

S submarines were the only boats available for training future officers and crews at the Submarine Academy at Qingdao.

Russia provided documentation for Type 03 Whiskey submarines in 1954 and five built submarines in 1956–57, but only provided documentation for the Type 033 Romeo class.[4] From 1950 to 1975 the Chinese assimilated the simplistic Soviet Whiskey- and Romeo-class designs and produced more than a hundred submarines at numerous northern, eastern, and southern shipyards, as well as third-tier inland locations. Naturally these yards had the ability to perform all levels of repair, but most support came from facilities near the home ports. Twenty years ago Chuandong Shipyard in Fuling built Type 033 submarines. Wuchang Shipyard in Wuhan built three Song-class (Type 039) antiship-missile diesel submarines. Chinese diesel and battery plants produced the basic HM&E systems. The Soviet Type 37-D 4000 high-power (HP) diesels were manufactured in China and designated as MTU-12V 493 diesels. The Soviet 46SU lead-acid battery cells were upgrades from the 46S batteries on the S class. Type 03 and later submarines used 224 cells rated at a 6,600-ampere-hour charge, permitting the Whiskey to stay submerged for as long as two hundred hours.

In January 1959 the Soviet Council of Ministers ordered that documentation on a Golf SSB and an R-11FM naval Scud missile be provided to China. A Golf, without missiles, was towed from Komsomolsk Shipyard to Dalian in 1959. After the Soviet specialists were called home in August 1960, China finally completed the Golf on its own around 1966.[5]

The early Golf I model had a D2 launch system that could only compute launch location at an exact latitude-longitude position. The USSR withheld the Sark SS-N-4 missiles that were on Soviet Golf-class SSBs. Norman Polmar argues that no 350-mile-range "Serb" R-11FM ballistic missiles were provided by the USSR,[6] while Kenneth Sewell claims that seven R-11s were provided in 1959 or 1960.[7] It should be observed again that China frequently obtains what it needs without necessarily going through legal channels. This platform was never an operational fleet SSB, but was used for test launches of new Chinese missiles for future SSBNs.

China's first semi-indigenous submarine was a direct adaptation of a late-1950s Russian design. About eighty-six of the Soviet Romeo-class submarines, named Wuhan by Western analysts for the shipyard at which they first were observed, were produced in China between 1960 and 1984. The nomenclature for these submarines can be confusing, with the Chinese designations ES3B and Type 031 also applicable to this series.

Combat systems such as radar, sonar, and navigation were mass-produced from Soviet examples and drawings, or they were reverse engineered as needed. When Soviet aid and advisers were withdrawn from China in 1960, the PLAN had to be self-sufficient to maintain production and support of the 1950s-era submarines and internal equipment. The sighting of a Type 031 class in the 1974 Paracel Islands conflict with Vietnam was one of the few out-of-area submarine operations observed.[8] The state of PLAN submarine systems prior to the purchase of Kilos is summarized in Table 20.

Table 20. PLAN Submarine Systems, 1955–95

DESIGNATION	SYSTEM	DETAIL	SUB CLASS
Type 921A	ESM	2–18 GHz	033 Romeo
Khrom	IFF	C-band	All
Fakyel	IFF	C-band	03 Whiskey
L-4/2	Torpedo FCS	Analog	03 Whiskey
UPM-E	Torpedo gyro	Preset course	033 Romeo
Leningrad	Torpedo FCS	Electromechanical	033 Romeo
Murena	Torpedo panel	Preset/fire torpedoes	039 Song
RPN-47-03	Radio navigation	C-band	03 Whiskey
ARP-53	Radio direction finder	186–750 KHz; electromechanical	033 Romeo
Snoop Plate	Navigation radar	X-band, 22-km range	All
Kurs-5	Gyrocompass	Two liquid gyroscopes	033 Romeo
PZN-10	Turn machine	Calculate turn	033 Romeo
AP-2	Auto trail navigation	Project course on map	033 Romeo
Andoga	Integrated navigation	Digital	039 Song
R-670	Radio receiver	HF	033 Romeo
R-641	Radio transmitter	HF	033 Romeo
R-672	Radio receiver	LF	033 Romeo
R-673	Radio receiver	LF–VHF	033 Romeo
R-609	Transmitter/receiver	VHF	033 Romeo
R-680	HF/VHF receiver	1.5–60 MHz	039 Song

Type 035 Ming-Class Submarines

Several Western nations offered to sell China modern equipment for its anti-quated submarine hulls during the period from 1975 to 1995, when China decided to design and produce modern diesel submarines. In 1975 two improved Romeos, Type 035, called Ming in the West, were launched from Wuchang Shipyard in Wuhan. This ES5E hull was slightly larger in diameter, and a different propulsion plant was installed. A third variant followed in 1982, and although it was marketed for export, no buyers appeared, and no more export vessels were produced.

The Ming class was based on the traditional Romeo hull design, and the first two, hulls 341 and 342, were launched in 1975. In 1979 boat 341 was scrapped after a serious fire. China may have undertaken some redesign on this model because hull 343 was not launched until 1982. There were other periods when production of Mings stopped for several years, but eventually nineteen in total were built. The next hull was four meters longer, causing rumors of air independent propulsion (AIP) testing.[9]

Although China is secretive about military problems, submarine hull 418 is thought to have sunk in December 1959 with the loss of thirty-nine sailors, and a Type 033 boat was lost in an accident around 1993. The most publicized incident took place during April 2003 in the Yellow Sea, when design problems might have led to the loss of a Ming submarine. On 2 May 2003 the PLAN admitted that an entire crew of seventy sailors was killed by accident on hull 361. The typical crew of that type of boat is fifty-six, so there apparently were fourteen extra people on board for its mission. Photographs of the doomed Ming 361 taken in Shanghai during 1995 show that it had flank array sonar panels, which indicate that it was an upgraded submarine that received a French TR-2225 passive tracking system.

After the fatal accident, the submarine was towed to port. The PLAN has been concerned about the capability to raise a submarine from the ocean bottom. In 2000 and 2001 China sent representatives to submarine rescue conferences and international submarine rescue exercises. The PLAN held meetings with Canadian and British deep-submergence rescue vehicle (DSRV) companies, but no actual sales were announced.[10] This suggests that 361 probably suffered its accident on the surface. No information about what happened was released, but the most likely scenario was that seawater seeped into the batteries, creating a toxic environment that possibly killed the entire crew while the craft was on the surface. The 361 was later reactivated.

On 13 June 2003 it was announced that two North Sea Fleet vice admirals (fleet commander Ding Yiping and political commissar Chen Xianfeng) were replaced and six other officers were demoted for the submarine's loss, and improper "command and control" was stated as the reason. This raises the possibility that a weapon launched from another platform, either during tests or in the midst of an exercise, might have accidentally hit 361. Of course, this is pure speculation, and until China releases more data the causes of this accident will probably remain obscure.

Type 039 Song-Class Submarines

Several Chinese submarines were copies of Whiskey or Romeo Soviet-designed diesel submarines, but the first truly indigenous diesel submarine design was launched from Wuchang Shipyard in August 1994. This new Type 039 Song class is modern in appearance with a seven-blade propeller, streamlined hull, and stepped sail. These all indicate an attempt at modern high performance and quieting features, although later versions would remove the stepped sail to decrease turbulence.

The cost to produce modern diesel submarines was so high that a special Chinese budget request was submitted in 1993, but only a quarter of the requested amount was funded. The first hull of the Song class started sea trials in 1995, but the integration of Chinese, Russian, and imported systems such as the French TSM 2225 sonar and the German diesel engine is blamed for serious system design and operational problems on the lead boat, and there were reports of high noise levels while operating.[11]

It was several years before a much-redesigned second Song submarine, the 039A type, was launched. The step front of the sail was replaced with a streamlined, more rectangular sail with fairings into the hull, which had undergone major modifications as well.[12] The usual rectangular water intake vent holes were replaced with a continuous bow-to-stern streamlined cover over the vents, similar to the intake vent design on the Han SSN.[13]

This was the quietest Chinese-designed submarine, and it launched several types of missiles while submerged. For example, tests of the submarine-launched Strike Eagle Number 8 Model 3 (CY-1) antisubmarine missile were held in the East China Sea area on a Song during 1997.[14] This Chinese effort to obtain a submarine ASW rocket capability would be unnecessary after future 636 Kilo deliveries included the Russian Club-S submarine ASW rocket. The antisurface-ship YJ-1 missiles, which launch through the torpedo tubes, were probably replaced by longer-range YJ-2 missiles.

Type 041 Yuan-Class Submarines

Internet photos of two Yuan submarines, called the Type 041 class, were unexpected when these boats were launched in December 2004 from Wuchang Shipyard. Considering the long development time for new PLAN submarines of two to five years, it is probable that considerable Russian assistance was being provided. The Yuan is expected to be a hunter-killer submarine and is reportedly the first PLAN submarine to have an experimental AIP system installed.[15] If so, this could greatly increase its range and underwater operability. Propulsion is by German MTU-16V-396 diesels manufactured under license by the Shaanxi diesel factory.

The single skewed seven-blade screw was first used by China on the Song 039 class, and may be a Russian or Swedish import. In addition, the rectangular sail shape with diving fins and hump on the top of the hull aft of the bow sonar array is similar to the newest Russian Lada submarine. The unique hump on the Russian export model Lada, and on Russian navy type 1695, are not on any other country's hull shape except the Yuan.

Other obvious differences are the stern rudder and flood hole intakes configuration. A review of its dimensions show the Lada has a compact 60-meter length, whereas the Yuan has the typical PLAN 72-meter length. Both submarines have six 533-millimeter torpedo tubes, and Russian references state that the Shkval is 533 millimeters in diameter, has a range of 15–20 kilometers, and has a speed of 195 knots.[16] This means that stories that appeared in 2001 that Shkval was 650 millimeters in diameter are incorrect.[17]

First-Generation Nuclear Submarines: Type 091 Han and Type 092 Xia

Since Soviet advisers departed China in 1960, the Chinese have had to design new nuclear propulsion technology by themselves, copying the teardrop-shape single-screw Albacore hull. The hull for the first Han nuclear attack submarine was laid in 1968 and launched in December 1970 at Bohai Shipyard, located in Huludao. The nuclear reactor was activated in July 1971, but this lead boat took seven years to complete, not becoming operational until 1974. This hull number, 401, seemed to have experienced technical problems, which likely led to such a long work-up. Some references did not include hull 401 as an operational submarine prior to its decommissioning in 2003.[18]

The keel for the second Han, hull 402, was laid in 1975 and became operational in 1980. An inadequate nuclear cooling plant required dry-docking for system modifications, with technical assistance provided by West German engineers in the 1980s. Hulls 403, 404, and 405 were lengthened 8 meters, but Western analysts doubted China's declaration that the additional space aft was to allow the stowing of YJ-1 or YJ-2 antiship-missile launch tubes. Later, this was discounted because the missiles could be launched from the torpedo tubes.[19]

Han nuclear attack submarines feature modern French Thomson-Sintra DUUX-5 passive sonars that can track three targets with a twenty-minute B-scan history display. Despite all of the naval activity in China's East Sea Fleet and the submarine flotilla in the South Sea Fleet, three remaining Hans seem to be based in the North Sea Fleet. This placement likely countered the previous Soviet naval threat, and also made use of the deeper operating waters in the north.[20] This would change when China built an underground nuclear submarine shelter near Yulin on Hainan Island around 2005.

The Han design was lengthened and made into the Xia SSBN. The Xia, which looks very much like the USS *George Washington* or a Russian Yankee-class boat, was completed in 1981 after twenty-five years of design and development. It carried twelve JL-1 SLBMs, called CSS-N-3 by Western analysts, which Xia launched successfully in 1988. The single-stage solid-fuel missile resembles a Polaris A-I, and is credited with a range of between 2,700 and 3,600 kilometers (1,700–2,250 miles).[21]

Second-Generation Nuclear Submarines: Type 093 Shang and Type 094 Jin

The second-generation SSN Project 093 and a new SSBN Project 094 were both built at Bohai Shipyard in Huludao. Numerous reports of Russian help persist, but the Russians deny direct involvement.[22] The project Shang appears to be similar to the Soviet Victor III submarine class, which had many advanced systems combined with quiet noise levels and high-speed performance.[23] It has 533-millimeter torpedo tubes with the capability to launch antiship and land-attack cruise missiles. The HN-1 and HN-2, with ranges of 600 kilometers and 1,800 kilometers, respectively, were operational in 1999–2001, and a new HN-3, similar to the U.S. Navy Tomahawk, with an estimated range from 1,200 to 1,800 kilometers, became operational in 2002.

The project 094 features twelve long-range (8,000 kilometers) JL-2 (CSS-N-4) SLBMs that have completed testing. The Second Artillery Corps, which is the primary PLA nuclear missile service, during June 2005 reportedly fired a JL-2 missile from a submarine, estimated to have a range of up to 8,000 kilometers, which is sufficient to hit targets in the United States; the JL-2 is a submarine version of the DF-31 land-based missile and has Global Positioning System (GPS) guidance.[24]

Meanwhile, sea testing of a more capable multiple independently targeted reentry vehicle (MIRV) payload submarine-launched ballistic missile, called the CSS-NX-4, used on the 094 SSBN, proceeded at a steady pace. No additional nuclear ballistic-missile submarines were built, although Western naval experts had predicted a total of three to twelve nuclear ballistic-missile submarines, with 16 tubes on the Xia follow-ons. However, initial work on the installation of C-801 antiship missiles began around 1981 on a Type 033 hull. Six ship-to-ship missile tubes installed aft of the sail were elevated to fire. This design, called Project E5SG, was not repeated and probably was a beta test for improved Han nuclear attack submarines with ship-to-ship missile capability. Belarus has reportedly sold a sonar communication system to China for 094 that was used on Soviet SSBNs. The navigation and fire control computers were mechanical-analog with synchro dials and range counters, again based on early Soviet designs.

Type 877 and Type 636 Kilo-Class Submarines

A factor not included in the published PLAN annual budget is the cost to procure foreign weapons. During the 1980s Kilo submarines cost $240 million each.[25] In 1993 China ordered four Kilo submarines. The first two Russian Kilos ordered—the earlier exported version, 877EKM, dating back to 1985—were delivered in 1995. Nearly all of its systems from HM&E up to combat were generations ahead of what was on all previous PLAN submarines. For example, Russian naval radio-electronic equipment after 1975 included Carat digital computers developed in Kiev. The sonar and fire control advanced from analog vacuum tube technology to the use of 100,000-operations-per-second digital computers. China obtained Russian TEST 96 wake-homing and TEST 71 wire-guided torpedoes with the Kilos that were ten to thirty years newer than their Yu versions.

The second two Kilos ordered were the much improved and lengthened Project 636 model; these were delivered beginning in 1998. The increased length allows for more freshwater and compressed air tanks than in the original 877EKM Kilos. The new submarines have improved propellers that run more quietly with a two-knot increase in submerged speed. The 636 Club-S antiship missile (ASM) and submarine ASW rocket and an increased snorkel range of 1,500 miles make it far more lethal than the 877EKM was.[26] Meanwhile, the troublesome 1,000 kilowatt Type 2D-42 diesel generators were replaced by more complex turbocharged Type 4–2AA-42M diesel generators from Elektrosila rated at 1,500 kilowatts each.

The Uzel fire control system tracks two targets automatically or three contacts manually for engagement, and the MGK-400 EM sonar is an active/passive system that performs all functions digitally, including beam formation. The 30-degree active sector mode detects submarines at twelve kilometers, and the passive array, with double the array elements of the MGK-400, can detect surface ships at twenty kilometers. The intercept array detects from one to sixty kilohertz, and it can automatically track four contacts and attack two simultaneously.[27] Equipment includes a newer Russian MVU.110Z combat information control system, a new Appasiouata EMK-1 navigation system, an MGK-400 sonar, and an MG-519 mine-hunting sonar. These two newer Chinese submarines were built at Komsomolsk na Amur, in the Russian Far East, which would make future repairs more convenient, if needed.

Instead of the eighteen months of training for 636 submarines that Iran and India had obtained, China restricted training to only nine months. Only the officers for the two 636 crews were trained in Saint Petersburg in 1997, and the enlisted men were trained at the home port in Xiangshan.[28] The Chinese are blamed for longevity issues involving the Russian T446 batteries installed on some Kilo submarines, but other customers such as Iran and India have had similar problems. Increased reliability was achieved by replacing the Russian batteries with ones made in India and Britain. New Russian T476 batteries recently installed in the next-generation 636 Kilos are expected to last five years, which is closer to Western standards.[29]

In January 2003 a $1.5 billion contract was signed for the Russian delivery of eight more new 636 type Kilo submarines; the eighth was received in early 2006. They were built in shipyards in Saint Petersburg, Severodinsk, and Nizhniy Novgorod. The first four Kilos did not include the 3M54E1 tube-launched antiship cruise missile (ASCM) with the SS-N-27B Club-S weapon system. Chinese negotiations to have the first four Kilos upgraded to 3M 54E ASM failed in December 2009 because the two parties could not agree on where the upgrade would be made—in Russia or in China.[30] The SS-N-27B Sizzler ASCM can be "launched while submerged and travels over 100 nautical miles to make a very low-altitude, evasive, supersonic attack intended to defeat the U.S. Aegis defense system."[31]

Russia has stated that the 636 Kilo Club has a range of 300 kilometers (188 miles) and a speed of Mach 0.6 to 0.8.[32]

China's Submarine Support

Several types of support vessels have been built for a submarine fleet that numbered around a hundred vessels for decades and now has about fifty to

sixty. The most capable of these are the three Dajiang-class 10,000-ton submarine support ships, built between 1978 and 1980 by Hudong Shipyard.
Prominent features include two huge cranes and two 35-ton DSRV embarked.
The Chinese DSRV can rescue twenty-two crewmen from a claimed depth of
six hundred meters, and it became operational in 1989.[33] In addition to the
two submarine rescue submersibles forward, this ship features a hangar and a
helicopter deck for two Zhi-8s aft.

The DSRVs in the Chinese fleet include the French-built SM-358, or copies of it. The 5,800-ton Dazhi, 5,000-ton Hudong, 4,000-ton Dalang, and
2,800-ton Dadong classes are other heavy-crane-equipped submarine support
vessels. In addition there are a few smaller 1,100-ton Dazhou-class vessels
and a former T-43 minesweeper with a "J" bow identifier for submarine support without heavy cranes.

Submarine command, control, and communications (C3) relies heavily on
seven verylow frequency (VLF) stations located at Changde, Datong, Fuzhou,
Lüshun, Ningbo, Yaxian, and Zhanjiang.[34] All Chinese submarines have at
least one HF whip antenna for normal traffic. The North Sea Fleet and East
Sea Fleet headquarters at Qingdao and Ningbo have links to the submarines.
The 1st Submarine Flotilla is based at Qingdao, home port of the Han SSNs.
The South Sea Fleet headquarters is colocated with the VLF site at Zhanjiang,
and the fleet's two submarine flotillas are based on southern Hainan Island.
Recent Internet sources indicate that the 2nd Nuclear Submarine Flotilla is
now based in the South Sea Fleet, with two 093 SSNs openly berthed at piers
in Yalong Bay in September 2010.[35]

There is a lengthy history of Chinese confrontations and conflict in the
South China Sea (SCS), including the seizure of the Paracel Islands from
South Vietnam in 1974, the construction of an airstrip and base on Woody
Island in 1978, combat against Vietnam at Johnson South Reef in 1988, and
the 1995 occupation of Mischief Reef. China has constructed harbor facilities at Gwadar in western Pakistan and upgraded Myanmar port facilities
on Hainggyi and Sittwe in 1994. The PLAN naval warship bases at these
locations, which naval writers have called the "string of pearls," were established for sea line of communication (SLOC) support and other Indian Ocean
operations.[36] They also would serve to link the PRC with Saudi Arabia, its
most important source of oil in the Middle East.[37] In fact the only two current PLAN external naval bases to support submarines or ships is tiny Woody
Island in the South China Sea and the Myanmar port facilities.

To operate submarines effectively, personnel must understand the ocean
bottom and acoustics. China has many ships dedicated to oceanographic
research with special complex equipment. Much of this gear, such as side-scan

sonars, has been provided by Western vendors. The ten large Xiang Yang Hong–series ocean research ships vary in size from 15,000 tons down to 1,000 tons. Ten other oceanographic research vessels run about 3,000 tons each, and many other smaller vessels are equipped for ocean surveys.

Maritime research ships have been important for testing China's latest missiles. During 1976–77 several 10,000-ton PRC research ships cruised into the South Pacific conducting communications tests, and in 1984–85 the Xiang Yang Hong 10 and J-121 visited Antarctica. The command ship *Yuan Wang* had many modern antennas and domes, possibly obtained during the two-year CIA-China joint operation that monitored Soviet missiles in western China. The PRC sent eighteen ships, including six guided-missile destroyers and at least two large "space event ships," plus two refueling vessels, to sea to support the 12 May–10 June 1980 CSSX-4 ICBM tests. The missile target area was over 4,200 miles south of the China coast.

Several very large universities and research laboratories support oceanographic and acoustic theory, modeling, and at-sea observations. One of the largest is the South China Sea Institute of Oceanography, located in Guangzhou, which designs sea instrumentation. Shandong University, which awards higher oceanography degrees, also provides support for this effort.

The PLAN's submarine force's shore support infrastructure has evolved greatly from one dedicated to just supporting the early generation ex-Soviet diesel boats. China now has submarine designs that receive limited assistance from imported technology, and its next-generation nuclear submarines are encountering greater support problems. A new base at Xiangshan for Kilos and the basing of sophisticated Sovremennyy guided-missile destroyers at nearby Dinghai make this area a central complex for Russian advisers to conduct training and maintenance of advanced Russian systems.

China has a wide range of indigenously produced torpedoes, based on either Soviet or U.S. models (see Table 21). The torpedoes initially deployed on all Chinese-built submarines were the straight-running Yu-1 (Yu means "fish"), which were based on the old Russian 53–51 straight-running torpedoes provided with the original Soviet submarines sold to China. The first number in the Russian designation is the diameter in centimeters; the second number is the year of design. Soviet RAT-52 air-dropped rocket torpedoes were provided to China in the 1950s, but Russia discontinued their use in the 1960s due to their inaccuracy. The PLAN may retain the Yu-2 on Il-26 naval bombers.[38] The Chinese-built Yu-3 electric homing torpedo is a copy of the Soviet SET-65, which was operational around 1967, and the Yu-4 electric passive was based upon the SAET-60 Soviet torpedoes, operational in the same time frame.[39] In 1996 Russia provided advanced TEST-71 and TEST-96

Table 21. Chinese-Manufactured USSR/U.S. Torpedoes

DESIGNATION	SOURCE	TYPE	RANGE	SPEED	PLATFORM
Yu-1	53–51 antiship (USSR)	Straight	9 km	39 kts	PC/sub
Yu-2	RAT-52 antiship (USSR)	Gyro	A/C height	58 kts	Air
Yu-3	SET-65 ASW (USSR)	Pattern/homing	15 km	40 kts	Sub
Yu-4	SAET-60 antiship (USSR)	Active/passive	13 km	42 kts	Sub
Yu-5	Antiship (USSR)	Wake home	18 km	45 kts	Sub
Yu-6	MK 48 (U.S.)	Wire guide	26 km	55 kts	Sub
Yu-7	MK 46 Mod 1 (U.S.)	Active/passive	6 km	43 kts	Air/surf

wire-guided electric torpedoes and 53–65KE wake-homing antisurface-ship torpedoes, but five years later they had not yet been test-fired.[40] The last two Yu torpedoes are copies of the American MK 46 and MK 48 models, and the Chinese technicians had difficulty converting American measurements into the metric system so they could use their tools.

China frequently includes technology transfer and future production licensing in such deals. Even if these arrangements were not made, China's record of copying unlicensed hardware or software is well known. For example, in 1997 Kazakhstan reportedly sold forty high-speed Shkval torpedoes to China without the necessary K-10 fire control system.[41] Since the Shkval has a short range of 15 to 20 kilometers and a speed of 195 knots, a fire control solution required for torpedoes with slower and longer range run times may not be necessary.[42] The Ukrainian OJSC SIC Kiev Automatic Plant exported an underwater rocket control system for Shkval-E to China at an unspecified date.[43] When these new torpedoes are operational in the PLAN, they will be serious threats to U.S. Navy surface ships that still lack an active kill anti-torpedo defense, even in 2010.

In addition, China faces unique difficulties in supporting complex Russian high-technology electrical and combat systems on imported Kilo submarines. Russia has repeatedly negotiated unsuccessfully for Kilo repair and maintenance contracts, since China now does this work at Hudong Shipyard.[44] The availability record of these Kilos indicates improper maintenance is at fault.

By contrast, other countries that use the Kilos, like India, do have Russian technicians performing maintenance.

The burden of servicing complex modern submarines rests heavily on the PLAN organization of shipyards, maintenance, repair, operations, and training. The time lag from receiving modern submarines and systems and assimilating them into the battle force is many years. This is complicated by the fact that China made no attempt to colocate or integrate modern Russian system training, support, or repair with the existing Chinese submarine support infrastructure, and appears to have gone out of its way to keep the Russian advisers isolated. It could be a decade before China's imported Russian submarines and complex systems will be completely incorporated, but four Kilo submarines have already been moved to Yulin on Hainan Island.

PLAN submarines historically did not operate at sea very often, and then usually in coastal waters. Two examples of fleet submarine command and control (C2) in the Yellow Sea provide conflicting arguments on the issue of effectiveness. On the positive side, from China's point of view at least, in 1994 a Han SSN, as mentioned previously, reportedly located the USS *Kitty Hawk* carrier battle group, and several F-6 naval fighters' on-site assistance showed effective PLAN communications, navigation, and control. More recently, in November 2006, a Chinese Song submarine "stalked" the *Kitty Hawk* before surfacing within firing range.[45] Not until 1999 did all three Chinese submarine fleets conduct operations off the eastern coast of Taiwan. Recently both submarine and antisubmarine operations have increased. Normally short coastal cruises have increased to forty-five days and sixty days for diesel and nuclear submarines, respectively. Foreign intelligence estimates for lengthy PLAN submarine cruises for 2006 put the chance at zero. The number increased to six for 2007 and doubled to twelve for 2008.[46]

Chinese Submarine Bases in the North Sea Fleet Area

The modernization of the PLAN's submarine force and the increase in its blue-water operations are related to the support basing for its nearly sixty diesel boats, seven SSNs, and three SSBNs. As mentioned earlier, the PLAN's submarine force is divided among the three fleets. The North Sea Fleet headquarters in Qingdao was formerly the base for the Imperial Japanese Navy (IJN) Submarine Squadron 3 in northern China. China began construction on its first submarine base at Qingdao in 1952. Fu Jize, a PLAN officer, established the Submarine Institute in 1953 and commanded the first PLAN submarine squadron created a year later, when the first four submarines were received by China. Qingdao was made the North Sea Fleet headquarters in

1954 and was equipped with a Soviet-furnished HF station command link to operating submarines. Fu Jize also commanded Chinese-built test ranges for PLAN weapons and a diving school with a deep dive tower to support the 1940-vintage Soviet boats.

Although many senior PLAN officers initially had army backgrounds, the Qingdao submarine school trained a core of submarine professionals. Qingdao served as a primary base for diesel Whiskey- and Wuhan-class submarines, but it was too exposed for the planned nuclear submarines. In 1968 a giant hardened sea cave was reportedly blasted out of rock at an inlet not far from Qingdao.[47] In the following years commercial satellite photos showed an unidentified naval base under construction along the isolated mountainous coast about ten miles north of Qingdao. The *Kanwa Defense Review* stated in May 2006 that an underground SSBN/SSN tunnel existed at the base, which was called Zhanggezhuang.[48] Detailed satellite photographs of the finished base had already appeared in print during the winter of 2006.[49]

In 1984 China reportedly began construction of a second nuclear submarine base near Lüshun. Xiaopingdao is a tiny town with a harbor and a few piers visible in satellite photographs midway between Lüshun and Dalian. The berthing and support for these valuable nuclear assets are probably dug in below the hillsides surrounding this village.

Because of reliability and radiation safety concerns, the Nuclear Submarine Repair Team was established at the sheltered base. This nuclear repair team was initially formed in Qingdao, and was dispatched to Huludao to support the first SSBN test launches in June 1988. Diesel submarines are supported by the 10,000-ton Dajiang-class submarine support ship J-121, based in Qingdao. Submarine operation support is reflected by a major oceanographic research institution, the Ocean University of Qingdao, dating back to 1924. The university owns 3,500- and 2,500-ton research vessels and has twenty-one research institutes. Its facilities include a large naval medical hospital, with an emphasis on deep-sea diving. In 1998 a "prevention and rescue" diving facility was added to the Qingdao Submarine Institute. The Chinese Hydrographic Office is also located in Qingdao.

The second northern submarine base is the restricted security facility of Lüshun, which was called Port Arthur when it was under Russian control and Ryojun under Japanese occupation. Japan gained this major Russian naval base by winning the Russo-Japanese War in 1905. It was also Japan's main naval base in northern China (called Manchukuo from 1932 to 1945) until 1945. After World War II Russia based surface warships and a submarine flotilla in Port Arthur until it was turned over to China in May 1955.

The Soviets trained the first group of future PRC submarine crew members at Lüshun beginning in 1951.[50] Lüshun is the site of one of the VLF stations that communicate with distant Chinese forces, including submarines, and has dry docks and repair yards dedicated to military vessels. The closed port provides security for submarine missile tests, and the Chinese Song guided-missile submarine (SSG) was usually based there for testing. When the Soviet Navy had its powerful Pacific bases north of China, the city was the focus of coastal defense for the PLAN's North Sea Fleet.

Although adequate submarine support is available in the home ports, major overhauls and repairs are usually accomplished at the shipyard that built the submarines. Bohai Shipyard in Huludao is the primary northern submarine construction yard and the only yard to build nuclear submarines. Bohai Shipyard features three docks; the largest is the Taishan floating dock, which is 250 feet long and holds vessels up to 120,000 tons. Huludao is also the site of the Naval Test Base, consolidating four naval test facilities. A Soviet-Chinese accord was signed in 1957 for the construction of Base 23, which is the site of SLBM test range number 2, used by the Golf SSB in 1982.

Chinese Submarine Bases in the East Sea Fleet Area

The East Sea Fleet headquarters are in Ningbo, southeast of Shanghai. The PLA established the Shanghai-Wusong Garrison in May 1948, a year before the Nationalists were driven from Shanghai. Shanghai is listed as the main naval base for the East Sea Fleet, and Wusong, at the mouth of the Huangpu River, was the East Sea Fleet headquarters. There are numerous photos of submarines berthed in Shanghai and Wusong, but neither is officially a PLAN submarine base.

Three clustered submarine support bases are located about 150 to 200 kilometers south of Shanghai, at the port cities of Ningbo, Xiangshan, and Dinghai. One of the most important submarine bases is at Xiangshan, which is home to the most modern PLAN diesel submarines, the Type 877EKM Kilos and the newer Type 636 Kilos from Russia. None of these imported submarines is based at the North Sea Fleet, while several have been observed at Hainan. The equally isolated port of Dinghai on the island of Zhoushan has been listed as a submarine base for many years. Dinghai is also home port for many frigates. The submarine flotilla VLF antenna command facilities are in nearby Ningbo, which is the East Sea Fleet headquarters, and has also been listed as a submarine base. Ningbo is the center for command and control of the East Sea Fleet submarines.

The crew of the first Kilo received in early 1995 was trained in Saint Petersburg, but the second and third crews were trained in Xiangshan by Russian submarine engineers. Many standard references state that the Chinese Kilos have support and training problems that keep them from being operational. This has been verified by several reports that two of the Kilos were observed moored and idle for long periods at Hudong Shipyard in Shanghai but not being worked on. But a 1998 report from Taiwan, stating that a Chinese submarine transited the strait undetected, also hints at equally successful Kilo operations. The East Sea Fleet also had eight submarines deployed in the 1996 Taiwan Strait crisis. Chinese diesel or nuclear submarines are not rated as well as 636 Kilos for quietness to avoid detection. Although submarines are commonly berthed at nearby Wusong, the building, repair, and overhaul work is largely done at Shanghai shipyards like Hudong or Jiangnan. One updated Song 039A SSG is based in Hainan, so vessels of this class are no longer based only at one site.

Chinese Submarine Bases in the South Sea Fleet Area

The South Sea Fleet headquarters is at Zhanjiang, in Guangdong province just north of Hainan Island. The Nationalist forces under Chiang Kai-shek did not take Hainan from the warlord who controlled Guangdong until 1926. Hainan Island was not used as a military base site or even exploited industrially until the Chinese puppet government under Wang Jingwei allowed Japan to occupy it in February 1939. The Japanese built ore mines and rail lines to its harbors for shipments to the homeland, a military air base, and naval bases at Haikou and Yulin.

Yulin was a Japanese submarine base with support for IJN submarine squadrons 4 and 5 by their respective submarine tenders. The Japanese departed Hainan in 1945, and a major typhoon in 1946 destroyed most of the mines, rail lines, and naval base structures. The Chinese navy did not begin repairs of the damage until 1957, even though the PLA's Fortieth Army took Hainan from Nationalist forces in May 1950. The initial PLA effort was on the air base at Haikou, with a visit by the PLAAF commander in June 1952. The only distant South Sea Fleet naval communication link in the mid-1950s was an LF station in Zhanjiang.

PRC naval activity in the south was nearly nonexistent through the 1960s. America's Far Eastern fleet dominated the South China Sea in the late 1960s and early 1970s, but in the 1980s Soviet Charlie- and Echo-class guided-missile nuclear submarines (SSGN) based in Vietnam cruised the surrounding waters.

Submerged submarine communications were enabled by 1980 via VLF transmitters at Zhanjiang and on southern Hainan in Sanya, near Yulin. By the early 1970s, after the U.S. Navy left the Gulf of Tonkin, Yulin had become home to a diesel submarine flotilla. Although submarine construction in the East Sea Fleet yards dates from the early 1950s, the first South Sea Fleet–built submarines from Huangpu Shipyard, near Guangzhou, date to the late 1960s. The growth in number and increased activity of the Hainan submarines was indicated by the reported participation of possibly one Type 03 submarine in the Paracel Islands occupation during 1974.

In the 1980s the 10,000-ton submarine tender R-327 *Yong Xing Dao* was providing support for Yulin-based Type 033 boats. China completed three SCS high-power radio navigation sites in 1989, and one certainly would have been in Hainan, probably at Yulin. This base is restricted, but many tourists visit the beaches of Sanya, separated from Yulin by the merchant ship mooring harbor facilities. The airport at Sanya has been expanded, and Lingshui is a major air base for China's naval F-8 interceptors.

Haikou is the most well-known city on the island and a busy tourist airport arrival and departure point. The city is a major commercial shipping port but not a submarine flotilla base as once thought; only a speedboat flotilla is based there. Major repairs and maintenance for Hainan-based submarines are performed at the Guangzhou submarine construction yards in southern mainland China. The Huangpu, Donglang, and Whampoa shipyards in Guangzhou all built Type 033s. In addition to the three Dajiang submarine support ships, China has about eight other submarine rescue or support vessels distributed at various submarine bases.

It is possible that a forward submarine base could only be available on Woody Island, but Japan had several forward submarine support bases during World War II in the South China Sea.[51] India suspects that a naval base that China began to construct in 1992 in Myanmar is intended to support PLAN submarines. Speculation that Chinese assistance to Myanmar on Hainggyi Island in the Irrawaddy River opening to the Bay of Bengal could be a future PLAN submarine base seems unfounded. PLAN signal intelligence or warship replenishment support seem more likely purposes for the aid.

Although China's submarine forces are gradually taking on a greater role within the PLAN, they still have vulnerabilities. While there are eight or more identified submarine bases for the three fleets, the majority of repairs are still done elsewhere in the respective submarine building yards. Through the 1990s the largest number of submarines was in the northern fleet facing the USSR, but the numbers are now shifting south for possible Taiwan or SCS operations. The newer-class submarines based at Yulin included Song, 039A,

636 Kilo, and upgraded Han SSN, which was very different from the old diesels previously based there. Finally, in the 1990s, Chinese submarines can largely cruise at will in the disputed SCS area. This freedom allows the PLAN to support Chinese island or oil field claims, or engage in future Indian Ocean SLOC operations.

All of China's major submarine bases were originally built by Germany, Japan, or the USSR and inherited by the PLAN. Although the nuclear submarines initially had protected facilities in the North Sea Fleet, in the 1990s China built similar hidden submarine tunnels in the south for SSN or SSBN units. These tunnels, each with several entrances, are at Yalong Bay near the Yulin submarine base.[52] In 2008 the prototype 093 SSN and 094 SSBN were observed in the Yulin hard shelter area.

Of the dozen or so large Chinese shipyards that launch warships, six have produced submarines. The most advanced submarine yards are at Huludao and Wuhan. The other submarine building yards are at Jiangnan, Guangzhou, Whampoa, and Wuhu. All of them can perform quality repairs, overhauls, or upgrades of submarines. However, any nuclear submarines being used in the South China Sea may possibly have to return to the Huludao shipyard in the north for major repairs.

Conclusions

China's future blue-water navy appears to be firmly linked to a robust submarine force. In particular, the next generation of indigenous Yuan SS, Shang SSN, and Jin SSBN have been augmented by Kilos from Russia. A real test for PLAN submarine support occurs when the Kilo submarines need to be overhauled. Will China have to continue to send Kilo submarines to Russia for major repairs and overhauls, or will it be able to do the job at one of its own shipyards? If the Kilos require Russian technicians for servicing, or perhaps even need to be returned to Russia for major repairs, strict limits would then be put on purchasing naval platforms from abroad. Kilos have been observed in covered repair pens in Shanghai since 2007.

To date, Chinese efforts to create a more robust submarine force have been reflected in a more active use of these capabilities to test its neighbors' resolve. For example, on 10 November 2004, a Type 091 Han SSN entered Japanese territorial waters southwest of Okinawa. The submarine was quickly spotted and was tracked by Japanese maritime forces as it moved submerged in Japanese sovereign waters for two hours before moving northwest back toward Chinese waters. The Han's action caused Japanese Self-Defense Forces to go on alert for only the second time since World War II.[53]

Following a Japanese protest, China's vice foreign minister Wu Dawei offered an apology for the incident on 17 November 2004, claiming that it was due to "technical error."[54] However, it is more likely that China was testing Japan's response, as well as trying to insert a wedge between the United States and Japan, since the two countries differ on their interpretation of international law when it comes to transiting through island channels to move from one area of international water to another. In this case the PLAN submarine was following standard U.S. practices.

The submarine picture is further complicated by the fact that several Western nations, including the United States, have tried to sell new-construction or in-service diesel submarines to Taiwan. Retaliation by China in the form of threats to stop trading with those nations caused most to back down. Taiwan could still purchase additional submarines, however, and it has implied that it might use its position on Itu Aba (Taiping) Island in the Spratlys to conduct a submarine counterblockade against China should the PRC elect either to attack or blockade Taiwan. Liang Kung-kai, head of Taiwan's Ministry of National Defense's Department of Strategic Planning, stated that "if war broke out between Taiwan and China, Taiwan's submarines would definitely have the ability to make ambush attacks against China's oil tankers in the South China Sea."[55]

Any way one looks at it, China's procurement of additional modern Kilo-class submarines for the PLAN, development of second-generation nuclear attack and ballistic-missile submarines, and continued production of improved indigenous diesel boats present a growing threat. This potential threat is especially grave when China's coastal defense and amphibious capabilities are taken into consideration.

——6——
Coastal Defense and
PLAN Amphibious Capability

The interception of a U.S. Navy EP-3 signals intelligence (SIGINT) reconnaissance aircraft in international airspace off Hainan Island in April 2001 highlighted the activities of the PRC coastal defense forces, which have in the past been low profile and largely remain so today. In fact, such interceptions and intrusions over Chinese waters and coastal areas have occurred for decades, as with the former Soviet Union. In addition to the expected PLAN assets, a surprising array of nonnaval units is integrated into offensive and defensive coastal military roles. These units include coastal air defense as well as nonmilitary maritime forces from a variety of paramilitary organizations.

The PRC had no Coast Guard until 1998 and crews are People's Armed Police (PAP) under the Maritime Safety Administration (MSA), but many functions of a typical coast guard are controlled by other agencies. The MSA now consists of about 150 vessels that augment many PLAN auxiliary, mine-laying, minesweeping, or amphibious-warfare vessels that were not designed for coastal defense. Fleet and air defense headquarters are colocated with air traffic control, the State Oceanic Administration (SOA), the Civil Aviation Administration of China, and scientific headquarters. This highlights the close control and coordination of these assets by the PRC to meet coastal defense requirements.

Inclusion of these additional sensors, aircraft, and ships greatly increases the capability of Chinese coastal defense beyond the PLAN order-of-battle listings commonly used. Coastal defense forces also have been used to infringe on another nation's sovereignty. This includes intrusions into Japanese waters by northern units. Tensions over the Chunxiao oil and gas fields in the East China Sea threaten to undermine Sino-Japanese relations; during September 2005, "Beijing dispatched war vessels at least twice to the area in an escalating dispute."[1] Unarmed auxiliary vessels and then frigates initially intruded in 2004. On 22 January 2005 a single Sovremennyy DDG was spotted by a Japanese Maritime Self-Defense Force (JMSDF) P-3 in the Chunxiao gas field.[2] It returned in August 2005 with a five-ship surface action group. In April 2010, China sent eight warships and two submarines to hold a military exercise in the vicinity of Japan's Okinotori reefs in the East China Sea near Okinawa.[3] On 8 September 2010 a Chinese trawler rammed the 1,349-ton Japanese coast guard cutter *Yonakuni* off the contested Diaoyu Islands, and forty minutes later rammed the 180-ton cutter *Mizumi*. China strongly objected to the arrest of the captain, who was charged with obstruction in a Japanese court. Japan claims that there are usually about 160 PRC vessels illegally fishing inside the thirty-mile limit in Diaoyu waters.

There have also been aggressive PLAN operations in the South China Sea around the Spratly and Paracel islands by southern fleet vessels. Intrusion into the Philippine-claimed Spratly Islands in the SCS started with paramilitary research vessels in 1980 and ended with a large navy exercise in 1989. Scientific vessels operated around Johnson South Reef in March 1988, resulting in its seizure in October by modern PLAN frigates and amphibious ships. In February 1995 China seized Mischief Reef by force with PLAN warships and marines. Although there have been several territorial disputes with other nations since then, Mischief Reef was the last PLAN gunboat diplomacy.

On 4 December 2007 China announced that all of its claimed territory in the South China Sea would be administered as a separate district within Hainan province called Sansha. This huge new city administration manages the three island archipelagoes of Paracel Islands, Spratly Islands, and Macclesfield Bank even though China's sovereignty over these islands remains in dispute. The use of vessels other than PLAN warships for coastal military missions seventy-five miles from southern Hainan is discussed later in this chapter.

On 8 March 2009 the U.S. Military Sealift Command (MSC) research ship *Impeccable* was surrounded and aggressively harassed and endangered by five Chinese vessels. These included an intelligence ship, an SOA vessel, a Bureau of Fisheries vessel, and two Chinese fishing trawlers. A fact that was not in most news reports was that the *Impeccable* had a PLAN frigate cross her bow and was buzzed a dozen times by a Y-12 twin-engine patrol plane in the SCS on 5 March. The MSC ship *Victorious* was also interfered with by two Chinese Bureau of Fisheries vessel in the Yellow Sea on 4 March 2009. Thus, of eight Chinese vessels in these coordinated anti-ocean-surveillance operations, only one was a PLAN warship. Evidence that China is upgrading its coastal defense vessels is provided by transfering Jianghu frigates 509 and 510 from the PLAN to coast guard duties in 2007.

There have been positive steps by China to lessen tensions and cooperate with other SCS nations. China did meet with Association of Southeast

Asian Nations (ASEAN) members in January 2000 regarding international law and Spratly region disputes. This resulted in China and ASEAN members signing a "Declaration on the Conduct of Parties in the South China Sea" in November 2002. The protocol stressed restraint by signees in not seizing uninhabited islands or reefs in the SCS. In 2003 China and the Philippines had discussions on petroleum exploration and increased trade and investment between the nations. In March 2005 petroleum companies from China, Vietnam, and the Philippines signed a tripartite agreement to limit joint petroleum exploration in the Spratly Islands and the SCS.

Examples of Coastal Defense

The first PLA coastal artillery positions were established at Qingdao in November 1950. The April 2001 EP-3 incident raised public awareness of U.S. surveillance and PRC coastal air defense interceptors. In fact, China's actions against U.S. coastal reconnaissance flights date back to the downing of an RB-45C by a PRC MiG-15 fighter in December 1950.[4] By 1959 seven U.S. aircraft had been shot down by fighters, and two had been downed by antiaircraft fire in 1952 and 1953. The first known reconnaissance aircraft downed by an SA-2 SAM was a Taiwanese RB-57D in October 1959. Between 1962 and 1967 Chinese SA-2s downed five U-2s flown by Taiwanese pilots. From 1964 to 1970 nineteen U.S. drones were shot down, two of them in March and August 1965 over the Lingshui air base in Hainan.[5] For various reasons, such as the advent of electronic intelligence (ELINT) and photo reconnaissance satellites, the shooting down of reconnaissance aircraft has decreased dramatically since the 1970s.

However, the PLAN is flexing its muscles in other ways. With post–Cold War Russia shrinking its submarine fleet and greatly reducing operations, the western Pacific had become fairly quiet. In September 1994 China began its largest coastal defense exercise to date. Known as East China Sea Number 4, it featured more than fifty large warships, including nuclear submarines. On 27 October 1994 the USS *Kitty Hawk* had S-3 Viking antisubmarine-warfare aircraft searching 450 miles northwest from the carrier's location west of Kyushu, Japan. A Han SSN was spotted at periscope depth just east of its home base, the North Sea Fleet headquarters of Qingdao. This provided a unique opportunity for U.S. ASW training as well as for obtaining good tapes of the sound signature of the Han class. As the *Kitty Hawk* continued its route to South Korea, the Han headed southeast, and two days later it came within only 21 miles of the carrier. The fact that a Chinese SSN closed within almost 20 miles of a U.S. aircraft carrier without being deterred was without precedent. The submarine was subjected continuously to the routine air platform tracking tools, from magnetic anomaly detection to active and passive sonobuoy patterns.

On 28 October the Chinese North Sea Fleet commander scrambled several naval F-6 fighters to intercept one of the tracking U.S. S-3 Vikings. As the SSN closed to surface escort zones, it was prosecuted by powerful SQS-53 sonars as well. The North Sea Fleet headquarters was in obvious control of air and submarine assets and knew the location of U.S. air and surface forces from shore radars or other sensors. A Chinese official later told a U.S. attaché that appropriate defensive actions would be taken when Chinese airspace and territorial waters were violated. Because the entire incident occurred farther than twelve miles from the Chinese coast, the U.S. Navy claimed it was outside of territorial waters. However, China's exclusive economic zone (EEZ) territory extends two hundred miles from shore, and China claims shallow areas of the East China Sea and Yellow Sea as sovereign territory. According to Beijing the U.S. forces may have been inside China's EEZ. The United States does not recognize the EEZ as sovereign territory, not only for its obvious impact on the concept of freedom of the seas, but also because this two-hundred-mile zone even includes part of the Korea Peninsula within its arc.

Harassment of U.S. aircraft by F-8 interceptors has also occurred, such as with an RC-135 reconnaissance aircraft in April 2000 over the East China Sea and the well-publicized collision with the EP-3 near Hainan one year later. Meanwhile, close monitoring of the MSC survey ship *Bowditch* by a PLAN frigate in March 2001 forced the U.S. vessel to depart the area. Two months later the same ship was buzzed by a PLAN long-range patrol aircraft in the Yellow Sea, even though an Aegis cruiser, the USS *Cowpens*, was escorting it at the time.

More recently, September 2002 saw renewed Chinese actions against the *Bowditch* as Y-8 and Y-12 coastal patrol aircraft buzzed the ship as it operated in the Yellow Sea sixty miles off the coast but within China's self-claimed—but as yet internationally unrecognized—two-hundred-mile total exclusion zone. Chinese intelligence-gathering vessels also approached the *Bowditch*, but they did not interfere with its passage.[6] While a two-hundred-mile EEZ is consistent with the UN Convention on the Law of the Seas, sovereign exclusivity is not, a fact that China tends to ignore when it works in its favor.

In March 2009 China aggressively reacted to the presence of the MSC auxiliary oceanographic ship *Victorious* in the Yellow Sea and the *Impeccable* in the SCS. The *Victorious* was interfered with by a Chinese Bureau of Fisheries vessel on 4 March in international waters off Qingdao. On 5 March the *Impeccable* had a PLAN frigate cross her bow at a dangerously close

range and was buzzed a dozen times by a Y-12 twin turboprop south of
Hainan. These normally clandestine operations became headline news when
five Chinese vessels harassed the *Impeccable* and even tried to cut her towed
array cable. The crew of the *Impeccable* had to use fire hoses to thwart the
Chinese attempts. Only three months later, on 11 June 2009, a PLAN submarine hit and damaged a towed array from the USS *John McCain* off of Subic
Bay during international exercises. It was called an "inadvertent encounter."[7]

Photo 7. A Chinese trawler attempting to snag the MSC ocean research ship *Impeccable*'s
towed array seventy miles south of the new submarine base in Yulin, Hainan, in March
2009. Source: U.S. Navy

Air Defense (AD) Zones

China divides its top-level air districts into AD zones. Each zone comprises sec-
tors and subsectors, which can consist of individual radar sites, AA guns, and
also missile batteries. Although it appears that naval air interceptors would
be better at performing over-water navigation and interception, in the eastern
fleet area PLAAF fighters are often used because their airfields are closer.

Larger patrol aircraft also have been used for spotting offshore contacts.
The first two of four PLAAF modified Tu-154M ELINT aircraft are based
in the Nanjing Military District. Additional units are expected for North Sea
and South Sea Fleet duties. Y-8X maritime patrol versions of the Russian
four-engine turboprop An-12 reportedly have shadowed U.S. P-3Cs off the
coast beyond F-8 range.

Coastal area radars also are the heart of China's Observation Communication Force, which may be under naval rather than air force control. In 1986 the California company ITT Gilfillan reportedly sold China Falcon coastal defense radars with an operations center. From 1994 to 1995 China procured from Russia six to eight S-300 SA-10Bs, and in 1998 it obtained the more capable SA-20A, which is rated among the best area defense SAMs in the world. Russia has sold between twenty-seven and thirty-five point defense Tor SA-15 surface-to-air missile sites to China since 1997. China is now producing the HQ-9 SAMs that have much S-300 technology, which along with SA-20 batteries now protect Beijing, Shanghai, and Hong Kong, the PRC's three major cities.[8] Ten new long-range SAM sites, probably a mix of Tor and HQ-9 SAMs, were installed in 2010 near Qingdao.[9] Other coastal areas have older Russian AD radars, such as the SA-2 Spoon Rest, and massive long-range yagi search radars, including Cross Slot and Moon Cone. Chinese-designed JY-series three-dimensional coastal radars are the 350-kilometer-range JY-8 and the lower-level JY-9 150-kilometer-range gap fillers. China introduced the indigenously designed Type-796 air route surveillance radar that is solid-state and features anticlutter and moving target indicator displays, and antistealth metric radars have been imported from Czechoslovakia and the Ukraine.

Prototype and developmental Chinese OTH radars have been identified since 2001. A later over-the-horizon, backscatter (OTH-B) site was situated near inland Xiangfan. The area of coverage is estimated to be from Japan to the Philippines. The latest is an over-the-horizon, surface wave (OTH-SW) site at Shenchang on the Chinese coast northwest of Taiwan. It is physically similar to the Russian OTH-SW site at Nakhodka, suggesting Russian assistance in its construction and development. It is thought to have a 60-degree arc, and 300 kilometers would be a conservative estimate of its range. These are not PLAN facilities, but the assistance they are capable of providing to the PLAN in targeting distant hostile naval ships with land-based ballistic missiles is obvious. The South China Sea is reportedly under surveillance by a Chinese OTH-B radar with a range of 700 to 3,500 kilometers in a 60-degree arc.[10]

The employment of dual-use exports is a key element in China's coastal air defense. U.S. and European high-technology companies have sold China long-range tracking radars for key east coast airline routes, which happen to be valuable military areas as well. In 1978 Thomson-CSF sold China six LP-23 long-range radars for the seven-hundred-mile-long corridor between Shanghai and Beijing.[11] The same deal included three TA-10 area radars for military bases in Shanghai and Beijing. Under the 1990 Marco Polo program, the European company Alenia sold five primary and eleven secondary air traffic control radars destined for eleven airports along the eastern coast of China. Although Western radar exports are sold to "civilian" air organizations, 85 percent of PRC airspace is still under PLA control.

Patrol Craft (PC)

PLAN warships and auxiliaries are not primarily blue-water vessels, so most of their exercises and operations are in coastal waters. If detection and interception of air or surface intruders is considered a primary coastal defense mission, then the few dozen large-destroyer-type units are too valuable to be used for such tasking. Meanwhile, the approximately forty frigates could barely meet radar and communication equipment needs for such coordinated work, although a frigate was sent to drive off a U.S. survey ship.

Although there is a large number of Chinese PC, their equipment capabilities are limited to navigation radar, visual detection, and HF radios. Table 22 lists weapons and sensors deployed on board PLAN PC. Most Chinese naval units spend the bulk of their time in port, and they largely have missions other than surveillance. Among the hundreds of fleet units, less than two dozen Russian-style auxiliary general intelligence (AGI) and intelligence ships are properly equipped for surveillance and evaluation to alert coastal defense assets. The only PC with 45-36A 457-millimeter torpedoes were the fifty copies of the Soviet WWII P-4. The P-6 and all later PLAN craft would have the standard postwar "53 series" 533-millimeter torpedoes.

From the early 1960s through the mid-1980s, the Type 037 Hainan-class patrol boats were the most numerous PLAN vessels, with more than a hundred built by 1960. The Type 037 had an HF Soviet sonar, 5-tube ASW mortars, and depth charges (D/C) for ASW. This equipment would be retained on the thirty follow-on vessels of the Haiqing class, except newer 6-barrel mortars replaced the older model. Both had Pot Head radars and the single-barrel 37-millimeter guns were replaced with a twin 37 millimeters, but no gun FC was provided.

In the late 1960s 147 Huchuan hydrofoil 533-millimeter torpedo boats with 14.5-millimeter AA machine guns were produced. The most numerous patrol craft were the Shanghai and Shanghai II, which numbered over three hundred in the 1980s. The ASW mission was dropped, although D/C racks were retained along with the 37-millimeter and 25-millimeter AA guns. The PLAN produced four multipurpose gunboats, called Haijiu, in the 1980s that were overly expensive and complex for the coastal mission. Each Haijiu possessed an ASW capability that had not been seen on a PC since the 1960 Hainan class, consisting of an HF hull sonar and associated ASW mortar and

Table 22. Coastal Patrol/Auxiliary Combat Systems

RADAR	PURPOSE	BAND	PLATFORM	PERIOD
Skin Head	Surface search	H/I	All	1948–60
Pot Head	Surface search	S	All	Post-1960
Round Ball	FC radar	I	Hola, Haijiu, Houjin	1965
Type 756	Navigation	C	Shanghai II	1962
MISSILES	**FUNCTION**	**RANGE**	**SPEED**	**WARHEAD**
CSS-N-1/2	SSM	25 km	Mach 0.9	500 kg
CSS-N-4	SSM	75 km	Supersonic	150 kg
MINES	**TYPE**	**DEPTH**	**BODY WT.**	**WARHEAD WT.**
M-3 mine	Acoustic	8–50 m	1,050 kg	240 kg
UDM-2	Influence	8–300 m	1,400 kg	800 kg
EM-12	Acoustic	8–200 m	570 kg	320 kg
GUN	**BBL**	**RPM**	**ELEVATION (DEGREES)**	**RANGE**
85 mm/50	Single	10	70	15 km
57 mm/70	Twin	230	85	13 km
30 mm/60 (manual)	Both	220	85	5 km
30 mm/60 (auto)	Twin AK-230	2,100	85	6.5 km
12.7 mm/70	Single	550	85	1.5 km
TORPEDO TYPE	**DIAMETER**	**RANGE**	**SPEED**	**WARHEAD**
45-36A	457 mm	4 km	45 kts	140 kg
SET-53 ASW	533 mm	4 km	35 kts	275 kg
53-56 pattern	533 mm	8 km	41 kts	400 kg
53-57 straight	533 mm	18 km	45 kts	305 kg

D/C. It had the ubiquitous Pot Head surface search radar and a large Round Ball FC radome for its 30-millimeter guns, while the Type 66 57-millimeter guns comprised the main battery.

The USSR provided several Osa boats with HY-2 Styx missiles and 25-millimeter AA guns in the 1950s. China manufactured two hundred copies, called Houkous, starting in the mid-1960s, which had the Square Tie

SSM radar and 25-millimeter AA guns. China modified the design into the Type 021 Huangfeng missile patrol boat (PGM) in 1969 and added Round Ball FC radars and associated AK-230 30-millimeter guns capable of firing 2,100 RPM, which were designated Type 69 by China.

In 1990 a new series of twenty to twenty-four Houxin-class boats were built with the more capable YJ-8 SSM, but the radars and guns were unchanged. In 1993 China introduced the expensive Type 520T Houjian class, the first patrol boat with a CDS, but only five were built. It had a Chinese-designed digital Type 88 FC computer and was fitted with weapons that included the YJ-8 SSM and 37- and 30-millimeter guns with an associated optical FC director. Rumors of a new series-production corvette, called 056, with four SSMs and helicopter, were confirmed in November 2010.

Type 022 Catamaran Houbei

In 2004 an innovative wave-piercing catamaran missile boat, the Type 022 Houbei class, appeared under construction at the Qiuxin Shipyard in Shanghai. It was based on an Australian catamaran hull design, since China had imported seven catamarans from Advanced Multihull Designs (AMD) Marine Consulting, located in Sydney, since 1993 for civilian use. Sea Bus International, a joint venture between the Australian firm and a company in Guangzhou, assisted in modifying the AMD 350 model. This was not a one-of-a-kind experiment, and model 022 was in production with over twenty hulls launched by four shipyards by 2008. A force of more than forty Houbeis has been built in 2009, making this the largest PLAN series production in three decades. A catamaran brigade from the East Sea Fleet completed full combat capability acceptance in July 2009, after a one-year work-up of all-weather, integrated training.[12]

Surprisingly, nearly all 022s are painted in colors used by the Chinese marine corps. The only difference is that the northern boats are painted blue, gray, and white, while southern boats have blue, gray, white and black camouflage paint. This design would not match any support need of the marine corps. These craft are obvious replacements for the obsolete Huangfeng and Hegu missile boats. Their inventory has dropped from a peak of 330 boats in 1985 to only a dozen still active. Lacking Band Stand guidance required by the C-803, the 200-kilometer-range C802A would be the logical SSM for these craft, but they are instead credited with having eight YJ-83 ASCMs.[13] The degree of modern automation on the Houbeis is highlighted by their crew of only twelve, compared to the twenty-six-man crew on the Huangfengs, which are of similar size. The Houbeis have four MAN Diesel 16PA6 diesel engines manufactured by Shaanxi Diesel Works. These 250-ton, 40-knot craft have high-technology HN900 data link and CIWS.[14] The 6-barrel Type 630 CIWS on the bow lacks the normal FC radar, but a small radar dish has electro-optic and LLTV backup trackers. Due to the craft's coordinated platform targeting link needs, it is surprising that Type 022 lacks a SATCOMM antenna, but this could be added, as the small FLS-1 SAM was in 2007. Two 4-barrel antimissile decoy launchers are on the bow, with unknown designation. The Houbeis are equally distributed among the three fleets, indicating a major littoral water role.

Naval references describing China's coastal defense craft list only the active fleet naval assets, not organizations that also directly support coastal defense. Use and control of allegedly civilian or nongovernment vessels are accomplished through direct government authority over and coordination of scientific, research, civilian, and educational assets to meet military needs, and to ignore such assets is a crucial mistake. In the past the best offshore visual detection platforms were the ubiquitous junks, which numbered in the thousands. When navigating into Hong Kong during the Vietnam War, U.S. Navy radar operators tracked groups of dozens of close-sailing junks as one contact. In the past, junks have been used to aid Chinese military actions, especially in the Taiwan Strait, where they provided concealment for PLAN warships. Junks seem to have been replaced by newer craft, but use of such nonmilitary small craft in any new cross–Taiwan Strait conflict should not be overlooked.

Photo 8. Two Type 022 Houbei serial-production catamaran missile boats. Note the blue and white colors, emblematic of the PLAN's marine units, on the craft at the left. Source: Kanwa

Maritime Border Defense Force

China's Maritime Border Defense Force (MBDF) is somewhat similar to a coast guard in organization, but not in function. Like the PLAN, the MBDF is divided into three militia groups. The northern MBDF group is made up of the Shenyang, Beijing, and Jinan military regions and is called the Shenyang MBDF. Shenyang MBDF vessels have the letter "S" in front of their unit number. This can be confusing because PLAN survey vessels also have "S" hull designators. The eastern MBDF corresponds to the Nanjing military region and is called the Nanjing MBDF. It is comprised of Jiangsu, Zhejiang, and Fujian provinces, and its vessels have "N" designators on their hulls. The Guangzhou MBDF guards the southern coast, and its vessels have "G" hull labels. The region used to include Hainan, but it is possible that Hainan and the SCS islands could now be reorganized under a separate defense control.

MBDF vessels are scattered among large and small ports, military exclusion waters, and other waters as required. For example, the Nanjing MBDF units include Huludao- and Shanghai II–class patrol craft, Yuling landing craft, utility (LCU), Yuqin landing craft, medium (LCM) N2332, two Youzhong-class cable ships, Fuzhou-class coastal tankers, and armed trawlers. The other two MBDF fleets have a similar mix of civilian vessels and former naval landing and patrol craft.[15]

The MBDF has four subcomponents: Customs Service, Marine Police, Border Security, and Border Defense. Because they provide state income, customs units usually have newer equipment and helicopters. Reports indicate, however, that many customs crews are staffed by PLAN members. Border Security units are also linked to the PLA's large PAP forces. In 2008 commercial fishing vessels of a Militia Offshore Support Detachment refueled and replenished PLAN warships off Zhejiang.[16]

Civilian Coastal Defense Units

Having had no coast guard equivalent until 1998, the Chinese government also uses groups that are allegedly civilian in nature to monitor coastal waters. Many similar organizations in the United States fill scientific or commercial functions, but the Chinese structure reveals a very military role. The State Oceanic Administration (SOA), for example, has three branches that closely parallel PLAN fleet structure.

The main SOA and PLAN headquarters are in Beijing, and the three regional SOA headquarters are also colocated with the respective PLAN fleet headquarters. A block diagram of SOA structure, with a ship-and-aircraft dispatching center that controls a brigade of marine surveillance ships and a brigade of marine surveillance aircraft, certainly parallels a military organization. China claims that the three SOA fleets are structured this way for oceanographic and scientific purposes. The only local variation is that the SOA South Sea Branch's surveillance vessels are in the SOA group designated 7th Fleet, whereas the SOA North Sea Branch and East Sea Branch surveillance vessels are in the SOA 1st and 4th Brigade organizations, respectively.

Another part of the SOA that could directly support coastal surveillance and tracking is the Marine Environmental Forecast Service satellite network. The headquarters is in Beijing, with primary coastal stations located in Qingdao, Shanghai, Guangzhou, and Haikou on Hainan Island. Two Antarctic observation stations were established: the Great Wall, in 1985, and Zhongshan, in 1989. The support for the stations was initially a 15,000-ton converted cargo ship, the *Jidi*, from 1986 on, until it was replaced by a new 21,000-ton icebreaker, the *Xue Long*, in 1994. SOA utilizes both Chinese and U.S. National Oceanic and Atmospheric Administration/Tiros ocean surveillance satellites.

In addition to the other nonmilitary naval craft that patrol around key ports and coastal areas, several major oceanographic centers and universities are located at SOA and PLAN control centers and ports.[17] They have more than two dozen research vessels that have operated in sensitive areas and supported naval activities in the past. These ships provide innocuous cover to various government/military missions.

When China's and other nations' claims on SCS islands and fishing rights conflict, there is no single Chinese maritime organization to provide protection for Chinese fisherman, so various civilian organizations provide "fishing administrative ships" to patrol those disputed areas. In March 2009 the Maritime Safety Administration (MSA) sent protective vessels from the Fishery Administration Bureau, the International Maritime Organization (IMO), Fisheries Law Enforcement Command (FLEC), and the China Marine Surveillance (CMS) to the SCS. On 16 May 2009 China issued a ban on fishing in SCS waters, and sent eight boats there to monitor and enforce compliance by other nations' fishing fleets. In November 2009 a FLEC 4,450-ton Dalian-class retired navy submarine rescue ship, the *Yuzheng-311*, made its maiden voyage south from a Guangzhou shipyard. After a typhoon in late November, two fishery administration ships, a helicopter, and a warship were sent to the SCS to rescue survivors from Chinese fishing boats that sank during the storm. Dozens of smaller vessels from Guangzhou, Shanghai, Guangxi, and Beihai also routinely patrol the SCS fishing exclusion zone for intruders. For example, the *Yuzheng 45001* from the Guangxi Inspection

Team, built in 2001, patrolled disputed SCS waters from 2007 until March 2009, which is an extraordinary cruise.

Amphibious Forces

PLAN amphibious operations and the development of specialized amphibious craft will be presented here in several phases encompassing the 1950s to the present. China inherited a large number of landing craft in 1949, when the Nationalists abandoned the following former U.S. Navy ships and craft: twenty-six landing ships, tank (LSTs), fourteen landing ships, mechanized (LSMs), and two hundred landing craft, medium (LCMs). Eleven of the LSTs were used immediately as cargo ships. To augment the abandoned Nationalist vessels, the USSR provided about seventy-five 70-ton T-4-class LCMs in the early 1950s. From 1949 to 1952 China took many coastal islands from the Nationalists, including Zhoushan in 1950. The Fortieth PLA Army finally captured Hainan in May of that year. PLA troops in small craft were repelled with heavy losses from the offshore islands of Jinmen (Quemoy) and Matsu in August and September 1958. It is possible that the high losses inflicted by dug-in Nationalist troops on the PLA soldiers, who were using junks instead of landing craft, caused the naval branch to create a cadre of amphibious-trained troops, if not a trained marine corps.

When the PLAN was established in September 1950, there was no mention of a marine corps. The Chinese marine corps was founded on 9 December 1954 and was disbanded only three years later. When the Paracel Islands were taken by force from South Vietnam on 19 January 1974, amphibious-trained soldiers and sailors were used. Vietnam had tacitly controlled the Paracels for decades, since these islands had previously been claimed by France. The South Vietnamese navy had four vessels facing eleven Chinese vessels, including landing craft, at Duncan Island. The victorious PLAN lost one of four Komar missile boats and one of two armed trawlers. Vietnam lost a PC, and their destroyer escort, radar picket (DER) flagship, and two high-endurance cutters (WHEC) cutters were damaged in the thirty-five-minute battle. In addition to reports of MiGs being deployed, on 20 January four additional warships arrived from Hainan.

The Central Military Commission of the PRC re-created the marine corps under the PLAN in May 1980 in Anding County on Hainan. Surprisingly, it seems the PRC had no formal, dedicated marine uniform and service badge until 1994, but PLAN officers mention having previously served in marine corps duty tours.

It is nearly impossible to determine the actual number of Chinese marines during the early 1980s. Manpower estimates for an alleged fighting force of five divisions varied among analysts by the thousands for any particular year. However, the numbers they gave for amphibious vessels assigned to the marine corps were strikingly similar. Many of those vessels were used for transport, barracks, workshops, and other nonamphibious roles. Estimates on the number of tanks in the two tank brigades varied from only a few to as many as six hundred.

The first marine corps brigade was established in Hainan in May 1980, and a second 5,000-man marine brigade (the 164th) was established in Zhanjiang in 1991, although references have conflicting force-level estimates. With an increasing need for a credible force to intimidate Taiwan or other offshore islands, it would have been expected that the force would be based on the coast of southeast China on the strait facing Taiwan. Since the first brigade was based in Hainan, however, it seems that China was looking south for amphibious operations. Later events, such as the seizing of SCS islands and atolls, would lend credibility to that estimate of their planned use.

By the late 1980s there were some reports that claimed the marine corps had grown tremendously to three divisions, but a PLA reorganization begun in 1986 reportedly reduced the marines back to two brigades under South Sea Fleet command by the early 1990s. A heavy rapid-reaction force division intended for littoral offensive operations that could support marine missions was established in the Guangzhou Military Region in 1990. A major indicator that marines were truly constituted as a separate military organization under the navy was the introduction of unique white and blue camouflage for uniforms and equipment in 1994.[18]

The SCS fleet has always been the main amphibious force base, and in November 1995 one of the largest Chinese landing exercises was conducted there. Later, in March 1996, while Taiwan was having presidential elections, a series of missile "tests" led to the U.S. decision to send two carrier strike groups to western Pacific waters off Taiwan.[19] Meanwhile, a major amphibious landing exercise was held in Fujian province, adjacent to the Taiwan Strait, which was intended to intimidate and affect the election results. These amphibious troops were not naval marines, as claimed in press photos, but were from the infantry divisions of the PLA's 31st Army Group in Fujian. Three of these divisions are trained in amphibious landing operations.

Amphibious Ships

From 1962 to 1972 China built 45 Yuqin class LCMs. Construction started on 320 Yunnan-class LCMs and 23 Yuling-class landing craft, utility (LCUs) in 1972–74. Table 23 summarizes the characteristics of all amphibious craft as well as patrol boats by class. Indicators that the PRC is serious about having the capability to invade Taiwan have appeared recently with reports of cross-strait training of officers, such as this:

> The students and the officers and men taking part in the exercise put out to sea and made the crossing together, and it was just like a battlefield situation. Because the waves were very high, during the crossing, which took nearly 30 hours, everyone was drenched, and they experienced firsthand how those leading men on the front lines organize and command things, give psychological guidance, and carry out wartime political work and dynamic wartime management. They underwent a test involving foul conditions and environments, prevailing over the waves, seasickness, vomiting, and other such difficulties.[20]

The first large amphibious ship designed and built in China was the 4,100-ton Yukan-class LST in 1979. This means the government decision to design and build the LST came years before construction could begin at Zhonghua Shipyard in Shanghai. The Yukan was 20 meters longer than U.S. Navy LSTs and had 500-kilograms less full load weight. Like the American LSTs, the Yukan LST carried five tanks, plus a few vehicles and troops, but only seven were built from 1980 to 1995, indicating this was not exactly a high-priority program.

Table 23. PLAN Missile Craft/Amphibious/Gun Craft Types, 1968–2008

TYPE	MISSILE CRAFT	TYPE	AMPHIBIOUS	TYPE	GUN CRAFT
021	Huangfeng	067	Yunnan	025	Huchuan
037-2	Houxin	068	Yuchin	062C	Shanghai-2
520T	Houjian	069	Yuqin	037	Hainan
024	Houku	072	Yukan	037-1	Haiqing
022	Houbei	073	Yudao		
		079	Yuling		
		071	Yuzhao		

A large 20,000-ton Type 071 landing platform, dock (LPD) under construction in Dalian since 2004 was launched in December 2007. Named the *Kunlun Shan*, it was hidden from sight under cover next to the carrier *Varyag*. It has a large helicopter deck that can carry two large Z-8 troop helicopters and a well deck that holds four landing craft. It has a crew of only 120, compared to the crew of 396 on the *San Antonio*–class LPD, which is an interesting anomaly. Does it mean more automation or less mission functionality on the Type 071?

The construction of Qiongsha-class troop transports of 2,150 tons that can carry 400 troops began in 1980. Two Qiongshas were built as hospital ships for amphibious landing casualties and stationed in Hainan. This indicates that preparation had begun to use the amphibious ships and marines for opposed landings in the South China Sea. In 2008 a helicopter-carrying 10,000-ton Type 920 hospital ship named the *Daishanduo* (Peace Ark), hull number 866, was commissioned and based in the South Sea Fleet. The ship and its crew of 428 completed operational training in May 2009. This ship and the LPD that was launched the year before have been portrayed as an attempt by the PLAN to add disaster relief capability. This analysis was supported when the LPD was deployed to Somalia in July 2010. In August 2010 the hospital ship left Zhoushan to begin an eighty-seven-day deployment for humanitarian operations to five Middle East and African nations. In 1980 construction also began on four 1,460-ton Yudao-class LSMs, while in 1991 construction began on six larger Yuting-class LSTs, ending in 1996. These were 4,800 tons loaded and carried ten tanks, four LCUs on which 250 troops would debark, and two medium-size helicopters. This is more than twice the load of the earlier Yukan-class LST. Construction of Yutings ended around 1995, but in 2000 China began a new construction run of Type 072 Yuting-class LSTs, known as the Yuting III; nine of these have been built. Table 24 summarizes amphibious construction during three time periods.

In 1988 China occupied several islands in the Spratly chain, but no amphibious landings under fire were required, since the small islands and atolls were unoccupied. In 1995 China expanded its areas of control to an island claimed by the Philippines. The barren Mischief Reef in the easternmost Paracels was occupied in late 1998. Philippine air photos in November 1998 showed two Yuting-class LSTs, numbers 934 and 991, and two Yuting LSTs with different hull numbers in December 1998. These vessels make regular supply runs from Hainan to the Spratlys, a common function for PLAN amphibious ships and craft.

Hovercraft have a unique ability to carry troops across the water-sea interface and move over land. The first Chinese military assault landing craft, air cushion (LCAC), Type 722 Dagu, was built in 1980, and the 65-ton proto-type was decommissioned that same year. Production of the 6-ton Project 724 Jingsha II series followed in 1994. The Jingsha II has British hovercraft fea-tures, such as two large ducted airscrew propellers aft. Around 1998 Jingsha hovercraft, carrying ten marines, were observed exiting from Yuting LSTs. These 40-knot LCACs have been prominent in multiple amphibious exer-cises for several years. A new model LCAC named Yuyi was revealed when it swam out from LPD 998 en route to antipiracy duty. Recently launched in Shanghai, July 2010 was its first public exposure. It looked exactly like the 88-ton U.S. Navy LCAC design. The copying of the U.S. design was unex-pected. Russia and Ukraine had heavily marketed their LCAC products in China, and it would have seemed more likely that the Chinese craft would have more closely resembled those vessels.

Table 24. Three Eras of PLAN Amphibious Landing Craft/Ships

PERIOD	YEAR	TYPE	CLASS	NUMBER	TONNAGE	SOURCE
Phase A	1948	LST	1100	26	1,600	U.S.
WW-2	1948	LCU/LCI		100	300	U.S.
	1948	LSM	LSM-1	50	740	U.S.
	1950	LCM	T-4	75	70	USSR
Phase B	1962	LCM	Yuqin	50	85	PRC
	1968	LCM	Yuchai	30	85	PRC
Craft	1968	LCM	Yunnan	235	130	PRC
	1972	LCU	Yuling	23	730	PRC
Phase C	1979	LST	Yukan	7	4,100	PRC
	1980	Transport	Qiongsha	4	2,150	PRC
Ships/Craft	1980	LSM	Yudao	14	1,460	PRC
	1995	LST	Yuting	18	4,800	PRC
	1995	LCAC	Jingsha	30	5	PRC
	2000	LSM	Yuhai	15	800	PRC
	2006	LPD	Yuzhao	1	20,000	PRC
	2009	LCAC	Yuyi	4	88	U.S copy

In the past the PRC has claimed that there are two marine brigades based at Hainan totaling seven thousand men. Although the PLA and the PLAN have always had several hundred landing craft since 1949, many amphibious landings have primarily used junks or auxiliary craft. Since the 1980s, the LSTs have carried naval-uniformed marines during mock exercises held for the media. The actual landing forces tend to be specially trained army troops, rather than PLAN marines. In fact, to date LST, LCU, and LSM have mainly been observed performing logistic support functions.

In 2004 photos appeared of a radical new Houbei-class twin-hull, high-speed catamaran missile vessel, numbered 2208, that went into series production at several shipyards. Chinese marine equipment and uniforms have a unique blue and white camouflage pattern, whereas PLAN ships were always gray. The marine blue and white paint seen on Houbeis is illogical, unless the craft would assume a landing fire support mission. Another PLAN conversion, which took place in 2003–5, has equipped 053H frigate 516 with additional new modern 100-millimeter guns and replaced the HY-2 SSMs with five 50-cell, 122-millimeter stabilized tactical rocket launchers for shore fire support. These Type 89 launchers, based upon the Russian BM-21 design, have a forty-kilometer range.[21]

Photo 9. The 22,000-ton Type 071 LPD *Kunlun Shan*, lead ship in its class, in Dalian Shipyard. It was commissioned in 2007 and deployed to the Gulf of Aden with CNET 6 in July 2010. Source: Kanwa

Conclusions

As this chapter has shown, most of the PLAN coastal patrol craft are simple mass-produced designs. Attempts to produce more sophisticated, multifunction Haijiu PCs in 1980 and Houjian PCs in 1996 only delivered four and five units, respectively. Therefore, it could be some time before China builds a large force of more modern patrol boats. The Houbei catamaran missile boats are currently the only craft in mass production. It is interesting to note the different approach to littoral warfare craft taken by the USN and the PLAN. The U.S. Navy strategy is based on the littoral combat ship (LCS), which has three possible mission packages, compared to China's serial production of high-technology catamaran missile boats and sophisticated VLS frigates. In four years there have been only two U.S. LCSs, while China has constructed about fifty 022s and 054As.

In the meantime the PLAN marines corps, although under the PLAN, appears to be completely separate from the PLA or PLAN sailors. It has its own amphibious vessels, although they are observed frequently being used for logistics missions. This makes it difficult to say whether China has a credible amphibious force if the PLAN were to be ordered to invade Taiwan or any other coastline. Clearly the marines do have a number of modern ships and craft to launch a limited landing. They will have the number of men required to be carried onto and charge a beach under fire, but historically the bulk of any such invading force has been PLA soldiers or sailors with amphibious training.

Even though regular troops, not special marine forces, might be making any future crossing to Taiwan, the Chinese marine corps needs to be watched carefully, especially in the South China Sea. According to reports about China's creation of Sansha township, "Shock waves were felt immediately throughout the region: both Vietnam and Indonesia formally protested China's unilateral and preemptive move."[22] Seen in this context, the recent production of additional large amphibious landing craft, like the Yuting IIIs and LPDs, could indicate plans for large and distant landings.

—— 7 ——

The PLAN Air Force (PLANAF) and China's Future Aircraft Carrier

There is a widespread misconception that China has no naval air force to speak of, that the Chinese government does not give it priority, and that China lacks the capability to build or support a credible naval air power, with or without an aircraft carrier. As this chapter will show, in recent years China has been developing larger multipurpose ships with blue-water capabilities, making the lack of a carrier an increasingly large barrier to new naval missions. This makes building an indigenous aircraft carrier a priority goal.

Though the great majority of military equipment circa 1950 and afterward owned and operated by the PLANAF is of Soviet manufacture, the Chinese navy has made enormous strides to upgrade its antiquated flying forces. Following the collapse of the USSR in 1991, a PRC top priority has been upgrading its air force, strategic missiles, and naval forces, generally at the expense of the ground forces of the PLA, except for quick-reaction forces. This is the opposite of the PLA ground force dominance of military priorities during the Mao years. This change in priorities had been borne out in PRC conscription laws, in which service in the air force and the navy was four years, and the army and second artillery was three years. This changed in 1999 when all conscripts served for only two years and then no longer received technical training.[1]

The PRC is grappling with an inherent conflict of relying on foreign imported avionics technology versus developing a state-of-the-art domestic manufacturing base. China is continuing its long-term commitment to advanced avionics research and development both for internal use and for export, and foreign technology is one source feeding that endeavor. China has demonstrated the capability to design and manufacture a variety of civil and military aircraft that indicate that its aircraft industry has finally matured. However, nearly all export models, and many aircraft flown within China, feature imported avionics suites.

Outside of China's closest friends, the aviation military export market has been slow to materialize. China has yet to convince customers that its lower-priced units are comparable in quality, technology, and service support to those of its more mature Western or Russian competitors. The nation does have a large avionics education, research, and production infrastructure in place, but the only candidate naval aircraft are largely imported, especially for carrier deck landing duties. The only state-of-the art naval aviation radars or jet engines manufactured are copies of foreign designs.

Early History of the PLANAF

The first PLANAF aviation school was formed in Qingdao on 31 October 1950. The highly regarded Dalian and Shanghai naval academies also would include aviation specialties in that early period. Additional naval aviation training schools would later be established in Dachang, Jinxi, and Mudanjiang, which is the site of Naval Air Headquarters. The first naval air regiment was formed in 1952 from a battle-proven F-5 (MiG-15) unit back from People's Liberation Army Air Force (PLAAF) service in Korea. In 1954, as a result of a major reorganization, the naval air assets had control moved from the military districts to the three fleet headquarters.

The PLANAF's earliest naval aircraft were provided by the USSR. For naval reconnaissance and torpedo attack, China had received twin-engine Tu-2 bombers. In the mid-1950s the Soviet Union built a dozen Be-6 seaplanes specially for the PLANAF. Moscow also provided plans and assistance so that Mi-4 helicopters for SAR or ASW could be produced by license in China as the Z-5 from 1958 until 1979. Some twin-jet Il-28 naval bombers provided in the 1950s were reverse engineered by Harbin Aircraft Manufacturing, with production beginning in 1966 as the H-5. Chinese naval air F-5s (Mig-17s) and F-6s (MiG-19s) successfully shot down American reconnaissance aircraft in the 1950s and 1960s and participated in over-water Taiwan Strait air battles against Nationalist aircraft. By 1969 the PLANAF numbered about four hundred aircraft.

Due to the abrupt cooling in Sino-Soviet relations during the late 1950s, the PLANAF was forced to become independent for its modernization efforts. Even though the Vietnam War was heating up, China began to rely more and more on French imports. Aviation factories in Harbin experienced prolonged development delays because of the Cultural Revolution beginning in the mid-1960s. In 1976 Harbin tested a four-engine turbo-prop seaplane boat hull replacement for the Be-6, designated SH-5, which entered service at the

Tuandao Naval Air Station in Qingdao in 1986. Seven of these aircraft are still active.

This period saw other locally produced PLAAF aircraft being modified to meet the more stringent naval missions. The Q-5 ground attack aircraft entered PLAAF service in 1965, followed by a PLANAF variant in 1980 that included a long-range radio, a newer engine, and a water survival kit. Meanwhile the Chinese reverse engineered the Tu-16 for the PLAAF and designated it H-6. It is doubtful that the USSR provided an actual Tu-16 bomber, production licenses, or documentation. One of China's friends probably provided a Tu-16 illegally. A special navalized H-6D version was certified for PLANAF use in December 1985, including over-water navigation, special fire control, and sensors for launching two C-801 ASM. That same year, China modified a long-range (2,500-kilometer) four-turbo-prop Y-8 transport (an An-12 copy) into an MPA variant. Onboard equipment included a Litton APS-504 surveillance radar, new navigation and communication systems, infrared camera and detectors, and sonobuoys.

From 1978 to 1986, twelve naval auxiliaries had helicopter landing pads and could carry helicopters on board. Six had only helicopter decks, and six also included helicopter hangar facilities. The first PLAN helicopter landing on a ship occurred in January 1980. The year 1985 marked the first license copy of the French Sud SA-321 Super Frelon boat hull helicopter by Changhe Aircraft Industries Corporation, which was called the Z-8. The Z-8 helos were carried by two naval auxiliaries for the landmark 142-day Antarctic cruise in 1985. The prototype warship helicopter deck trials were on the DD 105 Luda II destroyer whose aft 130-millimeter gun mount had been replaced with a two-helicopter hangar and flight deck in 1987. The twin-engine Harbin Z-9A, which was a licensed copy of the Aerospatiale SA-365N Dauphin, was the first PLANAF warship helicopter. After receiving the initial order of eight Ka-28s in 1998, the PLAN received nine more in 2009. Reports that the PLAN had twenty-four Ka-28s prior to 2008 seem inflated and may actually total all foreign helicopters that can be deployed on warships.

Since 1970 China has greatly increased shore-based naval air capabilities and has conducted shipboard helicopter missions. Naval air supported South China Sea combat operations for Duncan Island in the Paracel (Xisha) Islands in the 1970s, and noncombat support increased from supply helicopters up to naval air reconnaissance. During this period, the PLANAF increased the number of aircraft from four hundred to seven hundred, and may have doubled in size from 15,000 to 30,000 personnel or more.

The Avionics Industry

A look into China's aircraft and avionics history offers some insight into what can be expected in the future naval air force. When the Communists took over China in 1949, the country had no avionics factories. The first effort to create them did not occur until 1951, when the Soviet Union needed a local avionics capability to repair Korean War battle damage and to support the number of aircraft provided to China during the war. To accomplish this, China's Soviet mentor sent twenty avionics experts to train an initial cadre of a hundred young Chinese technical students.[2] The next year the first three avionics repair factories were opened by converting existing plants to the new task. Horse sheds located on a Chinese army base were converted into machinery shops and became the Taiyuan Aeronautical Instruments Factory.

In 1953 China's first Five-Year Plan called for expanding the nascent avionics industry to five plants, making them capable of licensed production. Five new avionics plants were built in Shaanxi province. By the next year, China's first effort to go beyond repair and on to copy production began in Taiyuan; in 1954 the PRC's first avionics research and development (R & D) training institute was opened.

Early in the 1950s the government initiated a plan to establish a research institute, six aircraft repair core factories, and twelve production plants. By 1959 four aeronautical electrical apparatus factories were built at Tianjin, Xingping, and Beijing.

The second Five-Year Plan mandated that China develop five more avionics factories.[3] The disastrous Great Leap Forward devastated China's industrial base from 1958 until 1960 and China's five-year avionics goals were not met for eight years. In 1965, fearful of a possible Soviet or U.S. attack on its coastal cities, China began relocating coastal factories farther inland to an area designated as the third line. These plants were not situated in major cities but in far, remote mountainous areas.[4]

In the early 1960s the original avionics factories started evolving from vacuum tubes to transistor and then later to microcircuit technology. Even though 6 Shanghai avionics plants were relocated inland, 10 major aviation plants remained in Shanghai. By the mid-1970s the China Aviation Industry Corporation totaled 111 enterprises. To be able to design new aircraft or indigenous avionics, three research institutes were combined into the Beijing Institute of Aeronautics and Astronautics, and by 1965 China had formed eleven aeronautic secondary schools.

From 1958 to 1963 the Communist Party tried to build thirty new aviation schools, but the Cultural Revolution later closed or merged thirty-eight schools. In the late 1960s specialized aeronautical research institutes were established for design. The desire to create in-country design capability drove the production of new avionics electronics and armament research schools in 1972. By 1975 China once again had thirty-six aeronautic R & D institutes and six aeronautic programs at major universities. The Third Plenary then expanded beyond internal research and development to encourage foreign imports and technical exchange. By 1980 China had included electronics and computers in avionics design as well as in the products themselves.

Attempts to Reverse Engineer Foreign Systems

China began its institutional avionics efforts by reverse engineering Soviet designs in duplicating the Soviet TU-16 bomber. Autopilot technology is a good example, as Chinese avionics engineers successfully replicated Soviet AP-5 autopilots used in China's H-5 and H-6 bombers. In 1958 the Aeronautical Automatic Control Research Institute began a complete redesign of this unreliable and inaccurate unit. The new version, called the KJ-3 autopilot, was produced by the Lanzhou aeronautical instruments factory nine years later.[5] Flight control systems have advanced to the Type 622 system that features triple redundancy with large-scale integrated circuits, digital computers, microprocessors, and embedded built-in test features.

After relying on copies of the MiG-15 through MiG-21, known as the J-4 through J-7, for nearly twenty-five years, China produced the indigenous J-8 design in 1980, based on the prototype MiG E-152A Finback, which featured entirely Chinese-manufactured avionics.[6] These systems included the KJ-12 autopilot, the HZX heading/attitude reference system, the Type SM-8 optical gun sight, and the Type III rocket ejection seat. The Chengdu plant improved Soviet single airspeed and altitude air data systems by fitting them with miniature servos to supply many of the flight parameters for the J-8.

In 1980 an updated J-8I fighter had the Type SR-4 air intercept radar replaced with an improved Sichuan Type 204.[7] Unreliable Nanjing YB-20B hydraulic pumps were later replaced with improved ZB-34 hydraulics. The older direct current (DC) power system was replaced with a more capable Hubei alternating current (AC) power generator and new DC-to-AC static converters, and a new Taiyuan head-up display (HUD) and digital flight computer were also installed on the J-8II.[8] Future J-8II/F-8II upgrades would replace many of these Chinese avionics with more advanced foreign imports.[9] However, the 1989 Tiananmen Square boycott ended the Grumman upgrade to the J-8II. This would have been a milestone of military technology transfer to China, consisting of an LN-39 inertial navigation system (INS), pulse

Doppler look-down air intercept radar, HUD, and data computer with a 1553B data bus.

The J-8IIM flew in a 1996 air show with the Russian Phazotron Zhuk multimode air intercept radar linked to Vympel AA-10 and LY-60 air-to-air missiles, an FC computer, a Xi'an INS, and the GPS via an ARINC 429 data bus. Power generators were upgraded to 15 kilovolt amperes to handle the additional avionics. An export F-8IIM was similarly upgraded, reportedly with Israeli assistance.

A Chinese helmet-mounted look-and-shoot sight, similar to those on the Russian Su-27 fighter aircraft, was displayed by the Luoyang Electro-Optical Equipment Research Institute in 1996. The purchase of forty-eight Su-27s with licensed production by Chinese plants included a full array of state-of-the-art onboard avionics. Meanwhile, modern Russian Sukhoi upgraded naval aircraft have put the PLANAF on a par with most modern Western naval air, and ahead of many of its Asian competitors.

In 2005 Russia signed two contracts to supply 250 AL-31F engines for Su-27 SK and Su-30MKK aircraft to China. That year China had two regiments (fifty aircraft) of Su-30 MK2 stationed at naval air bases in the eastern and southern fleet naval districts. The PLAN Su-MK2s and PLAAF Su-30 MKKs are superior to F-15s and F-16s, requiring the first-production F-22 Raptors to be based in Guam in 2007.[10]

Other Foreign Imports

Despite government policies promoting domestic avionics, Chinese upgrade programs for military and civil aircraft have relied heavily on foreign imports. The Chengdu factory, for example, began the J-7M aircraft design in 1981 and delivered it in 1985. An export version, the F-7M, named Air Guard, was produced jointly with GEC. It featured a GEC-Marconi Type 956 HUD weapon aiming computer, Sky Ranger ranging radar, air data computer, altimeter, digital IFF, and AD-3400 VHF/UHF radio. A later upgrade, called F-7MP, was exported to Pakistan with a Collins AN/ARN-147 VHF omnidirectional inertial landing system, automatic direction finder (ADF), and digital distance measuring equipment.[11]

The PLAN certified a maritime patrol version of the Y-8 with U.S. radar, navigation and communications, submarine detector, and sonobuoys. U.S. firms also provided a major civilian Y-8 upgrade, including a Collins VHF radio, automatic direction finder navigation and Litton search radar, and British Searchwater radars.

Two competitive upgrade offers to the A-5 attack model emerged in 1988. France proposed an improved HUD, laser ranger, and inertial navigation system (INS), while Italy recommended ranging radar, an MS-1553B data bus, a HUD, and navigation-attack system upgrades to the A-5.[12] In the mid-1990s GEC-Marconi upgraded the F-7MG with Sky Ranger multifunction radar, navaids, a HUD, and a computer.

China's F-8IIM Finback export fighter aircraft featured a new multifunctional HUD similar to that incorporated in the J-8IIM, including a Xi'an INS/ GPS and multimode air intercept radar. In 1996 the newest F-8IIM Finback combat aircraft upgrade flew with a modern Russian multimode Zhuk-8 pulse Doppler radar, multifunction displays, a hands-off target assignment system, and an integrated electronics countermeasure system mixed with indigenous technologies.[13]

Beijing is engaging in other joint ventures to manufacture Western avionics. Examples include the Allied Signal Aerospace partnership with China National Aero-Technology Import and Export for auxiliary power units and with Shanghai Avionics for radar and radios. Rockwell is also part of a joint venture for developing and producing GPS/INS systems. Meanwhile, Chengdu Aero-Instrument Corporation is jointly producing Honeywell air data computers, and reportedly Collins also has several production team deals in China. If these ventures succeed, then it may allow China to push itself into the global avionics market.

Recent History of Chinese Naval Airpower

During the past two decades, events along China's lengthy coastline would show the need for the PLANAF's naval air capabilities and so would sometimes push the high-technology limits of Chinese industry and imports ahead of the PLAAF. For example, the drive for naval air access to the South China Sea was helped by the completion of a 7,874-foot runway on Woody Island during the 1990s. A January 1999 satellite photo showed fuel facilities under construction for naval aircraft.[14]

From the 1960s up to the 1990s, Chinese interceptors have consisted mainly of Soviet MiG-15s to MiG-21s indigenously upgraded in engine and airframe and with imported Western avionics. The J-7III and J-8II interceptors are so different from their MiG-19 and MiG-21 ancestors as to qualify as nearly new designs.

The most modern Chinese interceptors included Russian Su-27 and Su-30 series Flankers. Russia manufactured twenty-four Su-27s, plus two two-seater trainers, at the Komsomolsk factory in 1992 and flew them to the Wuhu Air

Base west of Shanghai. One part of the sales agreement required that China would not base the Flankers in northern China, where they could oppose Russian forces. China reportedly has broken this agreement and has moved Su-27s to bases near the Russian border.

Photo 10. A PLAN flight support crew next to their Russian-made Su-30, which is painted in Chinese colors. Source: Kanwa

Negotiations for a third batch of thirty-eight Flankers stalled when China wanted to produce the aircraft in-country. A batch of Su-30 aircraft and anti-ship missiles were bought in 1999, and most of the thirty-eight upgraded Su-30MK2 naval aircraft are stationed at Luqiao in the Nanjing Military District.[15] An additional twenty-four Su-27s are based at the Suixi Air Base in southern China. China has a total of seventy-six Su-30MK regular and upgraded models.

Russia also reported that China had entered into negotiations for the carrier-modified version of the Su-30, designated Su-33, in 1997, which finally ended unsuccessfully in December 2009. After the delivery of the first batch of Su-27MK2 aircraft, negotiations have dragged out for years for a second batch. The Chinese are asking for avionic upgrades beyond what Russia wanted to provide. This is understandable, since China reverse engineered two Russian Phazotron ZHUK radars, which are being produced by the Wuxi 107 Institute, and China's J-11B is an illegal copy of the Su-27UBK or Su-27SK. China installed Russian AL31FN turbofan engines on their J-10 fighters, which Russia then forbid them to export. China illegally copied the AL31FN engines as the WS10 engine. The WS10 engine has serious quality problems but is being installed in the J-11Bs. In 2005 negotiations for upgrading the earlier Su-27SK and obtaining a new Su-30MK2 were still pending. In 2009 Sukhoi stated that new technology would not be sold to China, due to that country copying technology and competing with Russia on sales. An upgrade of the Chinese Su-27SK would include an air-to-air refueling probe, an enhanced multifunction fire control, and a longer-range ASM.

Russia believes the Chinese carrier program will need the Su-33 or Su-35.[16] The major difference between the Su-33 and Su-27 is the addition of nose canards and folding wings for carrier stowage on the Su-33. As of December 2006 a contract for sixty single-seater Su-33 airplanes and forty two-seater Su-33 UB upgrade models had yet to be confirmed.[17] By October 2008 negotiations for the purchase of fifty Su-33s were still ongoing because China wanted to buy just the new Su-33 radar technology, but Russia wants to sell complete aircraft. The Su-33 export deal finally ended in failure in December 2009 because Russia wanted to sell forty aircraft and China would buy only four.[18] After obtaining a prototype SU-33 from the Ukraine a couple of years ago, Shenyang has built a copy called the "J15" as a folding-wing carrier aircraft. The PLANAF J15 began flight tests at Shenyang in September 2010. China is building a flight test center at Yanliang in Shaanxi province, complete with a ski jump flight deck, copied from the naval air test site in the Ukraine.[19]

Two of the most advanced Chinese fighters were obtained for the PLANAF's needs, ahead of the PLAAF, which also sought them. Intended to replace the ancient H-5 bomber, the indigenous JH-7 attack bomber looks similar to the Su-24, with the pilot and the weapons operator sitting side by side for all-weather, low-level attack missions. The JH-7 entered PLANAF service in 1993 with Xi'an-produced WS-9 copies of tile Rolls-Royce Spey engines. It has been further promoted by Xi'an as the Fighter-Bomber China (FBC-1), first displayed at the 1998 Zuhai Air Show. The FBC-1 avionics are very modern with a JL-10A multimode radar that tracks up to fifteen targets, the Blue Sky forward-looking infrared (FLIR)/radar navigation pod and FLIR/laser targeting pod, and the triple fly-by-wire system, all made in China. The other plane is the very capable Su-27, which has been assigned to naval air bases. The first regiment of 30 Su-MK2s was delivered in 1992 and a second regiment in 1996. Shenyang is producing two hundred Su-30MK2s under license as the J-11; the first was delivered in February 1999. At least one regiment is based at the Sanya Naval Air Station, in southern Hainan, for SCS operations.

One key need for interceptors is an airborne early warning (AEW) aircraft. Bidding was intense among three nations to provide a modern, long-range airborne early warning radar for China. The United Kingdom marketed the Searchwater radar by Racal and the Marconi Argus radar, Israel proposed the

Phalcon radar, and Russia offered the Ilyushin A-50 Candid airborne early warning aircraft. China contracted for the Israeli radar on Il-76 aircraft that were bought from Uzbekistan.

Beginning in 1990, Israel was reportedly assisting China in installing solid-state L-band conformal array antennas on a Yun-8 transport. Such an airborne early warning asset would be useful over land or at sea to detect air targets and to vector fighter aircraft. When Israel installed an airborne warning and control system (AWACS) radar and aerial refueling rig on an Il-76, the United States insisted that the AWACS radar and other electronics be removed before delivery to China, forcing cancellation of the deal in 1999.

Several years of negotiations with Russia to sell its A-50 AWACS to China ended in 2002. Since then, China has received a few Il-76 bodies from Tashkent, Uzbekestan. The Xi'an Aircraft Company has modified several, and two additional AWACS have been completed by Xi'an without an in-flight refueling capability. Two indigenous AWACS versions are competing with each other. One, developed in 2004, has a large dish antenna like the American AWACS; the other, produced in 2006, has a Swedish Saab EMB-45 tilted beam antenna. They are referred to as KJ-200 or KJ-2000, respectively, by China.[20] The Ilyushin Design Bureau denies providing assistance to the Chinese AWACS radar. This rapid development has allowed China to field several AWACS in 2007, prior to India's first. Russia had been bidding for AWACS deliveries to both nations for years.

In-flight refueling capability has been added to some fighters with the conversion of five H-6 bombers into refueling tankers. The Hongyou-6 aerial refueling aircraft were seen in public for the first time during the 1999 National Day parade. The PRC has reportedly agreed to spend US$1.5 billion for thirty-eight Il-76 Candid transport aircraft and Il-78 Midas refueling aircraft, which means that the Russian Su-30MKK multipurpose combat aircraft, after one refueling, will increase its maximum range to 5,200 kilometers, close to that of Hong-6 medium bombers. "It is exactly because of the presence of this miraculous 'force multiplying' effect that the Chinese military has decided to develop and possess large aerial refueling aircraft."[21]

After the Luda II helicopter prototype, naval air was integrated into warship missions with a helicopter on the five Jiangwei-class frigates and two Luhu-class DDGs, both classes launched in 1991, and the 6,000-ton Luhai-class DDG, launched in 1997. The later 052C Luyang-class DDG carried two Z-9A helicopters, and the 052B and 051C have only single helicopter hangars. The emphasis on the naval helicopter ASW mission was the reason for China's request for three Ka-27s for evaluation in 1993, which resulted in the procurement of twelve in 1999. These helicopters would enhance shipboard ASW considerably over the Z-9As. Their purchase was followed by the acquisition of nine ASW Ka-28 helicopters in 2009, after five years of delay. The helicopter contracts did not include automatic communication and navigation systems.[22] Another step toward air operations was taken when the 10,000-ton air training ship *Shichang* was launched in 1997. Its helicopter deck occupies all of the main deck except for a compact bridge structure forward. It is dedicated to training aviators in at-sea operations.

The first at-sea rendezvous of two PLANAF fighters with warships beyond five hundred miles from the Chinese mainland occurred in May 1986. As mentioned in chapter 6, in October 1994 the PLANAF showed itself able to meet the most challenging distant sea mission. A Han SSN was under intense countermeasures by air assets from the USS *Kitty Hawk*'s battle group off the Korean coast. The North Sea Fleet headquarters (HQ) sent some naval air F-6s out to the area to support their submarine. The F-6s successfully navigated out, found the carrier task group, and returned to Qingdao under positive control. This was another "first" for the PLANAF.

The infrastructure for training naval air personnel was added to the first Naval Aviation Engineering College at Yantai in the 1990s. The number of naval air personnel dropped from 40,000 in 1989 to 25,000 in 2005. The amount of discarded obsolete aircraft was offset by new-generation aircraft, so the number of naval aircraft remains at about 750. China's naval air force entered the twenty-first century with a new generation of ASW helos, an all-weather attack JH-7 regiment, at least two Su-33 regiments, long-range MPAs, air refueling capability, and land-based AWACS aircraft. The finale of this phenomenal growth might be China's first aircraft carrier, which has been a matter of speculation for some time.

China's Elusive Aircraft Carrier

To date China has towed four foreign aircraft carriers to its ports. Its goal has been to study or dissect these discards and learn naval construction details unique to carriers. In 1985 a dummy carrier deck was constructed at an air base north of Beijing for deck landing and handling trials using the J-8III. In 2008, on the roof of the long Number 701 Institution building, located far inland in Wuhan, there appeared a full size mock-up similar to the *Varyag*'s bridge and flight deck. This "Comprehensive Testing Platform" by the Chinese Warship Research and Design Center even has a model Su-33 and Z-8 helicopter parked on the "flight deck."[23] The Wuhan platform has a ski jump bow and gas turbine vents, which answers two questions under discussion: no catapult and no steam propulsion.[24] The first carrier bought was the 15,000-ton decommissioned RAN (Royal Australian Navy) *Melbourne*, which was towed to Dalian in 1984 for scrapping, but was studied by naval engineers for more than five years before being dismantled.

Photo 11. This full mock-up of a carrier deck and bridge is on top of the Number 701 Institution building, located far inland in Wuhan, for topside EMI testing. Source: Kanwa

Meanwhile, China has bought three former Soviet large carriers. China's claims that they were to be used as resorts or tourist hotels sound dubious. The *Minsk* was initially sold to South Korea for scrap steel. A Chinese company bought the *Minsk* from Korea and towed the 45,000-ton carrier to the Wenchong Shipyard in Guangzhou city in August 1998. The *Minsk* is now the centerpiece of a theme park in Shenzhen, called Minsk World. It is alongside a pier in Dapeng Bay, and until recently thousands of tourists have admired the PLAN aircraft parked on the flight deck beneath naval signal dress ship flags. During 2005, however, Minsk World Industries Company was declared bankrupt in a Shenzhen court, and the aircraft carrier was auctioned on 31 May 2006 for $16 million. It still remains at the Shenzhen Museum in 2010.

The second Soviet carrier was the *Kiev*, which was the same class as the *Minsk*. It was decommissioned and disarmed in 1995 and purchased in 2000. It is now anchored near Tianjin. It is the main attraction in the Tianjin North Sea Warship Recreation Park with other retired warships.[25]

Following the USSR's collapse, Nikolayev Shipyard in the Ukraine stopped work on the *Varyag*. In 1992 Chinese naval officials visited and bid on the 70 percent complete 67,000-ton carrier. The ship had no pro-pulsion engines or rudders. After the weapon systems were removed, China bought the ship for scrap in 1998. The *Varyag* was towed for 627 days from Nikolayev Shipyard and arrived at Macao in February 2002. China claimed the carrier was to be converted into a gambling casino. However, soon after its arrival it was towed from Macao to a pier at the Dalian Naval Base, arriv-ing on 3 March 2002. It moved to dry dock in June 2005. The bridge island structure is being worked on and electronics are being installed. It was also painted navy gray, which suggests it is considered part of the PLAN. During 2006 it was being intensely worked on in a high-security dry dock in Dalian. It was also reported on 9 January 2008 that to send a message to Taiwan the ship will soon be officially renamed "the Shi Lang," after the Chinese general who took possession of Taiwan in 1683.[26] After four years in the same loca-tion, the *Varyag* was towed to a different dry dock in Dalian for more com-plex internal work on 27 April 2009.

Photo 12. The Russian-exported aircraft carrier *Varyag* undergoing a refit in Dalian Shipyard in 2009. It is expected to be a training platform for the anticipated PLAN carrier. Source: Kanwa

There are rumors that China has obtained detailed drawings and speci-fications for one or two of the former Soviet carriers. Surprisingly, Chinese officers who have publicly advocated carriers in the press were skippers of frigates (FF 537) or destroyers (DDG 108). One would expect to have had heard such statements from naval air admirals, such as Li Jung in the 1980s, or Rear Admiral Ma Bingzhi, the PLANAF commander in the 1990s, which may show that the PLAN's top brass had been ordered not to talk about the aircraft carrier program. If there had been such a ban, it had been lifted by 2008, when a number of statements began appearing in the press about China needing a carrier and the ordering of catapults and tailhooks from Russia.

There have been many unconfirmed stories of other new carrier activities. In 1993 Beijing reportedly claimed that it would begin construction on two 48,000-ton carriers, which would be completed by 2005. Two years later reports reduced the size of the two carriers to 40,000 tons, but construction was said to begin in 1996. China had reportedly opened negotiations in 1995 to have the Spanish Bazan shipyard build two 23,000-ton carriers, similar to the 12,000-ton carrier built for Thailand. In 1996 China allegedly discussed buying the *Clemenceau* from France when it was replaced by the nuclear carrier *Charles de Gaulle*. In July 1998 Indian media claimed that two 40,000-ton carriers were being built in a shipyard at Dalian and even claimed the carrier construction was called "project 9935."[27] Finally, a picture circulating on the Internet from spring 2004 onward showed a large hull with an underwater bulbous bow and very wide beam in Shanghai and this picture was labeled as "a carrier."

To date, however, not one of these reports has come true.[28] In fact China's 2006 national defense white paper had two naval aviation changes that might predicate against a carrier: the PLAN cut the naval aviation department and put control of its naval assets directly under the area fleet commands.[29] Later white papers have reversed these moves and advocate China's need for carriers.

The most recent report that China is starting a carrier program contends that two 50,000- to 60,000-ton carriers will begin construction in 2009 and be completed by 2015.[30] The same unidentified sources predicted that the work would take place in a new Shanghai shipyard and that the ships would be deployed to the South Sea Fleet.

Aircraft Carrier Shipyard Factors

Although not substantiated by the presence of an actual aircraft carrier, the Dalian New Shipyard is considered to be one of China's shipyards that are most capable of building a carrier. This shipyard was established in 1894 and enlarged in 1990, with impressive dry docks and engine shops. Nearby Shenyang and Harbin have numerous plants making steel, hulls, and mechanical and electric equipment, assisted by a direct Shen-Da (South Manchurian) rail link from Harbin to Dalian. Considerable North Sea Fleet naval air facilities are also nearby.

The second choice would be the East Sea Fleet's Jiangnan Shipyard in Shanghai. Jiangnan, like Dalian, has built the most advanced warships and many large-tonnage naval vessels. Both the Dalian and Jiangnan shipyards have built the newest Luhu and Luhai DDGs, with French combat systems and Ukrainian gas turbines. Harbin Turbine has built Mashproekt GT-25000 gas turbines under Ukrainian license. Shanghai also has a variety of local sources for complex systems required by the carrier, plus a naval aviation school. The Shanghai United Electric Company is the largest producer of boilers, turbines, and generators in China.

A third less credible candidate could be the South Sea Fleet's Wenchong Shipyard in Guangzhou. This shipyard, in particular, has a 150,000-ton dry dock. Thus, there are capable yards located in each of the three fleet areas, although building an aircraft carrier at a Guangzhou shipyard would cause it to be isolated from the steel and electronic technology centers located farther north.

A major shift away from the traditional Shanghai shipyard structure along the Huangpu River in old Shanghai emerged in 2005. Jiangnan Shipyard established a modern new shipyard, including two 300,000-ton docks at the Waigaoqiao waterfront of the Pudong New District. The same year Shanghai announced plans to develop three of the Chongming Islands in the mouth of the Yangtze River. Changxing Island, closest to Pudong, will be the site of a giant complex of shipyards, many of which will be relocated from their old Shanghai locations. In June 2008 Jiangnan Shipyard was the first to relocate to Changxing, where it has four huge dry docks and nine outfitting piers. There will be a nine-kilometer tunnel under the Yangtze connecting Waigaoqiao to Changxing Island in 2010. These factors make this area the most likely new carrier construction site.

The question of how many years it could take China to have a full-deck catapult carrier at sea is important. The Soviet navy initially had only helicopter-equipped warships like the PLAN, and it took thirty years for it to evolve from Moskva (helicopter) to Kiev vertical or short takeoff and landing (V/STOL) to Kuznetsov (catapult launch). Examples of development time for previous new Chinese navy technologies provide another measure. From keel laying (1968) to operational capability (1974) for the first Han SSN was seven years; for the Xia SSBN, it was eleven years. It took another six years for a JL-1 SLBM to be launched. It took fifteen years until the first SAM surface warship (FFG 531) was operational. It was probably not entirely successful, as the CSA-N-1 was never installed on the second ship in the class

(FFG 532), and both ships were scrapped a few years later. It must be noted, however, that China has considerably reduced development and construction times in the last five years for new Luyang DDGs, 054 and 054A frigates, and Yuan diesel and Shang nuclear submarines.

Meanwhile, the largest and most complex naval support ship to date is the 21,000-ton space tracking vessel *Yuan Wang*, which took only four years to be built, but was similar to the Fuqing auxiliary oiler (AO) class being constructed in Shanghai during that same period. Based on these earlier examples, if the keel were laid in 2009, China could probably have a 20,000-ton helicopter carrier by 2015, or a 40,000-ton aircraft carrier with a full air wing operational by 2019. Western experts note that the time needed to build up a carrier task group would probably be a prime weakness. However, the new Luhu, Luhai, Luyang DDGs, and four Sovremennyys already delivered would appear to fill such a need. The operational requirements for American carriers are far more rigorous than China will likely need in the near term. So long as the aircraft carrier operates within adjacent regional waters, China's other land-based air assets could help provide local air cover. Any foreseeable conflict against a major naval power would probably be within Chinese-defined defensive zones.

Since 1982 China has claimed its right to an offshore First Island Chain defense zone running from the Kurils to Japan, Taiwan, the Philippines, and the SCS. A more distant Second Island Chain extended from the Kurils to Japan, the Bonins, and the Marianas to the Carolines. An ominous new concept, which has been termed "national interest frontier," for defining areas of PLAN influence, possibly beyond the old First and Second Line islands, appeared in early 2009. On 4 January the *PLA Daily* stated that "using maritime forces to protect national maritime interest is an important measure for the PLA Navy to safeguard the national interest of our country."[31] Since there is no international law on this concept, or even a Chinese definition for it, the implication this might have for Chinese government or naval strategy is a serious concern to other naval powers. During March and April 2010, for example, two Chinese flotillas conducted exercises beyond the First Island Chain.

Conclusions

Although China imports many foreign avionics units, several civil and military aircraft feature completely indigenous avionics suites. However, for PLANAF aircraft the Chinese seem to prefer Western, and lately Russian, avionics because the Chinese avionics industry is unable to provide the desired equipment.

Assuming that China wants to export its aircraft, then Western customers tend to favor avionics brands and product lines that they know and respect. While China's sales of surface ships have done well, Chinese shipbuilders have tended to sell the hulls to foreign buyers, who then go to other Western companies to buy high-technology electronics to install in the ships.

As for a Chinese aircraft carrier, the immediate need for one has been offset by China's use of offshore islands, which will be discussed at greater length later in this book. However, the development of aircraft carrier capabilities is clearly part of the PLAN's long-term plans, either as a status symbol or as an emblem of China's role as a major naval power. Other area navies, like India's and Indonesia's, which either have or seek to acquire aircraft carriers, would severely limit the PLAN's capabilities. These same powers, including Russia, India, and American allies such as Japan, Taiwan, and Korea, seem to surround China.[32] The life of a Chinese carrier against a U.S. carrier battle group would be measured in minutes, so China would use its carrier in other nonconfrontational scenarios. With more and more of its vital oil supplies coming from the Persian Gulf, China fears that its lengthy SLOC to Africa and the Middle East might be disrupted. Escorting oil tankers with Luyang DDGs or a supporting South China Sea escort group would be an asymmetrical situation favoring the Chinese carrier. For these reasons, if for no other, the PLAN's carrier program will most likely take place and must be watched carefully.

——8——

Antiair-Warfare (AAW) Radar and Weapon Systems

The PRC is supplementing decades of foreign-built coastal AD systems with new indigenous technologies. These upgrades include long-range radar systems, new SAMs, improved communications systems, and top-of-the-line Russian jet fighter aircraft. The PRC has also developed two variant models of AWACS.

This modernization effort is taking place despite the evaporation of the Soviet naval threat to Asia and the decline of the Russian army as a rival. These momentous changes have not stilled the Chinese expansion of air defense capabilities and assets, but have perhaps spurred them on since China now has a chance of catching up to and perhaps even surpassing its Asian neighbors.

Meanwhile, new radars continue to emerge from Chinese researchers who have honed their skills with years of work on air defense technologies acquired from a variety of nations. China also maintains its import pipeline with recent purchases of the latest Russian and Western radars available on the international market. As a result, China's coastal and shipboard AD has improved substantially over the past decade.

China's Air Defense Regions and Radar Systems

The People's Liberation Army's AD was a large and fairly modern asset in the 1950s and early 1960s. Over the past few decades, however, this force became obsolete, with no new medium-altitude surface-to-air missile entering service until 1986. Recent Russian S-300 high-altitude air-defense radars and missiles have rectified this, but portions of China's coastlines still do not have this asset.

From 1955 to 1985 China's mainland comprised eleven military regions. The nation consolidated these into seven in 1985, matching the air defense regions, each with its own regional control center. In addition, modern warships with three-dimensional radars and SAMs could be used as AD assets. In the mid-1960s completion of an underground cable network linking all major cities and air defense control centers to AD headquarters in Beijing ensured survivable communications, even after attack.

Open-literature estimates on the number of coastal Chinese surface-to-air missile sites, antiaircraft guns, radars, air defense troops, and fighter aircraft remain strangely static. In fact China probably has added at least fifty new surface-to-air missile sites in the last decade, with more than eighteen being coastal S-300 SAM sites.[1] The past three decades have seen considerable expenditures for development of modern Chinese air defense radars. The main center for the latest radar developments is the Nanjing Research Institute of Electronics Technology. Much of the microelectronics, millimeter devices, displays, and millimeter wave diodes are developed in Nanjing at the Electronic Devices Research Institute and the Institute of Technology Radio Engineering Department.

The new Type 408C long-range warning radar is a large VHF radar, needing eight vans to hold all of its equipment. It operates in two bands, from 100 to 120 megahertz and from 150 to 180 megahertz. Its 8-meter-by-16-meter antenna transmits 800 kilowatts.[2] The HN-401R long-range air defense warning radar has a similar double-rectangular antenna on a smaller scale. Only three vans are needed to contain all of this system. The 401 operates in the UHF band and puts out only 20 kilowatts. Although smaller and lower powered, this radar's detection range is still in excess of 300 kilometers (188 miles).[3]

Surveillance Radar

China's first surveillance radar was the JY-8. Still in use, this unit is a mobile van-mounted radar that also provides target acquisition and interception control. The system uses four vans and is fully solid-state except for its transmitter tubes. It has fifteen transmit beams and eleven receiver beams ranging from 920 to 1,210 megahertz. The three pulse repetition frequencies are 365, 500, and 600 hertz. The JY-8 has two transmitters and puts out 800 kilowatts with a detection range of 350 kilometers (219 miles). A modified version of the JY-8, designated JY-8A, reduces the range to 150 kilometers but provides good low-altitude detection.[4]

The JY-9 is another Chinese-built three-dimensional low-altitude search radar. It operates in the S-band with a 20-microsecond pulse, and it uses a cosecant squared antenna. Installers can set up the radar antenna on a lattice mast in only twenty minutes and its maximum detection range is 150 kilometers (94 miles).[5] China's HN-503 warning radar has the longest detection range of any of that nation's AD radars with a maximum of 646 kilometers (400 miles).[6] The operating band ranges from 150 to 170 megahertz with a very long pulse length of 430 microseconds. The pulse repetition frequency (PRF) is a relatively slow 230 hertz, and this radar is intended to support naval air interceptions at coastal sites.

A new three-dimensional radar is the Type 146-1A. This radar has a 430 microsecond pulse length and a detection range of 350 kilometers. The three PRF choices are 250, 500, and 1,000 hertz. Another three-dimensional radar, the JY-14 antijam radar with a range of 320 kilometers, has been exported to Venezuela and Iran.

An over-the-horizon (OTH) radar, possibly United States supplied, has been reported to be operational in northern China since the early 1980s. It was intended to monitor Soviet Far East forces that were threatening China. More recently China has completed a second OTH radar in the southern part of the country that overlooks the South China Sea, where China and other Asian nations contest ownership of various islands. The frequency-modulated and continuous high-frequency waves are transmitted in 4-, 8-, or 24-kilohertz bands. The twenty sets of 50 kilowatt transmitters put out 1 megawatt of power. The range is from 700 to 3,500 kilometers within a 60-degree arc of coverage, meaning that this radar can support SCS naval operations.

China applies an unusual REL designation to a design of air management radar located at all seven air defense region headquarters. The operating frequency is 1,250 to 1,350 megahertz with a 200-hertz PRF and a detection range of 360 kilometers. A navalized REL-1 radar is on the Luhu DDGs.

Chinese forces must also be able to correlate data from various sites and coordinate defense forces. The South West Research Institute of Radar in Duyun developed a mobile three-dimensional solid-state information-processing-equipment van. The equipment can track as many as twenty-four targets with either manual, semiautomatic, or fully automatic modes. There is a trend to low-altitude detection and importing antistealth radars such as the Kolchak radar from the Czech Tesla Company. China imported four sets of the Kolchuga stealth radar in 2002 and also the Iskra 36D6 stealth radar from the Ukraine.

Surface-to-air Missiles (SAMs)

China's first SAMs were the SA-2 Guideline missiles provided by the Soviet Union in the late 1950s. The People's Liberation Army manufactured these weapons and designated them HQ-2. The latest HQ-2B mobile battery of six missiles can attack more than one target at a time. It is effective from an altitude of 5,000 to 25,000 meters and out to a range of more than 40 kilometers, with improved electronic counter-countermeasures and warhead.

During the mid-1980s the PLA strove for an indigenous SAM design, designated the HQ-61. This missile appears similar to the U.S. Sparrow, but it is longer at 3.99 meters (13 feet) and heavier at 300 kilograms (660 pounds). The HQ-61 uses semiactive radar homing guidance and continuous wave illumination. This Mach-3 missile has a maximum range of 10 kilometers and 8,000 meters altitude. HQ-61A upgraded missiles have extended the range to 12 kilometers and the altitude to 10,000 meters.

China has fielded the HQ-61 in both a shipborne and a land-based system. The HQ-61 land-based copy of the SA-2 was redesigned for shipboard conditions as the RF-61 twin-rail surface-to-air missile by the China Precision Machinery Import-Export Corporation (CPMIEC), an arm of the Chinese Ministry of Space Industry. Examples include the Jiangdong FFG 531, which was launched by Jiangnan Shipyard in Shanghai in 1972 and deployed in late 1979, and the FFG 532, which followed two years later. The naval version is associated with a Rice Screen G-band phased-array three-dimensional search radar and two tracking/illuminating H/I-band Fog Lamp radars. The fact that the Soviet SA-2 SAM had previously been "navalized" by the Soviet Union on a cruiser should have reduced the risk, but the Jiangdongs were apparently unsuccessful. FFG 531 did participate in the March 1988 naval battle with Vietnam for Johnson South Reef in the Spratlys, as a gun ship.

Although these two ships were at sea for several years, the successful certification firings were not achieved until December 1985, which was eight years after commissioning. That is longer than the ship's active life, as one ship was decommissioned in 1994 and the other went to the Chinese Naval Museum. The Chinese designed a large 6-cell HQ-61 SAM launcher forward on the Jiangwei I, but it reportedly has a short 10-kilometer range.

China imported the French Crotale SAM and put it on the Jiangwei II, the Luhu, and Luda I MOD DDG 109. Luhu DDG 112 had an 8-round reload box aft of the launcher, and DDG 113 had reload rounds in below-deck hatches. Chinese copies of the Crotale SAMs in following ship installations were designated HQ-7. The associated FC radar is the French Thomson-CSF Castor II radar on top of the bridge. In 1999 the HQ-61 was replaced on the Jiangwei with the LY-60N SAM, which was designed by the Shanghai Academy of Spaceflight Technology. China bought two hundred Aspide AAM missiles from Italy and now produces the LY-60 SAM copy with a range of 16 kiloyards (KYD).[7]

One of the newest Chinese SAMs is the KS-1, which seems to be based on the British Rapier surface-to-air missile. The KS-1 has a range of 42 kilometers (26 miles) and can reach targets 25 kilometers (82,500 feet) high. The missile weighs 900 kilograms (1,980 pounds) and uses radio command guidance. The associated PAR is a new model with 360-degree coverage claimed. However, a photograph of the KS-1 radar shows it to be similar to the familiar Gin Sling radar.[8] Newer KS-1A upgrades have a 50-kilometer range and 27-kilometer altitude.

The imported Sovremennyys have two SAN-7 Shtil SAM launchers. High-altitude targets can be engaged at 32 kilometers, targets at less than 1,000-meter altitude at 18 kilometers, and cruise missiles at 12 kilometers.[9]

In 1993 China bought eight batteries of the Russian SA-10 Grumble (S-300 designation) anti-cruise-missile SAM, with launch vehicles, including very sophisticated Clam Shell acquisition and Flap Lid B guidance radars. Access to these radars will greatly advance Chinese AD radar technology, as the SA-10 is claimed to be comparable to the Patriot system. Negotiations were under way for an additional twelve batteries in 1994. The naval variant of the S-300, the SAN-6, is used as the VLS on the Aegis-style DDG 170. In 2001 a $400 million deal was signed for an unknown number of S-300 systems. The S-300 track radar 30NE6 was navalized, and was paired with the Russian VLS launcher on two 051C Luzhou area defense DDGs in 2006.

Naval AAW Guns

China's destroyers and frigates were described earlier in this book, but in this section the naval antiair assets of these platforms will be discussed in greater detail. This warfare area has always been considered one of the major weaknesses of the PLAN. From 1948 until 1980 small-caliber guns were the primary AA defense. Main battery guns that have high elevation angles and an increased firing rate are useful for surface or air warfare; these are termed dual-purpose mounts. The few ships with gun directors were for the dual-purpose large main battery guns.

In 1954–55 the USSR transferred four 1940-vintage Type 7 Gordy-class destroyers to the PLAN. They had four single-barrel 130-millimeter dual-purpose open-mount main battery guns, which were 1936-designed 130-millimeter/50 open gun mounts. These were limited to a 45-degree elevation and a firing rate of 12 RPM with no AA capability.[10] There was a KDP-4 Mina type (Four Eyes) optical FC director on top of the bridge for the 130-millimeter guns. The KDP-4 director had two 4-meter separated stereo-optic sights, one for target range and the other for water splash points.

The 130-millimeter/50 guns were totally redesigned by China for Jiangnan, Jianghu, and Jiangwei frigates in the 1990s, with dual-purpose automatic loaders, enclosed mount, 85-degrees elevation, and 25-RPM firing rate. The Ludas mainly had twin 130-millimeter/58 guns with elevation up to 80 degrees for AA use, with the Sun Visor and Wasp Head gun FC.

Photo 13. The aft dual-purpose 130-millimeter/58 turret on a Luda-class destroyer. Note the unusual replacement of the twin 37-millimeter AA guns at left by a SATCOMM antenna. Source: Kanwa

The newest Luyang DDGs have a further modernized 130-millimeter/56 single-barrel mount with a 60–80-RPM firing rate. These ships also came with two 76-millimeter AA and four single-barrel 37-millimeter AA guns with three small optic directors for the secondary batteries. In 1974 China installed four twin 37-millimeter/63 AA mounts, but no 76-millimeter guns, on the Luda class.

The USSR also gave four Riga-class frigates to China in 1956–57, which had a 1938-vintage open-mount 100 millimeter/56 with a 12-RPM rate and a maximum elevation of 45 degrees. The Chinese thereafter built their own version of the Rigas from 1964 to 1968, naming them the Jiangnan class, which had a single 100-millimeter/56 main battery with a Wasp Head optic FC director and a Sun Visor X-band FC radar mounted on top. They had twin 37-millimeter/60 and twin 14.5-millimeter/75 AA. The 100-millimeter guns on some frigates used the optic Wok Wan fire control director, which is a copy of the Soviet Wasp Head optic director from 1940.

The only modern dual-purpose main battery guns were the fully automatic 90-RPM French twin 100-millimeter/55 Creusot-Loire guns initially installed in 1985 on two Jianghu IV–class ships with Matra Naja laser/electro-optic (E-O) AA fire control. The French auto guns were copied by China as twin-barrel 100-millimeter/55 mounts on the Luhu, Luhai, and Jiangwei II classes.

The secondary and small-caliber naval guns were originally imported from the USSR and manufactured in China. The Ludas had four twin 37 millimeters and four twin 25 millimeters replaced with air-cooled 57 millimeters. The PLAN had no other water-cooled guns until the Sovremennyys were provided with 130-millimeter/54 AK-130 water-cooled twin-barrel mounts with a minimum 65-RPM firing rate.

The Soviet AK-230 twin water-cooled 30-millimeter mount was produced in China as Type 69 and on the Huangfeng in 1965 and on the Haijou and Houjian in 1987 and 1992, respectively. The unmanned Type 69 had a firing rate of 2,100 RPM and a 4-kilometer range.[11] The associated Bass Tilt FC radar was not included, so the PLAN craft had only an optical director. The Soviet CIWS AK 630 30-millimeter Gatling gun had a 5,000-RPM firing rate and a range of 4 to 5 kilometers. The Type 054 frigate is the first Chinese-designed warship with the AK-630 CIWS, having four per ship.[12] These were also on the first two Sovremennyys to be delivered. No PLAN warships received any of the Drum Tilt, Muff Cob, Hawk Screech, or Bass Tilt AA FC radars that were associated with the same caliber guns on Soviet warships. The only modern AA FCs available to the PLAN were the French Compagnie de Signaux et d'Entreprises Electriques (CSEE) Naja optronic director in 1985 and a model derived from the Dutch Goalkeeper in 2004.

China improved the Soviet-supplied 37-millimeter/63 guns for the newer PLAN frigates and DDGs. The Type 74 on Jianghu frigates and Type 76A covered-mount, twin 37-millimeter/63 modern mounts on Luda II, Luhu, and Jiangwei frigates are unique PLAN gun modernization and redesigns. China also modified Dutch 30-millimeter Goalkeeper CIWS Gatling guns, designated as Type 730, for the newest 052B, 052C, and 051C DDGs, and 054A frigates. The Goalkeeper fires at 4,200 RPM. The Chinese Type 730 firing rate is a reported 4,600 to 5,800 RPM, comparable to the Russian AK-630's 5,000 RPM. The U.S. Navy's Phalanx CIWS, with lighter 20-millimeter ammunition, has a firing rate of 5,000 RPM. The PLAN replaced the Goalkeeper tracking radar with a Type EFR-1 radar and the Dutch search radar with an OFC-3 electro-optic director mounted on top of the gun. The Chinese 730 EFR-1 with Rice Bowl 347 radar aft claims a maximum range of 8 kilometers compared to the Dutch I-band radar's 7 kilometers. The E-O tracker has a range of 5 to 6 kilometers.

The Jiangkai frigates and Luyangs all have the Seagull SSM detecting radar/data link (referred to as SR-64, Type 360, or 364). The CADS-N-1 Kashtan has two 30-millimeter Gatling guns flanked by eight auto-reloading SA-N-11 SAMs and integral E-O and radar trackers. Russia had never provided the modern gun/missile Kashtan to China, until the second pair of Sovremennyys, when the aft AK-630s were replaced by Kashtans.[13]

HQ-9 Vertical Launch System

The four Sovremennyy bought by China and the two 052B DDGs have the SAN-7 Shtil SAM with associated tracker and data link systems. China's AAW took a giant leap forward with the purchase of Russian systems, and the resulting technology transfer of Soviet-era equipment. By comparison, the U.S. Navy's MK 41 VLS, which was first installed on the USS *Bunker Hill* (CG 52) in 1989, had 32 missile cells with 61 usable missiles. Both SAN-6 and SAN-9 VLS systems featured round modules with 8 cells each.

Based on the recent acquisition of Russian SAMs and associated acquisition and track systems, it was expected that the first PLAN VLS on the 052C Luyang II was going to be either a Russian SA-6 or an SA-9 VLS installation. The PLAN HQ-9 VLS is totally different from both Russian VLS designs, although it looks more like the Soviet service ring modules than the American MK 41 VLS. They both use 8-cell circular modules. Chinese and Russian VLS both use the pop-up cold-launch design, which eliminates the hazardous hot air exhaust vents with ignition in the below-deck cells on the U.S. Navy MK 41 VLS. The Russian VLS cells have only one hatch and can fire only the one cell that is rotated under that hatch. The Chinese VLS has hatches for each cell, with no rotation needed, allowing possible simultaneous launches. The Chinese VLS modules each have 6 cells and the Soviet VLS has only one hatch and 8 cells.

The rationale that the Russian 8-cell modules were too large for the smaller Chinese DDG hull does not seem likely since the diameter of the Russian module is only 1.5 feet larger. Possibly China used the S-300 missiles, and Russia provided no naval SAN-6 equipment until the 051C Luzhou DDG in 2006.

The new Jiangkai II frigate has a rectangular 32-cell VLS that looks similar to the U.S. Navy's MK 41 VLS launcher. This has also been observed on the Wuhu-B hull 891 weapon research ship for several years.

Conclusions

Even though Russia is usually portrayed as the prime weapon systems source for the PLAN, in AAW the French and several other European nations have actually provided some of the most modern technology. The key to determining the overall efficiency and firepower of these platforms will be to gauge how well the Chinese have managed to make interoperable these highly divergent systems. PLAN combat system interoperability challenge is not just integrating Chinese-made platforms with Russian technology, but also the Russian ships, weapons, and sensors with European and indigenous Chinese systems. Similar integration problems facing China's attempts to increase its ASW abilities will be discussed in the next chapter.

9

Antisubmarine-Warfare (ASW) Sonar and Weapon Systems

I n keeping with its approach to incorporating blue-water-navy technologies for possible littoral uses, China is deploying a number of ASW systems. These weapons would support PLAN ships engaged in a wide range of potential conflicts against adversaries equipped with the most advanced submarines. As with most of China's military, these systems constitute a mix of legacy import technologies and indigenous developments.

Surprisingly, only four PLAN warships have variable-depth sonar (VDS) installed, and no surface ships have towed arrays, which are two of the best surface sensors. Not even any Chinese oceanographic research vessels to date have been observed with experimental towed arrays. There is a lack of evidence that the PLAN has bottom passive arrays utilizing sound channels, which could indicate that long-range ASW cueing has a serious shortcoming. The PLAN concept of ASW is limited to tactical ship defense rather than strategic distant-warning sensor systems.

Many Pacific naval analysts do not believe that China has a credible antisubmarine capability or that ASW is a priority in the PLAN's new ship program. In fact, it would appear ASW is a high priority in some new naval production. While it seems that the lack of a PLAN ASW flag-rank staff has been seen as an indication of a low program priority, the U.S. Navy went from seven ASW vice admiral (VADM) billets in 1964 down to zero by 1992.[1] Nobody claimed that meant ASW was unimportant to the United States. PLAN ASW platforms and equipment have been acquired, developed, and deployed on submarines, surface ships, and aviation platforms. Many sensors and weapons are imported, but this does not decrease the threat they can pose to enemy submarines. Indigenously produced Chinese sonars are also becoming more capable.[2]

Chinese Surface Ship Sonar Technology

The types of sonars equipping Chinese warships are a barometer of Chinese naval technology and antisubmarine capability. The evolution of Chinese sonar from old Soviet equipment to series production, to indigenous designs, to French examples, and finally to modern Russian vessels with sonar suites parallels general Chinese naval progress. Just as these systems have grown from secondhand equipment to indigenous designs, supplemented by up-to-date foreign technologies, so has the Chinese navy transitioned to a high-tech force designed to serve the nation's maritime needs. Table 25 summarizes PLAN surface ship sonars. Several references differ on the designation of the sonar on particular platforms, but the Russian book by K. V. Chuprin (*Voennaya moshch' Podnebesnoy*) was referred to in those situations. The sonar type is operationally important.

Table 25. PLAN Surface Ship Sonar Types

DESIGNATION	FREQUENCY	TYPE	DETECTION RANGE	SHIP CLASS
Tamir-11	25 KHz	Searchlight, search	5 km	Hainan
Tamir-2	30 KHz	Searchlight, attack	2.5 km	Luda, Shanghai, T-43
Pegas-2M	MF	Searchlight, search	8 km	Riga, Luda
Tamir-10 (SJD-3)	25 KHz	Searchlight	5 km[a]	Kronstadt
SS-12 VDS	11.5–14.5 KHz	Active	10 km	Haijiu, Zhi-9
SS-12 VDS	7–20 KHz	Passive	20 km[a]	Haijiu, Zhi-9
EH-5	HF	Keel mounted	5 km[a]	Jianghu I, II, IV
SJD-5	HF	Bow dome	4 km[a]	Jianghu III, V
SO-7H/ SJD-7	MF	Bow dome	8 km[a]	Jiangwei I, II
ESS-2 (export)	MF	Bow dome	12–28 km	FFG
DUBV-23 (SJD-8/9)	4.9–5.4 KHz	MF scanning, bow dome	8–22 km	Luda III, Luhai, Luhu, Luzhou, Luyang I & II
DUBV-43 (ESS-1)	4.9–5.4 KHz	MF VDS	20 km	Luhu, Luda III
MG-335	MF	Bow dome	15 km	956 E, 054A

NOTE: Unlike the radar-defined frequencies for HF to LF in Table 1, sonarmen consider LF below 2 KHz, MF 4–20 KHz, and HF usually 25 KHz and above.

[a]Authors' estimated values.

A number of modern Chinese ASW capabilities became operational in the mid-1980s, which is evidence of a decision to put considerable emphasis into upgrading ASW in the air, surface, and submarine platforms. In the late 1990s further modernization of these areas with new big-ticket procurements provided the PLAN with modern ASW weapons and sensors in modest numbers. China has not obtained new surface ship ASW sensors, fire control, or weapons since 2000, except for the Sovremennyy systems.

In 1954 the Soviet Union provided components for four Riga-class frigates that were built in a Chinese shipyard in 1958. These ships included Pegas-2 hull-mounted HF searchlight sonars. Starting in 1964 Chinese shipyards produced five more copies of this ship, with no Soviet parts supplied, called the Jiangnan class. There were sonars on 1960s-era Hainan and Haiqing PC, but they were deleted from the three hundred Shanghai PC in 1980, although for some reason the D/C racks were retained. Soviet furnished T-43 minesweepers had Tamir-2 sonars.

The Soviet Union provided two classes of patrol boats in 1955 that included sonar equipment. These included ten Kronstadt patrol craft equipped with Tamir-10 HF searchlight sonars. Based on these examples, Chinese shipyards produced fourteen more copies, including the sonars. The other class comprised four T-43 ocean minesweepers (MSO) equipped with HF Tamir-2 searchlight sonars. China's Wuchang and Donglang shipyards produced thirty-seven more T-43 sonars.

Chinese Indigenous Sonars

When all Soviet assistance and shipments ceased around 1962, Russia had provided about twenty-five sonar sets to the PLAN. China began developing its own indigenous sonars and produced around a hundred sets from 1975 until 1987. Because the sonar transducer dome, or fairing, is the only part of the sonar that is visible externally, observers can visually detect two levels of sonar design technology. In the earliest "searchlight" sonar, the transducer was on a shaft that was lowered from a sea chest inside the ship into the water, while later designs were lowered into a water-filled dome under the keel. This shaft was manually trained and the flat-faced transducer only transmitted and received sound in one bearing at a time, like a searchlight. The newer scanning sonar technology transmits sound around 360 degrees, and echoes are displayed on a plan position indicator cathode-ray tube (CRT). A bow dome device cannot be a hoist-lower unit because of tight space restrictions, and so it is assumed to be scanning technology. Small bow domes indicate that HF scanning equipment is present, and larger, more bulbous domes likely contain medium-frequency (MF), or even low-frequency (LF), sonar technology, if very large. The first Soviet scanning sonar was produced in 1957, but none was provided to China.

Two major events in China greatly retarded or stopped the normal design process of newer sonar-unique technology, such as audio and video scanners: the Great Leap Forward of 1958–59, and the Cultural Revolution, which lasted from 1966 until the mid-1970s. During the repressive atmosphere created by these events, no significant sonar improvements were made during the crucial period from 1965 to 1975.

China has several highly respected oceanographic universities. The first was established in Qingdao in 1952, and in 1958 the government created six naval research and development (R & D) laboratories, including for underwater acoustics and underwater weapons. In 1965 China expanded its old Bureau of Oceans into a vast network of facilities, research institutes, and forecast centers and bureaus called the State Oceanic Administration (SOA). By 1970 it created special underwater acoustic sites in the Bohai Gulf and the East China and Yellow seas. Technical institutes known to be involved in sonar design are Institute 715 in Huangzhou and Institute 706 in Beijing. Sonar manufacturing plants include the Jiangxin Machinery Plant, the Jiangning Mechanical Plant, and the Great Wall Radio Factory in Beijing.

Although there are no photographs of indigenous Chinese sonars on warships in open sources, an interesting photograph taken in 1978 inside the J-302 vessel participating in SLBM test shots showed a "splashdown monitoring team" manning a unit. With one large CRT in the middle and three smaller CRTs above, it looked like a sonar set, although the operator was not wearing a headset.

The first mention of a PLAN designation for a sonar was the EH-5 on the Jianghu frigates in 1975. The EH-5 was on twenty-two of the Jianghu frigates in variants I, II, and IV from 1975 until 1986. Jianghu III and V had SJD-5 sonar. Photographs also show an HF bow dome for the SJD-7 sonar on Jiangwei frigates. The Jiangnan V frigate had a sonar designated an EH-5A, which would appear to be an improved version.[3]

Hull Configurations Indicate Sonar Types

The Luda-class destroyers all had a raked bow with one centerline anchor housing. The Luhus had a bow and starboard anchor, while all later DDGs from Luhai through Luyang and Luzhou all had bow port anchors. The logic may be that bow sonars need bow anchors to clear the dome, but a port anchor is retained only for emergency use. Soviet references state that Ludas had an HF Tamir-2 attack sonar and a Pegas 2M search sonar that were searchlight technology, with keel-mounted hoist-lower domes. After 1990 French DUBV-23 MF bow sonar domes and bow stem anchors are common Chinese sonar architecture. However, some anomalies exist. For example, the sixteen Luda destroyers all had a raked bow stem anchor beginning with 1971, but China had only copies of Soviet keel searchlight sonars during that period. Chinese auxiliary ships have sharply raked bows with normal port/starboard anchor arrangements. A Luda was observed in dry dock with a large bow dome in 1987, three years prior to the date China reportedly received the first French MF bow sonar on Luda III. Many more Ludas than the single Luda III could possibly have MF bow sonars. The Chinese designation for DUBV-23 is SJD-8/9.

The next Chinese sonar designation was not evident until 1991 when the SO-7H (SJD-7) was installed on the Jiangwei I (FF 539 to 542) and Jiangwei II (FF 521 to 524) frigates. Photographs of Jiangwei ships in dry dock clearly show a medium-size bow dome, and models or drawings on display support this observation. This transducer location indicates that these Chinese sonars are the more modern scanning type. A Russian reference work states that the modern SJD-7 is on the Jiangweis.[4]

Because it seems that the Soviets supplied only old searchlight sonars, the question is how did China advance into a next-generation scanning design so quickly? A crucial issue is whether China received an example of a first-generation Soviet scanning sonar or designed its own scanning sonar from scratch. Examples of new naval equipment designed in China without foreign help usually involved many years of testing and work-ups before the equipment became operational. Often the technology was not even placed in production, indicating inadequate results.

It would appear likely, therefore, that China received a foreign copy on which to base its scanning sonar. The first-generation Soviet HF scanning sonar, called Titan MG-312, was developed in 1957 and installed on Petya and Kashin vessels in 1960. This sonar is referred to as one of several Herkules sonars, also known by the NATO designation Wolf Paw. The Soviet Union continued providing equipment to China until 1962, and it is certain that China had listed scanning sonar as a priority request. Because it is not considered an offensive system, the Soviet Union might have provided at least one set, possibly with drawings. This would have allowed China several years' head start to reach full production for bow-dome Jianghu frigates by the early 1980s.

China's designation for sonar systems installed on various surface ships is "SJD" followed by a unique number. The Kronstadt with Tamir in 1955 was

SJD-3, and SJD-2 was on the Luda III in 1992. French DUBV-23 MF sonars were designated SJD-8/9. It is possible that Luhu and Luhai are equipped with higher SJD numbers, but this is not confirmed. No doubt the logistics support, maintenance, and operator training are especially challenging due to the variety of old Soviet and modern French and Russian sonars, in addition to several indigenous searchlight and scanning sonars.

Post-1974 Imported Sonars

Beginning in the mid-1970s China opted to import modern sonars. These tend to fall into two time periods. France provided modern sonar equipment from 1974 until 1993. The second period, when China bought mainly modern Russian sonar systems, extends from 1994 to the present.

The first imported French sonars were two sets of the lightweight Thomson-Marconi SS-12 VDS in 1974. These can be used as a dipping sonar on ASW helicopters or as a variable-depth stern-mounted sonar on small ASW patrol craft. China must have made a high-level decision on antisubmarine shortfalls by 1980, because around 1986 several new ASW systems appeared. In 1986 the Luda II conversion and the Jianghu IV frigate put the first helicopter decks on PLAN warships. Haijiu patrol craft hulls 688 and 697 had SS-12 VDS replace the aft 57-millimeter guns in 1987. These sonars could have been copies of the two acquisitions from France. The workhorse Luda-class destroyers (DDs) had their first notable upgrade in 1987. The lead ship, DD 105, built in 1972, received facilities for two helicopters and 57-millimeter guns and a new bow sonar. This was known as the one-of-a-kind Luda II. What is not as well known is that another Luda, DD 131, was in a Shanghai dry dock with a large bow sonar dome in the same year but was not called a Luda II.[5]

China commissioned two large 4,600-ton Luhu destroyers, from Qiuxin Shipyard in 1993 and Jiangnan Shipyard in 1996 respectively. Still active, they feature modern French DUBV-23 surface ship scanning MF bow sonar, the DUBV-43 MF VDS, ASW torpedo tubes, French integrated combat systems, and an ASW helicopter. The DUBV-23 is a sophisticated 4.9–5.4 kilohertz multimode scanning sonar with six different active/passive and sector search modes. Although bottom bounce and convergence zone detections are possible, the surface duct range is from 10 to 15 kilometers. The associated DUBV-43 shares frequency, but can operate either with the hull sonar or search independently.[6] These sonars first appeared on the Luda III conversion in 1990. Luhus were followed by the 7,000-ton Luhai DDG in 1999 and the four Luyang-class warships of the PLAN, all sporting the DUBV-23.

China had licensed production rights from France for both sonars but only produced the DUBV-23 as SJD-8/9.

In 1998 Russia sold two 8,000-ton Sovremennyy missile destroyers to China that included the latest Soviet MG-335 MF Platina and MG-7 FC HF tracking sonars. In 1999 the first Sovremennyy DDG arrived from Russia. The Russian-imported sonars are significant because they were included as part of a full weapon/sensor suite, which should ensure that all the major components can operate with each other seamlessly.

Coincidentally, 1999 saw the PLAN's first fully coordinated surface, submarine, and air ASW exercise. The fact that it involved China's North Sea Fleet is no surprise because Qingdao and the Lüshun-Dalian complex are main centers of ASW bases and schools. In addition, Chinese submarine topographic units have been making underwater maps in the Yellow and East China seas for submarine training areas and operations since 1960. These would be good sites for sound surveillance hydrophones.

Surface Ship ASW Weapons

The USSR has always been especially parsimonious with surface ASW weapons for China. The PLAN ASW weapons for the Ludas, frigates, and patrol craft for two decades were Chinese copies of the Soviet BMB-2 D/C throwers, designated Type 64, and copies of Soviet short-range mortars. The Chinese Type 62 is a nontrainable 5-barrel 252-millimeter copy of the Russian RBU-1200, and the Type 75 FQF-2500 was a 12-barrel variant of the 16-barrel Soviet RBU-2500 launcher. These launchers were the standard ASW weapons until new imported ILAS-3 Italian triple-torpedo tube mounts, French A244S, and copies of Western MK 46 torpedoes appeared.

The RBU-1200 ASW rocket is a fixed-mount, forward-firing RGB-12 depth charge rocket fired from five 252-millimeter-diameter tubes.[7] The Soviets held back the 12-barrel RBU-6000 automatic-loading ASW launcher that had a 6,000-meter range and could be aimed for accuracy. The Soviets also withheld ASW homing torpedoes that could have been launched from PRC surface vessels, helicopters, or aircraft.

Previous evaluations stated that the PRC navy had only short-range, nontrainable RBU-1200 Soviet launchers, which were designated Type 62 or 81 when improved and produced by China. This rocket was associated with the Uragan Fire Control.[8] Royal Navy visitors claimed 12-barrel RBU-6000 long-range launchers are on the Luda-class *Jinan* (DD 223), the Luda II 105 today, and the *Zhenjiang* (FFG 514). Table 26 summarizes PLAN surface ship ASW weapons. Luda destroyers and some new DDGs have 12-barrel launchers that look similar to the RBU-2500 launchers, designated FQF-2500 by the PLAN. These Type 75 launchers share the 212-millimeter barrels, but the RBU-2500 had 16 barrels and the FQF-2500 had only 12 barrels. These FQF-2500 launchers would still be manually loaded, with the same 2,500-meter range. The Soviet short-range RBU-2500's payload was 85 kilograms and the RBU-1200's was 70 kilograms.[9]

Table 26. Chinese Surface Ship ASW Weapons

DESIGNATION	ROUNDS	RELOAD METHOD	RANGE	PLATFORM
Type 64 D/C gun	2 projectors, racks	Manual	40–180 m	Destroyers, frigates, PC
Type 62	5 barrels/252 mm	Manual fixed	1,400 m	Luda, PC
Type FQF-2500	12 barrels/212 mm	Manual	2,500 m	Luda, Luhu, 052s
Type 81	6 barrels/252 mm	Manual	3,200 m	Frigates, PC
Type 87	6 barrels/252 mm	Manual	5,000 m	Jiangwei
RBU-1000	6 barrels/300 mm	Automatic	1,000 m	Sovremennyy
ILAS-3	3 barrels/launcher	SVTT	N/A	FF, DDG
ASW TORPEDO	SOURCE	SEARCH	RANGE	PLATFORM
Torpedo A244S	French copy	Active/passive	6,000 m	Jiangwei
CY-1 (ASROC)	American copy	Active/passive	8,000 m	Luda III, Jiangwei
Yu-7	Copy MK 46	Active/passive	6,000 m	Luda Mods, 051, 052/Jiangwei

In 1975 the Jianghu III series of new escorts introduced an upgrade to a launcher designated Type 81. This launcher had a 3,200-meter range, which was 1,800 meters longer than the Soviet RBU-2500. It is a mistake to assume that Chinese copies of foreign equipment do not have improved capabilities. The six follow-on Jiangwei frigates improved on the Type 81, having two 6-barrel mortars with a longer 5,000-meter reach; these were called Type 87.[10] The CY-1 copy of the American long-range ASROC has been mentioned in the chapter 2 and chapter 4 discussions of the Luda and Jiangwei classes. Obviously the Sovremennyy brought a newer generation of ASW to the PLAN. The Sovremennyy twin remote-controlled RBU-1000 6-barrel ASW mortar launches RGB-10 depth charge rockets 1,000 meters, controlled by a Burya fire control system.[11] This launcher weapon also has an antitorpedo capability.

Multiplatform improvements from the mid-1980s to the late 1990s indicate that Chinese government and naval leaders believed they faced an ASW threat. U.S. secretary of the navy John Lehman's visit to China in 1984 was intended to form a new relationship between the two navies in order to oppose the USSR. This plan included Chinese procurement of U.S. Navy weapons. Of all the potential naval weapons from which to choose, the MK 46 lightweight ASW torpedo was China's first choice in 1985 negotiations. This was a rare insight into the internal PLAN priority list of warfare needs. Reports that China received four MK 46 Mod 2 torpedoes in 1986 and converted them to metric production in 1987 are erroneous.[12] The MK 46 delivery was suspended after the Tiananmen Square sanctions, and the MK 46s were not delivered for several years. The MK 46 copy Yu-7 is the PLAN's standard surface ship ASW torpedo since the mid-1990s.

The modern ASW torpedoes and missiles with associated fire control systems resulted in fuller employment of the increasingly complex sonars.

Submarine Sonars

Chinese ASW efforts also include submarine platforms. The first sonar-equipped submarines acquired from the Soviet Union were four World War II–vintage S-class submarines with the MARS-12 passive sonar delivered in 1954. Two years later, components for the first of twenty-one Soviet Whiskey-class diesel submarines included the Tamir 5LS active sonar. This sonar, which was designated MG-10 Phoenix by the Soviets, had 132 audio transmission and receiver channels.[13] The Chinese assembled these kits in their own shipyards with Soviet assistance. China established a manufacturing plant for these sonars and produced more than a hundred, which were likely exact copies of the Soviet examples.

The MARS-12 passive arrays could have been slightly improved as MARS-24 sonars, indicating twenty-four instead of twelve transducer elements. This would provide twice the bearing accuracy and reduce beam side lobes. Chinese shipyards went into a large production run of the submarines, designating them as Type 031.

Chinese efforts to obtain more modern Soviet submarines and sonars were thwarted by the cooling of relations in 1960 when the Soviet Union began to pull back its military technicians and engineers. China did manage to obtain plans and drawings of the Romeo-class diesel submarine. This submarine had an Arktika active sonar and a Feniks passive array, allowing firing solutions to be reached without exposing the periscope. China's shipyards eventually produced eighty-four Romeo copies, designated Wuhan Type 033.

Table 27. Chinese Submarine Sonars/Weapons

DESIGNATION	SOURCE	FREQUENCY	MODE	RANGE	BOAT
MARS-12	USSR	25 KHz	Passive	15 km	S
Tamir-5LS	USSR	HF	Active	5 km	031
Feniks	USSR	HF	Passive	20 km	033
Arktika	USSR	3–13 KHz	Active	25 km	033
TSM-2233/2255	France	10 Hz–5 KHz	Active	25 km	039
DUUX-5	France	2–15 KHz	Active/passive	20 km	Han, Xia
MGK-400	USSR	LF	Active/passive	100 km	Kilo 877
MGK-400-EM	USSR	LF	Active/passive	110 km	Kilo 636, Yuan, 093, 094
MG-519	USSR	HF	Active	10 km	Kilo 877

TORPEDO	SOURCE	TYPE	SPEED	RANGE	BOAT
Yu-1 53-51	USSR/U.S.	Straight-run	39 kts	9 km	031
Yu-4A	PLAN	Active/passive	30 kts	6 km	All SS
Yu-4B (ET-31)	PLAN	Active/passive	35 kts	9.5 km	Export
E53-67	USSR	ASW homing	35 kts	10 km	Kilos
TEST-71	USSR	Wire guide	24–40 kts	15–25 km	Kilos
TEST-96	USSR	Wire guide	35 kts	25 km	Kilos
53-65 KE	USSR	Wake follow	45 kts	18 km	Kilos
Shkval	Kazakhstan	Straight-run	195 kts	15–20 km	40 units

CRUISE MISSILE	SOURCE	TYPE	SPEED	RANGE	BOAT
Ji-8 Mod 3	PLA	Antiship	Mach 0.9	42 km	Wuhan C

BALLISTIC MISSILE PURPOSE	DESIGNATION	FLIGHT	SPEED	RANGE	BOAT
Club-S 91RE1	Antisub	1-stage	Subsonic	50 km	Kilo 636
Club-S 3M54E1	Antiship	2-stage	Subsonic	300 km	Kilo 636
JL-1 CSS-N-3	Land target	Ballistic	Supersonic	3,600 km	Xia
JL-2 CSS-N-4	Land target	GPS guidance	Supersonic	8,000 km	Jin

Unlike the Type 031, the Type 033 bows did have a unique fez-shaped top-side transducer as on contemporary Soviet submarines (possibly an underwater telephone transducer), which indicated that current sonars had been obtained. The Arktika active sonar interfaced to a Leningrad analog FCS on 033 submarines. Since the mid-1990s, the standard PLAN ASW torpedo has been the 324-millimeter Yu-7, based upon the American MK 46.

China had several facilities that could contribute to the design and production of an indigenous sonar. The first leading-edge development challenge for Chinese naval construction was the Han SSN, built in 1974. Prior to this China copied Soviet submarines, destroyer escorts, and patrol craft. The Han had active SQZ-3 and passive SQC-1 sonars installed in 1970, but the systems were not certified until 1975.

The Dongfeng Mechanical Plant produced the SQ2-D sonar for diesel submarines. The Shanghai 22nd Radio Plant reportedly produced the SQC-1, but too little time seems to have elapsed for it to have developed the expertise to design and build a sonar more capable than the crude Tamirs known to be in production. In the 1970s China augmented more than sixty old Wuhan diesel submarines and their obsolete Soviet HF sonars with two new Type 035 Ming diesel boats containing a mix of French and Soviet sonars. Several important ASW improvements occurred in the mid-1980s. In 1983 two 033 diesel submarines were upgraded with the French DUUX-5 sonars (see Table 27). In 1987 the first Han-class SSN received a modern French DUUX-5 imported sonar, as did the single Xia SSBN around 1988. The following year saw the launching of the first of three new Type 039 Song-class attack submarines in Wuchang Shipyard with modern French TSM-2233 and TSM-2255 sonars.

The PLAN submarine force received its most modern ASW capability with the inaugural order of four Kilo submarines, which was followed by eight more. The first two imports were Russian 877E Kilo submarines in 1995. These quiet diesel boats had MGK-400 active/passive LF and HF MG-519 classification sonars with an associated MVU-110 or 113 digital combat system fire control suite.

The next two Kilos in 1999 were newer 636-class submarines with improved sonar and fire control. Two additional improved 636 Kilos followed in three years, but the sonar suites appear to have been nearly identical. The MGK-400 was improved to the MGK-400 EM variant with Uzel digital computers, double the transducer elements, and automated tracking.[14] More 636s have been ordered and are being built and delivered. Export Kilos include Russian E53-67 acoustic homing ASW torpedoes with wire-guided and wake-homing versions. Kilos are among the quietest and most modern

ASW submarines in the world. The newest PLAN nuclear submarines finally have Russian towed-array pods aft, a first for the PLAN.

Chinese Airborne ASW

Because China has no aircraft carriers in service yet, its fixed-wing naval air assets are all land based. However, land-based and shipboard ASW helo platforms have been expanded. Two new naval air ASW platforms were introduced in 1986. The Soviet An-12 transport, designated by China as the Y-8, was redesigned by Shaanxi Aircraft Company and equipped with Western ASW systems to become the first true PLANAF Y-8-X maritime patrol aircraft. It has an APS-504 search radar, an LTN-72 INS, and LTN-211 Omega navigation by Litton Canada, various Collins guidance and landing transmitters/receivers, and an IR submarine detection system. The weapons it carries include mines, D/Cs, and ASW torpedoes, as well as active/passive sonobuoy sensors.

In 1986 an original Chinese-designed Harbin SH-5 four-engine seaplane with an ASW mission reached initial operational capability at Qingdao's Tuandao naval air station. A magnetic anomaly detector stinger aft, sonobuoys, ASW torpedoes, and D/Cs show varied ASW capabilities. Meanwhile, and somewhat ironically, the U.S. Navy has converted ASW maritime patrol aircraft (MPA) for overland Tomahawk missions and to provide reconnaissance during the ongoing Global War on Terror.

Six Chinese destroyers and twelve frigates equipped with helicopter decks initially had Z-9 helicopters that were copies of the French Super Frelon, but only three of these had French ASW avionics, including the SS-12 dipping sonar. The first Z-9 dates from 1985, and there are now thirty-six units. In 1988 Thomson Alcatel, GEC Q Avionics, and Plessey competed for the helicopter ASW system contract.[15] Photographs of Z-9s with externally mounted torpedoes label the aircraft as ASW helicopters. China contracted with Russia for five modern Ka-28 Helix-A ASW and three Ka-28PS search and rescue (SAR) helicopters in the 1998 Sovremennyy deal. The PLAN negotiated for nine more Ka-28s in 1995, but did not sign the contract until 1999 because Russia would not include modern automatic navigation and Kobalt communication systems. China agreed to develop its own systems. Actual deliveries are probably more than twenty by 2010.

Soviet-era OKA-2 helicopter dipping sonars are 15 kilohertz with an active range of 5,500 meters and triple that range for passive detection. This helicopter has a next-generation Lira ASW system with a mission computer controlling all radios, radars, sonobuoys, dipping sonars, and ESM. Onboard weapons include Yu-7 (MK 46) torpedoes, Russian AT-1 active/passive acoustic homing ASW torpedoes, and PLAB 250-120 Lastochka D/Cs. It is possible the RAT-52 rocket-propelled ASW torpedoes, which were discarded by Russia decades ago due to problems, may still be carried by the PLANAF as Yu-2 torpedoes.

Conclusions

Based on forty-three original sets of sonar equipment provided by the Soviet Union, China produced over four hundred additional sonars for various classes of warships and submarines. Other ships are fitted with modern French sonars, and the new Russian sonar suites on Kilo submarines and Sovremennyy DDGs have been noted. The sonar types of a vast number of Chinese-designed combatants launched between those two known sonar installation groups are an interesting mystery. These numerous indigenously designed destroyers, frigates, patrol craft, and submarines total more than a hundred vessels, which means that China's indigenous ASW capability is quite broad. What is surprising is the two most capable ASW assets, VDSs and CY-1 ASROCs, are limited to only a few ships, and those are not the new-construction warships.

Potential conflicts that could entail submarine threats include the Taiwan Strait, the South China Sea, and SLOCs to Mideast and African oil sources. In the past China's expansion into the SCS has led to conflict with Vietnam and the Philippines, two other claimants to the Paracel and Spratly island groups, but neither of these countries currently has any submarines; Vietnam has reportedly ordered a number of Kilo submarines from Russia. Notably, of the six original nations with claims on these two island groups, only two—Taiwan and Indonesia—operate submarines. Chinese diesel and nuclear submarines have been observed in Japanese home waters and oil-drilling areas.[16]

China's expansion northeast or southwest would meet strong modern Japanese or Indian submarine forces. U.S. Navy submarines are a constant threat. Other countries of Southeast Asia with submarine-equipped navies could represent ASW threats to China, especially in the disputed waters of the South China Sea. These potential threats will be discussed at greater length later.

——— 10 ———

The South China Sea (SCS) and the Mine Threat

D
ue to the lack of aircraft carriers, an airstrip and sensors have been established on several small islands and atolls in the South China Sea. China has been seeking to network disparate assets to support its SCS claims. These facilities, which range from communications relays to radar units, demonstrate China's expanding regional reach and provide a rare glimpse into the country's military electronics technologies.

Meanwhile, to help ensure that it can blockade an enemy, or perhaps protect its own ports from invasion, the PLAN has a robust mining capability. Although mines are often spurned as being low-tech warfare, the history of naval warfare shows how effective they can be, especially in shallow waters along the littoral. Therefore, both a PLAN attack against Taiwan or an active defense strategy could utilize mining.

An overlooked PLAN capability is degaussing, which is absolutely necessary on surface warships to neutralize the effectiveness of magnetic mines. The PLAN's degaussing equipment and ships are based on the Soviet Union's program, which China has largely copied. Estimates of PLAN degaussing capability are analogous to Soviet capability twenty-five years ago, but with far fewer assets.

Hainan Island and SCS Bases

Hainan Island is an increasingly major focus for PLAN operations. China has been actively expanding south from Hainan Island since 1974, when it seized the Paracel Islands from the Vietnamese. Its activities continued in the 1990s with base construction on several Spratly Islands reefs. Locations of Chinese military electronics on the mainland are largely hidden. But basing facilities on the SCS islands and reefs make these sensors more observable.

Extrapolating from the types of electronics and facilities observed, Woody Island in the Paracels and Fiery Cross Reef in the Spratlys seem to be the main control links for PLAN activities from the Malacca Strait area to China's South Sea Fleet headquarters. The fact that Zhanjiang is the headquarters of the southern fleet indicates a major complex of tactical and strategic space and land-based long-range radars and communication in that area for SCS operations. Other armed Chinese islands or reefs are linked via satellite communications and radio to the local and fleet commanders. The electronics and combat systems of the Chinese aircraft, warships, and paramilitary ships greatly augment the island-based electronics.

The only electronic systems facing southward off the China coast are ones that involve offshore naval operations. For example, during the 1970s, China developed a large over-the horizon, backscatter (OTH-B) radar, sometimes referred to as "sky wave," facing toward the SCS. This experimental OTH radar had a 2,300-meter antenna and can detect surface ships as far away as 250 kilometers. A series of technical papers describing an over-the-horizon, surface wave (OTH-SW) radar in the early 1990s leads to the conclusion that its operational deployment north of Taiwan, might have occurred during that period.[1]

Although appearing to be a tourist island to the casual observer, Hainan Island features an embedded, but nearly invisible, military electronic infrastructure. The emergency landing of a U.S. Navy EP-3C at the Lingshui airfield in 2001 was a look into this secret world. Mainland Chinese governments prior to World War II virtually ignored Hainan, although there was a naval station at Hoihow (now Haikou) in the early 1900s. During the seven-year Japanese occupation in World War II, the island had an extensive military and industrial buildup. This included large coal and ore mines as well as the first railroads connecting to a new major Japanese submarine base at Yulin. Although today the locations of Hainan's long-range air search sites are classified, Japan had sites at Yulin, Basuo, and Haikou in 1944.[2]

Naval activities require precise navigation aids, and Hainan has extensive aids in place. Radio beacon navigation (RBN) Differential Global Positioning System (DGPS), or RBN-DGPS, are located at the southern ports of Zhanjiang, Fangcheng, and Luyu. The twenty-one DGPS systems are reportedly imported from Australia. In 1999 three DGPS beacon stations were activated at Sanya, Yangpu, and Baohujiao on Hainan using frequencies from 295 to 313 kilohertz. Three high-power RBN aids in southern China, at Sanya, Haikou, and Haifou, were operational in 1983. Sanya is the newly built-up submarine and DDG base.

American vessel traffic service (VTS) stations equipped with radar and computer tracking are manned and located on Hainan at Dongfang and in Haikou. The Haikou VTS controls traffic in the Qiongzhou Strait between

Hainan and the mainland.[3] A VTS station is also installed at the South Sea Fleet HQ in Zhanjiang.

Hainan certainly has one or more major ELINT stations, but references are usually vague or disagree on the details. Because of Chinese concerns about Vietnam, China probably built an ELINT site on mountaintops on southwestern Hainan. The most detailed description available discusses a large facility at the Lingshui air base on the southeastern coast. Built in 1968, and greatly expanded in 1995, an estimated one thousand signal analysts are located at this facility. Nearby, there is a large satellite downlink facility. It is allegedly an SOA site for receiving data from China's Antarctica weather stations, but may serve dual purposes by linking these intelligence centers with Beijing.

In 1965 the first high-power LF station was built on Hainan to support submarine operations in the region. The Yulin submarine base maintains VLF communications with submarines and surface ships in the SCS area. This may have been one of the first Chinese verylow frequency (VLF) stations, since construction activities had been reported from 1969 until 1982. It is uncertain if the VLF stations have replaced the LF sites. Communist nations like redundancy and old systems seem to be retained. Navigation charts showing Yulin stated that it is "closed to foreign commercial vessels" due to World War II mines in the approach, which may be just a convenient excuse to keep unwanted visitors away from these waters. There are large, underground, hardened tunnels at Yalong Bay, just east of Yulin, that can protect vessels from SSN up to Luyang-class DDGs, which are based there.[4]

The Importance of the Paracel Islands

The Paracel Islands (called Xisha Islands by China) were occupied by Vietnam until China seized them by amphibious assaults supported by naval warships in 1974. A 1980s photograph of a naval base in the Paracels shows a huge multiantenna array of sixteen yagi antennas aimed skyward with each antenna consisting of eight cross arms. This probable VHF giant array is not described or named in open-literature references. One publication with this illustration described it as a satellite communication antenna,[5] while another stated it was a Cross Slot early warning radar.[6] The antenna appears similar to a smaller truck-mounted 400-megahertz wind-tracking yagi radar designated Type 701 by China.

Woody Island, also referred to as Yongxing Island, is a classic example of how a crude "fisherman shelter" can grow over time into a significant military site. A helicopter landing pad was built within one year, which would have required ground-to-air links—probably the Ote Alenia imported radios used throughout China. As mentioned in chapter 7, in 1990 China constructed a 1,200-foot runway on Woody Island that was extended to 7,300 feet and finally to 7,874 feet.[7] This should be sufficient to handle heavier aircraft such as H-6 bombers or large transports for resupply. This facility probably houses a Chinese Type 791 X-band precision approach radar, which is based on the old Soviet Two Spot RSP-7. It has a 20-degree-azimuth and 6-degree-elevation antenna beam pattern and a cone-shape antenna for VHF and UHF air communications. A larger pier and airplane hangars augmented the island's single jetty, and fuel storage has been added. During June 2001 it was reported in the *Washington Times* that HY-2 antiship cruise missiles had appeared there.[8] If true, they would almost certainly require a long-range surface-search radar to detect surface ship targets. In mid-1995 a new SIGINT station entered service on Rocky Island, which is near Woody Island.[9] This station could support air or surface warning for air missions or ship targeting, especially since Rocky Island has the highest peak in the Paracel Islands.

The largest island in the Paracels is Pattle Island, which had a weather station when Vietnam lost it in 1974. The port facilities on Duncan Island, the second-largest island, are being enlarged, which could indicate increased military construction. Drummond Island, the site of a naval battle in 1974, is not known to have any buildings or electronic equipment. The only radio beacon south of Hainan is at Robert Island, which is only five hundred meters long. There are no modern DGPS navigation beacons in the Paracels, so this must be an older type installed in the late 1970s.

China's Spratly Island Claims

Another disputed island group claimed by China is the Spratly Islands (called Nansha Islands by China), which are several hundred miles farther south of the Paracels. The Spratly Islands were largely uninhabited until the recent construction, although Chinese fishermen probably visited them hundreds of years ago. In fact, during World War II Japan built a radio and submarine base on North Danger Reef, Tizard Bank, and Namyit Island, which are occupied by Vietnam and the Philippines today. Taiwan still controls Itu Aba Island, which is one of the most northern of the islands, and one of the few that is large enough to allow for an airfield plus has a supply of freshwater. During the 1930s the Japanese constructed a submarine base there.[10]

In the 1980s cruises in the Spratlys by Chinese nonmilitary fishermen and later ocean research ships were soon followed by warship visits. After civilian and scientific vessels reconnoitered the area in October 1987, China seized

Johnson South Reef from Vietnam on 14 March 1988. Three PLAN frigates—the Jiangnan-class 502, the Jianghu II–class 556, and the Jiangdong-
class FFG 531—sank two Vietnamese armed transports and captured an
LST. One hundred Vietnamese were killed or wounded. Experts differ if this
battle should be called "Fiery Reef" or "Johnson South Reef." Both islands
will be described. The naval battle was in Philippine-claimed waters in the
western Spratlys. A photo of a two-hundred-foot-long concrete building on
Fiery Cross Reef shows a standard naval HF yagi radar antenna based on the
Soviet Knife Rest. The Chinese copy, designated Bean Sticks, operates in the
70- to 73-megahertz frequencies with a range of about 180 kilometers. Two
other small ECM radomes on the building appear similar to the RWS-1 copy
of Jug Pair mounted on navy destroyers. Land-based ECM domes such as
these are not identified in references. Several whip communication antennas
and taller mast antennas are also on the roof.

Chinese radios may be connected to different antennas for different needs.
For example, R-series HF radios use a 4-meter whip for up to 25-kilometer
communications, and they use an 11-meter mast for ranges out to 40 kilometers. A long wire runs from a mast on one end of the building to the ground,
which would be an HF long-line radio antenna. A probable radio would
be the large 73-kilogram SR 109 synthesized receiver with a band from 10
kilohertz to 30 megahertz. It is suitable for radio signal surveillance and LR
communications. In addition to two roof-mounted 2.5-meter satellite communications (SATCOMM) dishes, there is a 4-meter dish mounted on a large
pedestal. This may be a meteorological weather antenna.

On Johnson South Reef, four octagonal huts initially were built on
wooden pilings. By 1989 there were two round cement towers on the ends
of a two-story white rectangular building on a concrete base. At one end is a
2.5-meter SATCOMM antenna adjacent to an 8-foot mast antenna, with two
more tall mast antennas on the roof. Chigua Reef has an identical building
structure with a wooden barracks added, which greatly increased manning
space. Subi Reef in 1997 had the typical wooden barracks structure and a
two-story building with one SATCOMM antenna. Two unusual features are
a huge round helicopter landing pad and a sturdy concrete bridge with arches
connecting it to the headquarters building. These are both unique to Subi
Reef.[11] Many of these island complexes retain small wooden huts on the end
of jetties, which would be a good location for noisy power generators and
hazardous toxic materials, such as extra fuel barrels for the power sources.

In 1988–89 several dozen Chinese warships conducted large naval exercises coinciding with the occupation of reefs in the Spratlys. In November
1990 China completed a lengthy hydrological survey with "research" ships

looking for oil in the Spratlys.[12] In the 1990s construction began on crude huts and octagonal wooden structures on wooden pilings. These were called "typhoon shelters" by the Beijing government.[13]

In 1995 China built its first structures on one point of the circular Mischief Reef, which is only 150 miles from the Philippines within waters both countries claim. In October 1998 these were expanded with three additional clusters of octagonal wooden structures. Each cluster of structures has a 2.5-meter SATCOMM dish aimed skyward. The northern and southern clusters had two-story concrete buildings constructed, which resembled forts with the usual SATCOMM and high-frequency (HF) whip antennas.[14] The southern building was about 36 meters long, and the northern building was 122 meters long. Many of the Chinese outposts sport a small tower on top of a two-story concrete building, which appears to be the electronics centers for communications, ELINT, and radars. This tower also appears to be where the duty officer would stand watches, and so might also be the command center.

Two years later major new additions to the electronic and weapon emplacements were completed. These included new piers, a helicopter pad, and several AA guns, along with an unidentified missile weapon system that might be the HY-2 or the newer C-801 anti-surface-ship cruise missiles. A white rectangular antenna appeared on top of the building control tower that "resembles a navy navigation radar, which would have a range of about 25 miles around the semi-submerged 'island.' It could be an imported Racal Decca 1290 Arpa radar or a Chinese Model 756 navigation radar with a dual X-band and S-band antenna."[15] Although small in size, if necessary these facilities could support future Chinese expansion throughout the area, and could perhaps even support a limited naval conflict in this contested region.

In June 2009 Indonesia seized seventy-five Chinese fishermen and eight vessels. In response the next month China sent seven vessels to conduct an exercise in protecting its South China Sea fishing areas. A new 2,500-ton fishery patrol vessel with a helicopter deck, Yuzheng 310, will be launched in early 2010.[16] More than a dozen vessels from different ports and under different maritime fishing/rescue organizations have rotated duties to patrol the Spratly and Paracel island groups. For example, in April 2010 FLEC Yuzheng 311 and 22 were relieved by two other Yuzhengs after six months patrolling the Nansha Islands. China is even now in the process of making these island chains an integral part of Hainan province and establishing Chinese tourist locations, even at military bases.

The PLAN's Mine-Warfare Operations

The PRC government has stated that it could blockade or close off the two major Taiwan ports by using intermediate-range ballistic missiles (IRBMs), but mines are cheaper, almost invisible, hard to clear, and so more efficient. Due to the negative reaction to a naval and airpower blockade or invasion of Taiwan, mines could provide the maximum gain with minimum investment and risk. Taiwan is outnumbered almost ten to one by the two hundred PLAN and paramilitary mine-warfare forces.

Rather than a unified naval mine-warfare command, the PLAN apparently has split minesweepers into various controlling organizations, which is unique to China. The oceangoing minesweepers (MSO), like the approximately fifteen active T 43s, are attached to the three navy fleet commands. There are still forty T 43 minesweepers, but many are now in reserve status. The location of the mine-warfare HQ with command over all units, if there is one, could be either Dalian in the North Sea Fleet area, or Shanghai in the East Sea Fleet zone. There was mention of a mine school in Dalian years ago, but there are large surface-warfare schools at both Dalian and Shanghai.

Most photos of mine vessels are taken when they are moored in Shanghai, but that could be said of many warship classes. There is believed to be one mine squadron in each fleet. The eastern and southern fleet HQ are probable mine squadron home ports, but mine vessel sightings at the northern fleet HQ of Qingdao have been minimal. Lüshun's location at the mouth of the Bohai Gulf suggests that it would be the likely home port for the northern mine squadron to protect Beijing.

Open information on PLAN mine warfare is limited to sketchy descriptions of the number of minelayers or minesweepers believed active. The organization or command structure is not mentioned. Based on known dates of construction of various mine vessels, the first Chinese minesweepers included nine coastal minesweepers (MSCs)—four former Japanese AMS-class 222-ton units delivered to Qingdao in October 1947 and five 350-ton former U.S. Navy YMS-class minesweepers delivered in 1948. A good estimate is that a formal mine-warfare group would have been created about 1954, with Soviet naval technical assistance, although a rudimentary group would have had loose control over the few foreign World War II vessels available since 1948.[17] The current mine-warfare vessels are summarized in Table 28.

The first postwar minesweepers, which were the beginning of a credible mine-warfare force, were four T 43 MSOs obtained from the USSR in 1955.[18] In the mid-1950s China began construction of first-generation harbor minesweepers in the Qiuxin, Zhonghua, and Jiangxin shipyards. China

Table 28. Mine Warfare Vessels

NR	CLASS	MECH SWEEP	ACOUSTIC SWEEP	MAGNETIC SWEEP	SONAR	TONNAGE	NOTE
1	*Wolei* MSO	Yes	Yes	Yes	Yes	3,100	Command
40	T-43 MSO	Yes	Yes	Yes	Yes	500	Ocean
8	*Wosao* MSC	Yes	Some	Some	Yes	320	Coast
80	Lianyun MSC	Yes	No	No	No	400	Trawler convert
10	Fushun MSC	Yes	No	No	Some	275	Shanghai convert
60	Type 312 drone	No	Yes	Yes	No	47	Remote control

soon began building copies at Wuchang Shipyard in Wuhan and Donglang Shipyard in Guangzhou. The first two copies were launched in 1956, and by 1976 twenty-three had been built. In 1960 Wuchang stopped production, but Donglang continued until forty were built.

Chinese mine countermeasure equipment on the T 43s include variants of Soviet TEM-522 magnetic sweeps, MT-1 sea contact sweeps, and acoustic-sweep-type BGAT or two BAT-2 towed units.[19] The Tamir-11 sonar on T 43s is based on the World War II–era HF searchlight Soviet Tamir sonar. Electrical power sources were one 25-kilowatt and two 75-kilowatt generators. Many of the T 43 minesweepers built have since been assigned duties as oceanographic ships, customs, or survey vessels, similar to the Soviet navy's conversions. In 1976 about twenty Shanghai II PC, named the Fushun class, were built for minesweeping; the last one was decommissioned in 1995. The seventy-odd smaller coastal and auxiliary minesweepers are assigned to various maritime district control roles. Typical are the 400-ton Lianyun-class sweeps that are designated with district letters, such as "J 141" under the Shanghai Maritime Military District or "E 303" for a Fushun-class 250-ton coastal sweeper. To reinforce the disassociation from the PLAN, these MSC letter designators would stand for submarine support (J) and diving tender (E) on fleet units. The coastal and harbor minesweepers are equipped with simple, mechanical sweeps that only counter crude contact mines.

Around 1980 the Chinese copied German remote-control Troika mine-sweepers, designated Type 312, and more than fifty were produced.[20] Although several PRC minesweepers have been marketed for export, the only sales were drones exported to Thailand and Pakistan. In 1988 the PLAN built one large 3,100-ton combination minelayer-minesweeper named *Wolei*. This vessel would serve in a command-and-support role in mine-clearing operations, but no additional units of its type were built. In 1988 China also built the 320-ton *Wosao* (hull 4422), designed for export, to be followed by eight more, but there were no customers. All Luda destroyers were built with mine-laying tracks and carry thirty-eight mines. The imported Sovremennyy DDGs carry forty mines.

Tensions with Russia and Taiwan made the North Sea and East Sea fleets' mine-warfare complement larger than that in the South Sea Fleet. Several naval conflicts with Vietnam in the 1970s and 1980s expanded the South Sea Fleet units. Warnings to mariners to avoid waters off Yulin in southern Hainan in the 1990s either cast doubt on the efficiency of PLAN minesweepers tasked with destroying fifty-year-old Japanese minefields, or represent a gambit to keep the area closed to outsiders.

Newer Mine Technology

There is little open information on a mine industry infrastructure in China. Plant number 884 in Taiyuan and a satellite facility near Houma in Shaanxi province began producing contact mines in 1958. The technology advanced to noncontact mines by 1965; all were initially based upon Soviet models. Naval civilian research facilities on demagnetization and mines are focused in Institute 710 in Yichang. PLAN mine-warfare testing was concentrated in Huludao, with other test facilities at Lüshun, Zhoushan Island, and Changshan Island, which is near the naval port of Yantai on the northern coast of Shandong Peninsula.[21] Dalian is the location of the mine-warfare school adjacent to the major Surface Warfare Officer School. Nearly all mine industrial facilities noted are in the North Sea Fleet area except for Yichang and Zhoushan. The Guangzhou district held mine-warfare training from March to September 2005 that encompassed classroom to at-sea exercises for new vessels and equipments, followed by 2006 and 2007 East Sea Fleet mine exercises.

China has thousands of M-1 ("M" for Mao) and M-2 contact mines based on old Soviet technology, but also newer magnetic and acoustic combination types. In 1953 China produced M-3 acoustic mines with a sensitivity range of fifty meters, which were copied from Soviet MDT models. The M-4 ship- and submarine-laid mine was based upon the Soviet aviation AMG 1 mine.[22] Western references on PLAN mines refer to L1–L4, which should equate to the Chinese M1–M4 name. In 1973 a deep acoustic L4 model was developed and improved in 1985 with solid-state circuitry. C-4 and C-5 noncontact pressure mines were fielded in the period from 1975 to 1977. The newest mines are the EM series. EM-11 and EM-12 bottom-combination fused mines with 320- or 700-kilogram warheads can be laid down to a depth of two hundred meters.

The Chinese export of EM-52 rocket-boost rising mines to Iran several years ago highlighted modern advances in PLAN naval mines. The EM-52 can be laid in waters up to 110 meters deep and has an electronic trigger for the 140-kilogram warhead.[23] The EM-55 rocket-propelled rising 533-millimeter-diameter mine can be submarine-launched from 50 meters depth, with a 140-kilogram warhead. The surface ship version has a 130-kilogram warhead and can be laid down to 200 meters bottom depth. Soviet ADM or MDM series mine copies dating from 1985 have 500- or 1,000-kilogram warheads that have air-, ship-, or submarine-launched variants. The latest cooperative Russian-Chinese mine is the PMK-2, called PMT-1 in Russia, which can rise from a depth of 120 to 1,000 meters.

The units to lay mines off of target areas, such as Taiwanese ports, would likely not be mine-warfare vessels, with several options available among other naval assets. About 150 maritime patrol aircraft (MPA) and naval bombers can carry several mines. For example, the H-5 bomber can carry six Chinese copies of the ADM-500 type mines and H-6 bombers can carry eighteen mines. All PLAN attack submarines can sow mines in complete secrecy. Earlier diesel attack boats carried twenty-eight mines, while the latest Yuan SS and Shang SSN each can carry thirty-six mines, and older frigates and the 60 Hainan PC carry thirty mines each. The 15 large Luda-class DDGs can carry thirty-eight mines, and the 24 older Jianghu frigates can carry sixty mines. However, newer model frigates do not seem to include mines among their weapons. The 180 old Shanghai II and Hainan PC still carry ten mines each. Of course, most of the mines that have been laid worldwide since 1950 have been by merchant ships, fishing trawlers, or junks, and China has thousands of such vessels available.

Degaussing Ships

One area critical to PLAN mine warfare that is little noted is auxiliary degaussing (ADG) ships. Russia had over forty such vessels scattered at all ports to support deperming of warships, submarines, and especially mine-warfare units, and one would expect that China would have adopted the Soviet philosophy. However, the Chinese did not use unique hull letters to designate such ships, as Russia did with the letters "SR" (for *sudno razmagnich-ivaniya*, or "ship demagnetizing"), so these Chinese ships are hard to identify.

Although three different class names have been noted, a common thread is the name "Hai Dzu," which is attached to five units. These vessels probably move around to meet degaussing needs in various ports that lack the capability. The six Yanbai-class degaussing tenders are enlarged Soviet T-43 mine-sweeper hulls whose generator output can deperm vessels up to 7,000 tons, but most PLAN units displace less.[24] Several photos of new Luyang DDGs and 054 frigates show cables around the hulls from bow to stern for checking on magnetic fields. In addition to neutralizing magnetic mines, degaussing is critical for magnetic compass calibration, especially for North Sea Fleet higher-latitude backup navigation.

The first Chinese degaussing vessels were four former American 387-ton landing ships, infantry, large (LSIL) that were converted in the 1950s. These probably carried sixty KSM-type accumulator batteries providing 10-volt external and 110 or 220 volts for internal coils, as in Soviet SR barges. Cable reels for 240-millimeter-diameter cables and magnetometers to measure vertical and horizontal fields would be required. By the mid-1960s additional ships were needed. Two Yen Fang–class and two 460-ton Yerka-class ships were built by 1980, but were decommissioned by 1990. By 1993 the four World War II–vintage LSILs were scrapped, leaving only three active PLAN degaussing ships. Three new 460-ton Yen Pai–class ships built in the early 1990s are the only remaining active degaussing vessels distributed among the three fleets since 1995. A degaussing building has been identified at the critical Yulin forward base.

Finally, China does have degaussing ships to neutralize magnetic mines. In the past the use of PLAN helicopters flying ahead of frigates to detect mines visually has also been noted. Although there are a limited number of such ships, in times of war the PRC has been known to use land railroads to quickly move numbers of small vessels for long distances for naval operations. This solution would be perfect for the many small MSC craft. One example of this tactic was the 1958 transport of Shanghai gunboats by rail from Shanghai to Fujian province in order to participate in the Jinmen and Matsu action.

Conclusions

China has built facilities on several islands and reefs in the Paracel and Spratly chains to back up South China Sea claims in disputed areas. Radar and SATCOMM links are common, but only Woody Island could be considered a true naval base. China is instead using many of its strategically placed offshore islands and linking their bases by a modern electronic communications network. Several outposts have helicopter landing pads and small-to-medium-size piers to receive personnel or logistic supplies via ships. These island outposts are not only adjacent to China, but have appeared off the coast of Myanmar (Burma) as well, and are clearly aimed at monitoring India. In 1993 a SIGINT station was established on Great Coco Island near the Indian navy's large base on one of the Andaman islands.[25]

The PLAN has realized the need for retaining a robust mining and degaussing capability. The PLAN's minesweeping forces are primarily littoral vessels. During PLAN fleet naval exercises over the last decade, however, PLAN oceangoing minesweepers have even been mixed in with coastal minesweepers, which shows how their missions overlap. While degaussing is not a romantic occupation, it is absolutely necessary for the PLAN to retain a viable mine-warfare capability.

The mission and purpose of the PLAN mine forces are mostly defensive, but could also be used for preemptive offensive mining operations off Taiwan, or perhaps against a South China Sea adversary. To carry off such a mission successfully, however, would require good communication systems and training, areas in which the PLAN may still be weak.

── **11** ──

Combat System Integration, Electrical, and Training Issues

H aving effective sensors, fire control, ordnance, and control systems is only part of the picture for building capable shipboard combat systems. The task that makes all of these elements work together is called combat system integration (CSI). Even in the United States, where defense contractors are given precise data on how to make their equipment compatible, making diverse equipment work with each other is a difficult task. This task is even harder for less-developed countries, like China, which rely heavily on imported military equipment that was never designed to be integrated with CDSs or LANs.

Many foreign navies rely on CSI to pull together shipboard combat systems that have components originating from different suppliers. If the integration is not done well, it can be very costly and take years to accomplish what should have taken months, making valuable warships unavailable for service. Newer European communication equipment, aggressively marketed at naval shows, might look attractive on paper, but making it work with existing systems can be a challenge. The result is best described as combat system dis-integration.

To use foreign systems successfully, however, also requires more thorough training. In recent years the PLAN has emphasized training, both on land and—more and more—at sea. It has also provided greater incentive programs for officers and sailors to excel in this area. Whether it has succeeded or not remains an open question.

Common Integration Problems

Since China does not talk about its problems integrating diverse systems or openly admit CSI problems when assembling a warship, one must study the history of delayed commissionings and equipment anomalies. Typical scenarios include having difficulty achieving multiship interoperability, problems operating a system that resulted from different nations teaming up on a design, and installing particular combat systems on only one class of ship. CSI problems may be far more common and widespread than many China analysts were aware.

These interoperability and incompatibility integration problems have arguably only gotten worse during the past ten years, since the PLAN has been purchasing or obtaining enormous quantities of high-technology foreign equipment from Russia or former Soviet republics without proper training. All of this foreign-made equipment must be absorbed into the PLAN, and sailors must be trained in how to operate and maintain it. In estimating the PLAN's capabilities, even the U.S. military often finds the proper use of technology in joint, combined, and coalition operations to be daunting; therefore, it should come as no surprise that poor interoperability is most likely a major tactical, operational, and strategic Achilles' heel of the PLAN.[1]

China has developed combat systems separately from hulls in the shipyard, and many new systems have taken several years from hardware delivery to reach combat readiness. The PLAN bureaucracy has not tackled this integration problem, but in 1992 a hundred Shanghai weapon vendor plants conducted a three-year survey and in 1995 implemented a reform plan in conjunction with the East Sea Fleet. Reforms included delivering documents with the hardware, allowing crew members into shipyards during construction, having crews participate in sea trial tests, and having engineers from the production factories make technical assistance visits to ships to provide maintenance training for crew members.

The problem China encountered with its Ming- and Song-class submarine combat systems is a case in point and was well known for years. The lead submarine combat system was still in redesign many years after commissioning, and the original combat system may have been completely replaced. The Songs lacked full mission-required integrated combat systems for many years after the problems were first noted.

Another example is China's SAM program. The first indigenous SAM was on the Jiangdong-class FFG 531, a modified Jiangnan frigate. It was a navalized SA-2 land SAM, designated HQ-61. The first class of Chinese frigates with surface-to-air missiles provides several clues about serious CSI problems. These include having many years pass from ship installation until initial operating capability, not installing HQ-61 on FFG 532, the second ship in the class, and having a very short lifetime from construction to decommissioning.[2]

Similar problems arise when several nations cooperate on a common new ship design, hoping to save money. CSI problems include disagreement on system selection arising from different mission requirements; disputes if one country believes it suffers from an unequal share of the cost or contracts; design and redesign dragging on for years, usually ending in a project cancellation; or the lack of a centralized decision authority.

China's recent purchases from Russia may have added to the CSI problems. Russia's post-1991 fleet inherited virtually all of its vessels from the USSR, which always was a very closed society—especially in military advances. The Russians especially did not disclose problems that occurred with new ship designs. For example, the first three Udaloy cruisers were launched from 1981 to 1983 with five cover plates where the three VLS launchers and two Cross Sword SAN-9 missile guidance radars should have been located. The SA-N-9 team of Fakel MKB and Altair NPO appears to have had difficulty with the new VLS design, as well as with the complex Cross Sword, which combined six antennas. Other Russian ships reveal more subtle combat system engineering difficulties: a new combat system might appear on only the first unit of a production series, or newer units might have more kilowatt power but weigh less than prior series.

For example, the Tarantul II missile patrol boats appear to be a failed SS-N-22 CSI attempt to replace the old SS-N-2C Styx surface-to-surface missile. A new Light Bulb missile data link and Band Stand targeting radar replaced the Tarantul I SS-N-2C Plank Shave radar. The most probable problem was that the SS-N-22 full system with fire control, missiles, and launcher was too large and heavy, which required considerable interior hull redesign.[3] By contrast, the PLAN's Sovremennyy and new Luyang DDGs now have the 3M80 SS-N-22, with a cruise ramjet and solid booster capable of Mach 2.4 speed and a maximum range of 120 kilometers.[4]

Perhaps because of its close links with the Russian navy, the Chinese navy has several ship classes with CDS design features that indicate a similar potential for integration problems. These features include being equipped with weapons, sensors, and control systems from many different nations; having many system designs that are copies manufactured in the host nation; and installation by a shipyard unfamiliar with ship- and system-unique difficulties. China is a major world navy that has bought Soviet vessels, as well as integrated systems from as many as eight different nations on one vessel. A Chinese shipyard may build and repair entirely Russian-class vessel types with mixed national sensors and weapons on board, and also vessels that are totally Chinese built and equipped. Increasingly, more foreign designs are being built in China today rather than fewer, since Chinese shipyards have the capability to manufacture many foreign systems. Meanwhile, new complex PLAN DDG and FFG designs built indigenously in fact have 60 to 70 percent of their foreign-designed equipment made by Chinese plants.

Shipboard integration problems can become apparent in a different manner. For example, builders of one new Russian warship intended for the export market were sued because of a three-year delivery delay caused by CSI problems. The customer claimed it was the Russian shipyard's fault; the shipyard blamed constant supplementary requirements added on by the customer; and the usual mix of different national systems added to the confusion.

The PRC is not relying exclusively on domestic technology to upgrade its fleet, and many ships use Western electronics. For example, the PRC has been producing a copy of the Decca 202 navigation radar for years, and in October 1984 purchased $15 million worth of Seafox integrated communications from Marconi. Another example of what may be foreign technology is the array of domes and antennas found on the Yuan Wang space event tracking ships. The parabolic tracking antennas, UHF antennas, huge yagi antennas fore and aft, and domed optical trackers are much like those on Soviet and American space tracking vessels. This impressive technology has definitely not been provided by the Soviet Union, so American aid during the era of Sino-U.S. cooperation is not out of the question.

Integration Problems Can Arise at Sea

Some instances of inadequate CSI are not detected until ships are launching weapons at sea. Mixing Eastern and Western systems tends to make it difficult for those systems to function together successfully. Design sources of systems on Chinese ships have been identified as being Russian, French, British, German, Dutch, Swedish, Canadian, Italian, and even American. Meanwhile, during the early 1990s, Russian ships were being replaced by Chinese vessels in the PLAN as part of a trend away from Soviet dependency. However, based on recent Sino-Russian joint exercises in 2005, it is more than likely that the PLAN will procure even more Russian systems in the future.

Even excluding shipboard systems that do not interface with combat control, such as propulsion or helicopter handling, China's Luhu-class DDG has sensors from six different nations that network with the Italian IPN-10 combat direction system. It uses a 10-megabit-per-second dual serial data bus connected to two CP-2000 series central computers. Systems on the distributed network can include Russian radars and fire control; hulls and VDSs from many different nations; Dutch navigation; Italian INS-3 ECM/ESM; and Indian radars.

Other good examples are China's Pauk patrol boats and Natya minesweepers, which are identical to original Soviet units. Many Russian, French, and other European systems are now produced in Chinese factories for installation on PLAN ships. Chinese shipyards produce several Russian warship designs, many under license. China's success in acquiring an indigenous capability to produce Russian warships has resulted in fourteen developing world navies buying these warships from China instead of Russia (see Table 29).

Some nations that used to be part of the USSR also have exported some critical systems to China. In 1997 Kazakhstan reportedly sold some of the much-feared Russian 195-knot Shkval antiship and antisubmarine torpedoes to China.[5] This is one of the weapons systems that Russia has not exported to China. It is doubtful if Kazakhstan provided full manufacturing or technical documentation; certainly the very sophisticated fire control computer was not provided. However, even the Shkval torpedo/missile fired from the 533-millimeter-diameter PLAN submarine tubes without a computer is still a serious threat. In addition Kazakhstan and Ukraine have sold China Kolchuga passive radars, rocket-propelled mines, and gas turbine engines for its new DDGs. A number of firms from former Warsaw Pact nations have been mentioned as illegal exporters, including the Tesla company from the Czech Republic, which sold Tamara long-wavelength antistealth radars to China in 2000. Israel has been in the headlines several times for leaking F-16 technology and AWACS radar technology to China, much of it originally from the United States.

Photo 14. Excellent details of topside communication systems, ECM, and radars on the Luhu-class DDG *Qingdao* while entering Pearl Harbor in 1997. The huge Hai Ying aft radar is unique to this class. Source: U.S. Navy

Table 29. Chinese Naval Exports

CUSTOMER	UNITS	CLASS EXPORTED
Albania	6	Shanghai II FAC gun
Albania	32	Huchuan PTH
Algeria	4	SAR craft
Bangladesh	4	P-4 hydroplanes
Bangladesh	6	033 Romeo subs
Bangladesh	4	Hainan PC
Bangladesh	12	Shanghai II
Bangladesh	4	Hegu
Cameroon	2	Shanghai II
Congo	2	Shanghai II
Egypt	4	033 Romeo subs E103, E104
Egypt	4	Shanghai II PC
Egypt	2	Hainan PC
Egypt	2	Jianghu II FFG E202
Egypt	6	Houku PGM
Guinea	6	Shanghai II PC
Iran	2	Catamaran PTG
Iran	10	Houdong PTG
Iran	10	Chinacat catamaran PTG
Korea	7	033 Romeo SS
Korea	8	Shantou FAC gun
Korea	5	Hainan PC
Pakistan	12	Shanghai II PC
Pakistan	4	Hainan PC
Pakistan	1+	Jiangwei II FFG
Pakistan	4	Huchuan PTH
Romania	3	Huchuan PTH
Sierra Leone	3	Shanghai II PC
Sri Lanka	7	Shanghai II PC
Tanzania	4	Huchuan PTH
Tanzania	7	Shanghai II PC
Tanzania	3	Yulin PC
Tanzania	2	Yuchin LCM
Thailand	4	Jianghu II FF
Thailand	2	Jianghu IV FF
Thailand	2	25T FF
Thailand	1	Fuqing AO
Vietnam	6	P-6 FAC torpedo
Vietnam	14	Shantou FAC gun
Vietnam	8	Shanghai II PC

Integration Links and Standards

The problem of integration is very real. U.S. electronics manufacturers adhere to American National Standards Institute (ANSI) standards while Russia and other former Eastern Bloc nations were covered by Council for Mutual Economic Assistance electrical engineering standards. Meanwhile, Europe follows European Committee for Electrotechnical Standardization rules. Although a European country, the United Kingdom has its own British Standards Institution electronic standards. More than a dozen organizations are involved in international electronic standards, and some apply to all of the nations that have equipment on Chinese naval ships. The higher-level international electronic standards in which most nations participate include the European electrotechnical standards group, as well as the International Electrotechnical Commission (IEC), which sets international standards for electrotechnical testing and certification.

Almost all nations with electronic systems on Chinese ships should either comply with or participate in IEC standards. Britain and other European nations all are under the European electrotechnical standards. Russia, Canada, and the United States, however, are the exceptions. The United States continues to be the real maverick in standards by retaining the inch-foot measures in a metric world. The same applies to power, with the United States using 115 volts and 60 hertz where most other nations selling naval equipment use 220 volts and 50 hertz, but the minimum standard for synchros and fire control is 400 hertz. The United Kingdom and Russia additionally meet IEC standards, and the vast majority of Indian naval electronics are British or Russian. Military systems in Europe also have North Atlantic Treaty Organization (NATO) Standardization Agreement (STANAG) requirements. STANAG 4156 deals specifically with serial data synchronization interface standardization.

The IEEE-488 Data Bus in the United States is called Gost 26003–80 in Russia, and the two share sixteen identical pinouts and data lines. One example of the dangerous possibilities created by dis-integration is an identical rectangular plug with sloped sides and twenty-five pins common to IEC-625 and RS-232-C. One has five volts unity; the other has twenty-five volts on the same pins; and the plugs mate perfectly. Although a simple problem to solve, this example merely shows how complicated it is to design electronic systems that are perfectly compatible on the one hand, and yet relatively simple and safe to use on the other hand.

Chinese Equipment Anomalies

China does not openly discuss its problems with CSI. When observing the Chinese combat systems on classes of ships, however, there are some anomalies that hint at equipment problems such as unexpected design or equipment changes to vessels. These anomalies, whether true or merely perceived, make it difficult to track the PLAN's real capabilities.

One of the most impressive radar antennas on a PLAN warship was the huge Hai Ying Type 518 air search radar. It dominated the aft 0-1 level of the Luhu vessels. The Hai Ying Type 518 was a navalized version of the L-band 1,220–1,350 megahertz REL-1 Chinese airport surveillance radar (ASR) used at several airports. It had a track and video data link range of 230 kilometers and detection range as far as 360 kilometers. For unknown reasons the follow-on Luhai DDG replaced this with the ancient 1953 Soviet-vintage P-10 Knife Rest air search radar in the metric A-band 0–250 megahertz frequency. It had a range of 180 to 200 kilometers at 75 kilowatts, and it actually was a minor upgrade to the even older Soviet Army 1948 P-8 Knife Rest A. An even more fascinating anomaly is that this Knife Rest antenna reappears again on the newest 052C Aegis-type DDG 170 in 2004. There is obviously some air search gap in even the most sophisticated and complex modern Chinese radars that this old relic fills.

Another example, the original Jiangwei frigate hulls 539 to 542 had a new 6-cell launcher just aft of the bow twin 100-millimeter gun mount. Naval references had differing claims on what type weapon was in those six cylindrical cells. Meanwhile, other references stated that it contained an undesignated SAM, which is now known to be the HQ-61B. This is similar to the same conflicting intelligence claims for the six forward SS-N-14 missile cells on the Soviet Udaloy cruiser. Some "experts" claimed they were ASW weapons, while others were certain they were SSN-10 surface-to-surface missiles. After the Cold War was over, Russia revealed the disputed weapon's specifications. It turned out that the SS-N-14 had both capabilities.

Yet the CY-1 missile is also somewhat of a mystery. It was allegedly an illegal copy of the U.S. Navy ASROC that was on only a few old Luda destroyers and Jiangwei frigates twenty years ago. Why was it not carried on the new-construction 051 and 052 DDGs or 054 frigates? Such a weapon is impractical unless the sonar sensor has considerable range and a sophisticated fire control computer for target motion analysis and ballistic-missile-thrust cutoff programming. There has been adequate time for this to be developed. The CY-1 seemed to be very alive in the submarine community with submerged antisubmarine rocket tests since 1997. The Club-S from Russia on Kilos has replaced that effort on Song submarines.

Another anomaly was the lengthening of the Han SSN 404 and 405 from 98 to 106 meters from the initial two hulls. The most popular, and most logical, belief was that this was to allow room in the hull for added cruise missiles to be carried, for either surface or subsurface launch against surface ships. This became a less likely explanation, however, when it became apparent that the cruise missiles could easily be launched from the existing torpedo tubes. The real reason for this design change, and even whether it is propulsion or combat system related, is still speculation.

Reports of new PLAN designs, usually supported by grainy Internet photos, have been common up to the present. The latest is the story of a new radically modernized Yuan Type 041 submarine that surprised the West when photographed completed at Wuchang Shipyard. Usually new PLAN submarine designs take several years to launch, and it looked strikingly similar to Russia's new Lada design. Meanwhile, Internet stories about the construction of large aircraft carriers in China have averaged about one per year for the last decade.

Naval Navigation and Satellites

China is making progress with integrating its naval navigation systems, including its long-range navigation (LORAN), various DGPSs and GPSs, and the ARGO and MAXIRAN MF and UHF systems. As these navigation aids continue to develop, Chinese ships, aircraft, and even precision weapons and missiles will become more and more accurate.

There is an extensive upgraded LORAN-A network from Korea all the way down to Hainan. The daytime ground wave effective range is from 650 to 900 miles, which extends out to Taiwan and Japan. Night ranges reach out to 1,500 miles using a one-hop sky wave. The coverage extends south of the Philippines.

China's other naval navigation aids include twenty-one DGPS radio beacons. The crucial eastern coast naval bases with DGPS are located, from north to south, at Dasanshan (near Dalian), Laotieshan (near Lüshun), Qinhuangdao, Beitang (near the nuclear submarine complex area), Dinghai (a major frigate base), and Sanya (adjacent to the major Yulin sub base). The field strength of the DGPS is 50 microvolts/meter at 50 kilometers. The PLAN ships can utilize satellite navigation (SATNAV) from both their own satellites as well as from foreign networks.[6] American and Russian global navigation satellite system (GLONASS) frequencies are included in Chinese SATNAV receivers, and American- and Japanese-built receivers are commonly seen on PLAN vessels.

The ARGOS-73 network is located in the East China Sea. It has a medium frequency of 1,600 to 2,000 kilohertz. It works on the phase comparison principle. There are five fixed sites and seven mobile shore sites. MAXIRAN is another East China Sea navigation network in the UHF 420–450 megahertz band with five fixed and six mobile shore stations. It uses a pseudorandom code and pulse correlation principle and the effective range varies from 200 to 250 kilometers.

Unlike the global American GPS or Russian GLONASS, China proposed Beidou, which means "Big Dipper," as a purely regional geostationary satellite navigation system in 1983. Tests showed that the two-dimensional regional precision of the Beidou system would be comparable to the three-dimensional American Global Positioning System, so the PRC agreed to fund the Beidou program in 1993. China launched the first two Beidou satellites in 2000 and the third in 2003. That year China bought into the European Galileo Joint Undertaking, which was intended to keep China from being a world competitor. These ranging satellites needed bulky two-way radios and had limited capacity. The next Beidou in middle earth orbit (MEO) was launched on 13 April 2007, still using S-band. In July 2007 China launched a different model Beidou with L-band signal structure and frequencies similar to the GPS, Galileo, and GLONASS. It is expected to operate for eight years and is limited to Chinese mainland coastal waters. The 2008 announcement that China would launch ten next-generation Beidou-2 satellites by 2010 caused consternation among competitors. The new satellite would have five open channels and five closed military channels, like the GPS. This made jamming of the Beidou-2 GPS impossible. This satellite is being followed by the next-generation GPS/GLONASS-compatible active Beidou/BD Star and Tianjan-A.[7] These new satellites have an expected mission life of fifteen years and will provide platforms for meteorological, natural resource, and marine observation, as well as geospace exploration.[8] In October 2009 China seemed to have retrenched on its plan to have thirty MEO and five geosynchronous satellites worldwide by 2030, settling for twelve regional satellites by 2012.

China launched its first successful STW-1 (from Chinese words for "experimental communications satellite") on a new Long March-3 rocket in April 1984. The third stage failed during the first attempted launch in January 1984. The next STW-2 was launched in February 1986. Later the designation Dong Fang Hong (DFH) was assigned to these satellites, so STW-1 is also DFH-2, which can cause confusion in the West. Four improved DFH-2As (with four instead of two C-band transponders) were launched from 1988 to 1990 as STW-3-5. At least nine communication satellites of three different types have been available for naval links as needed, with the SATCOMM control center located at Weinan. The first generation of orbiters was the five STW series, followed by three Chinasats. The next-generation Chinese-German Eurospace Sinosat-1, with twenty-four transponders, was launched in July 1988, but Sinosat-2 was not launched until 2005. China's STW and DFH series of communication satellites are C-band 1 to 2 gigahertz, and newer Ku-band satellites are 12 to 18 gigahertz and include the 14-to-30-gigahertz Chinese naval transmission band. Although designations are not revealed in open-literature sources, Chinese naval SATCOMM receivers are manufactured by the Lingyun radio factory in Baoji. With Russian long-range (LR) radios left at Lüshun and Qingdao being the first node in the fleet submarine command, the northern ports were the first with LR capability.

With the limitation of exposed SATCOMM antenna, the shore commanders could utilize the early STW/DFH series and later improved Chinasat links to high-value units. By the mid-1980s Chinese nuclear submarines utilized American very low frequency (VLF) Navstar and Omega system satellites for their onboard inertial navigation systems, and between 1984 and 1990 China launched five military communication satellites. This rapid growth was assisted by cooperative agreements with U.S. companies, although this was halted temporarily in 1989. During the mid-1990s President Bill Clinton authorized the sale of high-tech American communication satellites to China.

China launched its first HY-1A ocean color remote sensing satellite on 15 May 2002. The HY-1B followed in April 2007. The HY-2A is to be launched in 2010. China candidly has described using downlink data from Japanese GMS and U.S. Landsat, Nimbus-l, and National Oceanic and Atmospheric Administration satellites to provide ocean information. The Chinese Bureau of Oceanography upgraded ground stations to receive ocean color satellite data from foreign sources as well as its HY series.

The PRC launched its first weather satellite, Feng Yun 1A, in September 1988, but it failed after thirty-nine days. An improved Feng Yun 1B weather satellite was launched in September 1990. The most recent, Feng Yun 2E, was launched on 23 December 2008 and began operational monitoring on 22 May 2009. Two of the three Feng Yun 2 satellites are still operating in 2010.

Meanwhile, China's manned space program may also be used to benefit the PLAN's blue-water ambitions, and reports of a successful antisatellite (ASAT) capability have increased concerns throughout the region over the PRC's defense spending.[9] The most alarming Chinese space event was the launch of an ASAT in January 2007, which successfully intercepted a target satellite. The implications to the survivability of space-based naval command, control, communications, computers, and intelligence (C4I) for the U.S. Navy and other major navies could be very serious.

Communication Networking

Communication networking is perhaps the most crucial command component. It has been reported that the 716 Institute developed a first-generation C2 system of unknown designation. Claims of widespread distribution hint that this system could have predated the new post-1990 051 and 052 series DDGs. It could have been on newer 053H frigates and even possibly updated Luda ships. The system allegedly had two computers and a single display console. A Pentium central processing unit (CPU), compact peripheral component interconnect (PCI) bus, and Fiber Distributed Data Interface (FDDI) high-speed local area network (LAN) with 100 megabyte Ethernet somewhat date the system technology.

The first Chinese tactical communication links with characteristics similar to the NTDS were observed on the 4,200-ton Luhu-class DDGs in 1991. Initial TAVITAC CDS installations took place on DDG 105 in 1987, and other Luda models in 1987 could have tried the concept. The PLAN link frequencies of 225 megahertz VHF and 400 megahertz UHF are the same frequencies the NTDS uses and may be part of the Chinese tactical data link system, designated HN-900. Sovremennyy DDGs and Ka-25 helicopters are equipped with the A-346Z secure data link in addition to HF, VHF, and UHF radios. The PLAN is upgrading HF, VHF, and UHF communications to digital systems with Western imports and indigenous radio production plants. Some radars, such as Plank Shave and Strut Curve, can function as directional data link receivers. Western vendors have provided Chinese aircraft with the MIL-STD 1553B data bus, which has now been installed on all new 052 DDGs.[10] China has also used a Type W data link provided by France to non-NATO export customers, which is similar to TADIL-A.

Chinese data networking and integrated services digital network systems have advanced significantly in the nearly two decades since the first Chinese TAVITAC ship installation. The Chinese high frequency and ultrahigh frequency link frequencies are compatible with Russian navy systems. Some auxiliary general intelligence (AGI) and non-SSM ships now carry a Light Bulb antenna, indicating a functional change from a missile data link to a high-capacity communication link similar to a Link 16.

China has a long-range HF and VLF communication capability to support distant operations. The North Sea Fleet was the first to have submarine command links with long-range HF radios left by the departing Soviet forces at Port Arthur and Qingdao. The distant South Sea Fleet naval communication link was an LF station in Zhanjiang, with the first high-power LF station built in Hainan in 1965. By 1980 submerged submarine communications were possible via VLF transmitters at Zhanjiang and Yulin. Chinese VLF sites are 20.5 kilohertz, which is bracketed by Russian Pacific VLF of 18.1 kilohertz and 21.1 kilohertz. China currently has twelve VLF stations. The most valuable Russian imports of 956 EM DDGs, Su-30 long-range fighters, and Kilo 636 diesel submarines provided proven interplatform data links that Chinese technicians can copy or try to emulate on their indigenous PLAN platforms. Additionally, that will enable combined Russian-Chinese naval operations with common data links.

In the mid-1970s there were still three submarine bases with 1950s-vintage Russian LF equipment. Russian warship's shortwave R-630 series used 1.5–30 megahertz.[11] Four models used on surface ships, submarines, and shore stations shared the Mayak-1 exciter, which had 8 kilowatt burst or 0.25 kilowatt continuous power, that PLAN radios would have used.[12]

Chinese-Made Diesel Generators and Engines

Diesel generators provide electricity for all warships, and propulsion was diesel until Luhu. Chinese production of generators shows possible naval sources and also reveals the copying of foreign designs. The largest manufacturers of marine generators are the Shanghai and Harbin electrical machinery plants. The Shaanxi Diesel Engine Plant provides French S.E.M.T. Pielstick diesel generators and diesel engines for all Jianghu and Jiangwei frigates. In 2007 MAN Diesel & Turbo bought the French company S.E.M.T. Pielstick. The main switchgear and circuit breaker suppliers are Shenyang and Shanghai switchgear plants. The largest transformer and wire/cable plants are both in Shenyang. Meanwhile, NGK Insulators, in Nagoya, Japan, controls 90 percent of the Chinese 500 kilo-volt insulator market, which could be a possible bottleneck in times of conflict.

Modern marine diesels designed by Ishikawajima-Harima Heavy Industries are built at Hudong and other Shanghai shipyards, Shaanxi Diesel Engine Plant, and Dalian Marine Diesel Works. Henan Diesel Engine Industry in Luoyang is licensed to copy MWM AG high-speed diesels, and Sichuan Diesel Works and Dongfeng Diesel Engine Plant produce Sulzer four-stroke medium-speed diesels. Shaanxi Diesel Engine Plant 406 in Xi'an produces copies of Japanese Daihatsu medium-speed diesels and MAN Sulzer Pielstick medium- and high-speed diesels. Although MAN 16PA6 and 19PA6 diesel engines are on several PLAN frigates, Shaanxi may now manufacture more powerful MAN 20 V28/33D STC diesel engines with a 9,000 kilowatt output for new warships.[13] Dalian Marine Diesel Works and Hudong Shipyard manufacture copies of Sulzer and MAN B&W turbocharged low-speed diesels, and Yichang Marine Diesel produces Finnish Wärtsilä and Sulzer medium-speed diesels.

Wuxi Huaxiang Control System produces Siemans AG marine brushless synchronous alternators. Wuhan Marine Machinery Plant manufactures Japanese pumps, winches, deck cranes, electrohydraulic steering gears, and French electric deck machinery. Shanghai Navigation Instrument Factory produces German ship automation and Japanese Terasaki main switchboard control panels and starters.

The list could go on, but this sample shows that Chinese companies can produce many foreign designs for their warships.

The three largest PRC companies producing boilers, turbines, and generators are Shanghai United Electric Company (SUEC), Dongfang Electric, and Harbin Power Equipment. SUEC controls half of the Chinese market divided among nine major factories. The largest of these factories is the Shanghai Turbine Works, which manufactured China's first 600-megawatt turbine generator in 1956. Its most popular models are the 50-, 125-, and 300-megawatt turbine generators, as well as nuclear 300- and 600- megawatt plants. Other subsidiary SUEC companies specialize in boilers, switchgears, relays, porcelain, transformers, auxiliaries, and heavy machinery. The second major company is Dongfang Electric, in Deyang. It features pump turbines up to 550 megawatts, steam turbine generators up to 600 megawatts, and hydraulic turbine generators up to 320 megawatts. The third large company is Harbin Power Equipment. Its three subsidiaries are Harbin Electric (generators and AC/DC motors), Acheng Relay Works (power transmission/distribution), and Harbin Turbine (steam and gas turbine models).

It is obvious that the foundation for China's major electrical industries are in Shanghai and the northeast, both built by outside nations such as Russia and Japan. The same can be said for industrial transportation such as railroads, long the main mode of transport along with the rivers, which makes Manchuria one of China's most important industrial areas for the manufacture of heavy naval equipment.

Electrical and Mechanical Problems

Hull, mechanical, and engineering (HM&E) is an area overlooked in most naval technical assessments. Focus is typically on the sensors, transmitters, and armament, but all of these are reliant on robust electrical power.

The United States only exported five LM-2500 gas turbines to China, four of which provided the main propulsion for Luhu DDGs 112 and 113. This left only one for the following Luhai, which used Ukrainian-provided GT25000M Russian gas turbines. A recent Russian reference states that the LM-2500s are on both Luhus.[14] There is a story that the lead Luhu had to be returned to Jiangnan Shipyard because the engineering space did not allow for installation of the LM-2500 gas turbine, and had to be enlarged. Ukraine provided eight DN-80 gas turbines for Type 052B and 052C DDGs. There are indications that the Xi'an Aero Engine Works has achieved the ability to manufacture DN-80 gas generators instead of relying on imports.

As mentioned in chapter 4, the first PLAN warships were the Soviet Riga frigates, which were copied by China as the Chengdu class. These had only 450 kilowatts of generator power.[15] Details on the Luda destroyers' electrical power are not listed in naval references, but it is probably similar to the Soviet Tallinn/ Kotlin specifications. If so, then Luda electric sources should be two 400-kilowatt turbogenerators, two 200-kilowatt diesel generators, and one 100-kilowatt harbor/emergency diesel, for a total of 1,300 kilowatts.[16] The various types of power required by basic equipment such as a navigational radar is typical of the complexity. The Mius radar used 220 and 280 volts/400 hertz, and 220 and 380 volts/50 hertz.[17] Chinese warship equipment is normally 220 volts, alternating current (VAC)/50 hertz, with 400 hertz for modern electronics. Additional generators for different frequencies introduce weight and maintenance issues for technicians.

The amount of generated power required for warships is related to the complexity of their systems, more than their tonnage, as will be illustrated in following examples. The Jianghu I and II, built in 1975, had four 300-kilowatt S.E.M.T. Pielstick 16PA6V280BTC diesel generators and one 120 kilowatt diesel generator, for a total of 1,320 kilowatts. When a surface-to-air missile was added, turning Jianghu class into the Jiangdong class, more powerful diesel generators were added, making 1,720 kilowatts in total. To reduce unit production costs, a later Jianghu V was reduced to the basic 1,320-kilowatt level. The new-generation Type 540 Jiangkai frigates have over double the appetite for kilowatt power.

The 68-ton Hoku missile boat had 65 kilowatts of power, compared to the larger 134-ton Shanghai II missile boats that had only 39 kilowatts. The 500-ton T 43 minesweeper had 550 kilowatts. Auxiliary PLAN vessels provide interesting comparisons. The 3,000-ton research ship *Shijiang* required 1,065 kilowatts, compared to the 14,600-ton Fuqing-class replenishment/ support ships that need 2,480 kilowatts of power from four 620-kilowatt diesel generators.

The complexity of new warships such as the Luhu, Luhai, 052Bs, or 052C DDGs suggests great kilowatt appetites, but no information is available on electric generators. The Sovremennyy class has two 1,250-kilowatt turbo-generators and four 600-kilowatt diesels for 4,900 kilowatts of total power. Assuming Russian sales to China include HM&E support of Sovremennyys, such data on it could approximate modern PLAN warship power requirements for Luyangs. As for the early Kilos, although the sonar, fire control, radars, and electronic warfare all were highly advanced and complex systems, it seemed that the HM&E systems actually kept the two submarines from being operational for more than two years after delivery. The Type 2D-42 diesel generators, rated at 1,500 kilowatts each, were beyond the ability of the Chinese to maintain or repair, and they were returned to the Elektrosila plant in Russia for repairs.

Educational Reforms

To determine how well the PLAN is integrating foreign-purchased equipment into its indigenous systems, it is important to study the background of naval officers and judge the quality of their training. Not surprisingly, beginning in the 1950s, the PLAN's training was based almost completely on Soviet procedures and utilized Soviet training manuals. Even after the Sino-Soviet split in 1960, the PLAN continued to rely mainly on these earlier training regimes. More surprising, many of these Soviet techniques continue to hold sway to this day, especially with regard to the basic division of the subject materials into a common curriculum, professional techniques, and tactics. This Soviet-style training was especially important when the majority of China's naval recruits were uneducated peasants. In many cases basic literacy was a problem that had to be overcome during training.

During the past two decades, however, the PLAN's leadership has attempted to increase the number of college graduates in its officer corps. By the mid-1990s 85 percent of the officers in command of naval vessels reportedly had a college education. Many of the top-ranked officers are graduates from MA programs and some even have PhD's. This represents a huge change in the PLAN from focusing merely on training to emphasizing the general educational levels of the officer corps.

To increase even further the percentage of educated officers across the board, beginning in 1999 the PLAN began to recruit a thousand officers annually from nonmilitary universities and colleges. As part of a special "Captains Project," promising officers were sent back to college for advanced study, especially in the physical sciences and in engineering. In the "Project of Crack

Units," officer training in advanced weapon systems was emphasized, while in the "Thousand Generals Project," a thousand young officers, including many from the navy, were promoted to the rank of general or admiral on the theory that "these officers would [better] foresee the modernization program of the armed forces in the coming decades."[18] These kinds of incentive programs are becoming more and more common as China builds for itself and purchases from abroad more high-tech ships and advanced weapon systems.

In addition to technical training, during recent years the PLA has also attempted to toughen up training standards. In December 2005 the HQ of the General Logistics Department (GLD) launched a new staff officer appraisal system. The GLD awarded a gold cup, a silver cup, and a bronze cup in each of thirty categories to reward excellent staff officers based on their adherence to a pamphlet entitled *The Basic Knowledge for Staff Officers Working in the PLA General Logistics Department Headquarters*. In addition, the GLD's headquarters tests applicants on three subjects, including professional basics for staff officers, foreign-language skills, and computer applications. Selection of finalists for the excellent staff officer awards would depend on combining examination grades with a general evaluation.[19]

When it comes to technical training, however, even with all of its recent efforts China remains far below global levels, including those of its neighbors such as Japan, Taiwan, and India. The PLAN's task has been made more difficult due to the large range of equipment, both indigenous and foreign made, thus greatly complicating training. The lack of technical expertise on the part of Chinese sailors results in some computers being used as typewriters, which inhibits C3 missions. China has had "mixed results" solving this problem: "In training, the PLAN is still beleaguered with problems of inadequate training time, limitations in live-fire exercises, insufficient missile allowances, ineffective unification of command and control, and lack of integration of different weapon systems, etc."[20]

Recent international events have given China an excuse to conduct naval exercises. On 26 March 2010 a South Korean patrol boat was allegedly sunk by a North Korean submarine in the Yellow Sea. When the U.S. Navy announced joint ASW exercises in the Yellow Sea with South Korea scheduled to begin on 5 July 2010, the PLAN showed how live-fire exercises were effective tools for sea control. China did not want the USS *George Washington* (CVN 73) on the western coast of Korea, within striking distance of Beijing. From 30 June to 5 July the PLAN had live-fire exercises in the East China Sea, followed by naval logistic exercises on 17–18 July, delaying the scheduled U.S.-ROK joint ASW exercises. On 26 July China had missile-firing exercises in the South China Sea. The U.S.-ROK Yellow Sea

ASW exercise occurred on 25–28 July, but the U.S. carrier remained east of Korea allowing China to deny access.

Two positive examples of PLAN education and training are the Dalian Naval Academy for surface officers, established in November 1949, which underwent a major modernization and expansion completed in 1988; and the Submarine Academy at Qingdao, established in 1953.

Meanwhile, numerous technical schools exist for training enlisted personnel, but much of the advanced training occurs around Shanghai. The major training school for submariners is located at Qingdao, the major submarine home base in northern China. The longer enlistment periods for submariners provides some stability and a core of technical enlisted experience. However, in this field, as in so many others, China is undergoing enormous changes.

Personnel, Technical Training, and At-Sea Training

Enlisted men in the PLA Navy receive basic training at Shanghai, Nanjing, and Qingdao, then go on to shore duty. Since 2002 conscripts receive no advanced technical training. Their training base will provide basic technical training, and their operational base will provide general and on-the-job training.[21] Those assigned to ships attend a specialist school for several months. There are enlisted rating schools for electronic technician, radioman, and signalman at Shanghai; there are quartermaster, engineman, and gunnery schools at Nanjing. Training for electricians, in submarine operations, and for maintenance of torpedoes and mines is conducted at Qingdao. There is no sonar or ASW school listed, although the navy operates the Institute for Ocean Science Research, and the Beijing Institute of Acoustics works with transducers and underwater sound.

Prospective PLA Navy officers may attend four-year courses at either the Dalian Naval Academy or at the new Navy Service Arms Command Academy, established in Guangzhou in 2004. There are also officer candidate schools in Qingdao and Shanghai. Officers training for submarine and surface ship duty face a four-year curriculum with postgraduate follow-on training consisting of two-and-a-half-year courses for senior officers and four-year courses for junior officers at Nanjing Naval College. Officers may receive technical training at two schools: the Naval University of Engineering at Wuhan, or at the First Surface Vessel School at Dalian. Based at the Dalian Naval Academy, the training ship *Zheng He* has sailed 290,000 miles since 1988, during which time more than 30,000 cadets have received instruction on its decks. Cadets may also train with enlisted men at the logistics, radar, and coastal artillery schools at Jinxi Second Artillery College, or the engineering school at Harbin.

After technical school, graduates are assigned to ships. The PLA Navy continues their training by rotating officer enlisted teams through various departments so that sailors gain experience in several different billets. This training, made possible at least in part by long terms of conscription in the PRC, is probably superior to the limited, one-job Soviet approach. Because many of the combat systems are modern Russian equipment, China has minimal capability even to repair peacetime losses in port. Senior noncommissioned officers (NCOs) were previously the respected enlisted experts, but changes in modern ship systems have caused junior high-technology NCOs to be the new valued leaders. This is being rectified by retraining senior NCOs on modern systems, using junior NCOs and factory experts as instructors.[22]

While in-port education and training are important, so is time spent out at sea. The amount of at-sea training for PLAN warships and distant cruises are minimal compared with that of Western navies. It was in 1985, thirty-six years after the creation of the PLAN, that the first foreign cruise was accomplished by the coastal defense navy. The first distant multimission navy exercise occurred in 1991.[23] A couple of Ludas were at sea on operations much more than the others. DD 110 has been photographed many times at sea, and DD 105 is another ship seen at sea frequently, even before it was selected to be converted to helicopter operations as the Luda II. The Fuqing replenishment ship 887 and modern Luhu- or Luhai-class vessels have made two long-distance cruises to the United States since 1997. The first PLAN global cruise was in May 2002 by the Luhu-class destroyer *Qingdao* and the auxiliary oiler *Taicang*. In typical showing-the-flag cruises, Luhai 167, Luda 455, and Fuqing 887 visited Pakistan and Thailand ports in late 2005.[24]

After being unable to participate in previous Southeast Asian relief operations with other navies, China made its first out-of-Pacific deployment in anti-piracy operations off Somalia. On 27 December 2008 the first Chinese naval escort taskforce (CNET), made up of the 052C *Haikou* (DDG 71), the 052B *Wuhan* (DDG 169), and the *Weishanhu* (AO 887), departed Yulin, Hainan, for Somalia and four months of operations. On 2 April the 051B *Shenzhen* (DDG 167) and the 054A *Haikou* (FFG 570) departed Hainan to relieve the first two warships. They made the transit in eleven days, as the first group had, but the oiler had to remain on station. After two days of joint operations, the two DDGs departed Somalia and arrived back in Yulin on 28 April 2009.

CNET 3, from the eastern fleet port of Zhoushan, consisting of two frigates, 529 and 530, along with the other Fuchi vessel *Qiandaohu* (AO 886), assumed operations on 30 July. The CNET 4 frigates 525, 526, and 568 departed for the Gulf of Aden on 29 October 2009. They were the first ships to be deployed from the East Sea Fleet's elite 3rd Flotilla, which includes the four Sovremennyy DDGs.

Sending the CNET groups from different port areas distributed the deployment lesson, but the reduction from two large DDGs down to two frigates could have had several possible causes. Either the complex DDGs were overkill for the minimal threat the pirates posed to the mission or difficult to maintain, or the PLAN wanted a dramatic power demonstration with the first CNET. CNET 5, which departed Hainan in March 2010, had a balanced complement composed of DDG 168, FFG 568, and AO 887. The DDG was the first of its class to be deployed since CNET 2 in April 2009. CNET 6 departed Hainan on 1 July 2010 and returned on 7 January 2011, and contained a couple of surprises. Besides the usual DDG (170) and the AO 887 replenishment ship, the third ship was the new 20,000-ton *Kunlun Shan* (LPD 998). Five days out of Hainan, it revealed the first view of the new Chinese-built air cushion hovercraft, strikingly similar to the U.S. Navy's LCAC. Compared to the single Z-9 helicopters on DDGs or FFGs, which have a four-troop capacity, the two large Z-8 helicopters on the LPD can carry twenty troops each. The turnover from CNET 5 to CNET 6 in the Gulf of Aden took place on 14 July 2010.[25] En route to Hainan, CNET 5 ships visited Egypt, Italy, Greece, and Myanmar, marking the first visit by PLAN ships to that country.

China is reaping benefits for the PLAN from its investment in military aid and civil port facilities in the Gulf of Aden. The three replenishment ports used by CNET ships are located in Salala, Oman; Aden, Yemen; and Dubai, United Arab Emirates.[26] This is a sign of maturity and the use of soft power. Since their inception, Western navies have always made numerous overseas cruises and had rotation on stations. However, the trend in the PLAN is clearly to provide more at-sea training for its officers and crews during their second training cycle from March to June.

The peak-of-readiness preparation and evaluation are fleet exercises during the third training cycle from summer to October. The PLAN averages four to five exercises per year; about two-thirds of these are single-fleet exercises, with the East Sea Fleet having about twice as many as the other two fleets. Certainly the new DDGs would be the heart of ASW and AAW exercises.

Because of the clustering of the most modern Kilo and Sovremennyy units in the Zhoushan area, Russia established a maintenance, training, and support group there for the complex imported combat system weapons, sensors, and HM&E. While availability of such training is important to the PLAN's officers and men, it would be unwise for China to depend on it, given the fickle nature of previous periods of Sino-Russian cooperation.

Conclusions

Communications, integration, and training are a tough nut to crack for any navy, not just for relatively new navies like the PLAN. The real keys to the integration problem are naval training and documentation, which is difficult enough with a fully indigenous fleet, but almost impossibly complex when imported or copied foreign equipment is added to the mix.

What will undoubtedly make this task even more difficult and risky for China is that some of the core technology may have been acquired illegally. Several European nations have denied exporting many of the systems that have appeared on Chinese ships. Some of these systems may have been stolen or illegally bought from third nations or businesses, which means that they probably arrived without proper instruction manuals and without essential replacement parts. In fact the vast majority of these systems were probably sold under the table, either secretly or during low-profile transactions, so supporting documentation may be nonexistent.

Discussions have been held about ending the European arms embargo of China, which would increase even further the number of European systems appearing on Chinese ships (Table 30 summarizes many of those systems). While China has proven adept at copying sample equipment, complex systems have taken years to develop, and so have been difficult to produce. Moreover, once they have been produced, it has been difficult to train operators to operate and maintain many of these systems effectively. When the European systems are combined with the Russian-made systems, both those already in China and those that might be purchased during the coming years, the picture becomes even more complicated. It is reasonable to conclude, therefore, that China's military technology problems could increase over time, not decrease.

Table 30. Eurasian Systems on PLAN Warships

CATEGORY	EQUIPMENT	FUNCTION	SOURCE
Radios	Various	Comms	Germany
SSM	Exocet	SSM	France
Jammer	Alligator	ECM	France
Intercept	DR-2000	ECM	France
Search radar	DRBV-15	Surface search	France
Hull sonar	DUBV-23	Ship ASW	France
VDS sonar	DUBV-43/SS-12	Ship ASW	France

continued

Table 30. Eurasian Systems on PLAN Warships *continued*

CATEGORY	EQUIPMENT	FUNCTION	SOURCE
FC radar	Castor II	Ship gun FC	France
Sub sonar	DUUX-5	Sub ASW	France
Helo	Dauphin/Frelon	Ship helo	France
Diesel	S.E.M.T. Pielstick	HM&E	France
ASW torpedo	A-244	ASW	France
CDS	TAVITAC	Ship CDS	France
Sub sonar	TSM-2233	ASW	France
E-O FCS	Naja	Gun FC	France
SAM	Crotale	Ship AAW	France
100-mm autoload	Creusot-Loirs	Ship gun	France
Helo recovery	Samahe	Ship helo deck	France
Generators	Siemens	HM&E	Germany
Sub batteries	Unknown Designation	Sub HM&E	Germany
Comm radios	Redifon/Marconi	Comms	Great Britain
40-mm/37-mm CIWS	Breda	Ship AAW	Italy
Jammer	Scimitar	ECM	NATO
EW	Ramses/Rapids	ECM	Netherlands
Sub screws	Kockums	HM&E	Sweden
Sub screws	Wärtsilä	HM&E	Germany
ASW torpedo	Alenia	ASW	Italy
ASW tubes	ILAS-3	ASW	Italy
Torpedo	Shkval	Sub antisurface	Kazakhstan
Diesel	TB-83	HM&E	Germany
CDS	CTC-1629	Ship CDS	Great Britain
ESM	Newton-Beta	ECM	Italy
CDS	IPN-10	Ship CDS	Italy
Data link	TYPE W	Ship CDS	NATO
CIWS	Goalkeeper	Ship AAW	Netherlands
SATCOMM	Magnavox	Comms	Great Britain
Radar	Decca	Ship navigation	Great Britain
SAM	Aspide	AAW	Italy
SATCOMM	SNTI-1240	Comms	Great Britain
ESM	DR-2000	Submarine DF	France
ESM	DR-3000	Ship DF	France

——12——

The PLAN Fleet in the Twenty-first Century

The previous chapters have focused on the PLAN's sensors, platforms, and weapons, plus the shipboard combat systems that connect them. Knowing a modern navy's capabilities can provide vital clues in determining that country's intent, since technological factors can either allow for an offensive strategy threatening to other nations or can limit maritime forces to purely defensive strategies. In the PRC's case, does it intend to use its naval forces to attack Taiwan, for example, or will the PLAN be used to protect China's vital trade interests and national growth, a strategy common to any large nation with a huge coastline?

Although China has a history of isolationism and traditionally has been reluctant to participate in international treaties, the naval advances described in prior chapters have been tied to several agreements over the past decade. Following the USSR's dissolution in 1991, the 1996 Shanghai Five meeting led to the creation of the Shanghai Cooperation Organization (SCO) in June 2001. This linked China to Russia and other former Soviet states that China relies on for military aid and support.

Tension with the five nations with South China Sea claims that had resulted in prior conflicts was defused with the 2002 Declaration on the Conduct of Parties in the South China Sea, which bound the signatories against using force to resolve disputes. This helped China's relations with other Southeast Asian nations, which were enhanced further by a 2003 Chinese agreement to commit to the 1976 ASEAN charter.

In 2001 China started discussions with Russia to have an oil pipeline built from Skovorodino, in Siberia, to Daqing, but a formal agreement was not reached until February 2002. The pipeline was opened in September 2010 and will double the amount of oil moving from Russia to China, which previously was transported by slow trains. This pipeline reduces China's reliance on oil shipped via the sea from the Middle East. The possibility of an overland pipeline from Iran in the future promises to further ease China's reliance on shipping the oil that it needs.

Another recent example of cooperation was Beijing's December 2008 decision to send warships off the coast of Somalia to conduct antipiracy operations. Many nations, including the United States, welcomed China's decision as a sign of constructive international engagement. But other nations—India, for example—perhaps saw Beijing's decision as a more aggressive naval action, since it gave Chinese naval forces the perfect excuse to conduct exercises throughout the Indian Ocean.

This book has shown that following the 1991 collapse of the USSR China could skip over many stages of naval development by purchasing Russian equipment from Warsaw Pact countries and former USSR republics. Since that time China has had the luxury of picking and choosing from some of the world's best naval equipment offered on the open market, including from western European nations and America. With their new missiles, surface platforms, and submarines, the PLAN can better patrol and control the three dimensions of air, sea, and under the water. Given the PLAN's new capabilities, including anti-carrier IRBM developments, Chinese leaders have perhaps convinced themselves that a U.S. carrier strike group cannot intervene in a Taiwan conflict unopposed. Beijing is determined that China's March 1996 setback, when two U.S. carriers were sent to the vicinity of Taiwan, will not be repeated. Therefore, in terms of China's ability to support a policy of "sea denial," one cannot help but conclude that the PLAN already represents a potential maritime threat.

This said, China's Achilles' heel now, and for some time to come, will be the lack of full systems interoperability. Systems interoperability affects the speed of sensors to detect, decision makers to decide, and naval commanders to initiate operations, making time an important new "fourth dimension" in the PLAN's technological capabilities. While China will undoubtedly loom large as potentially the most important, as well as perhaps the most dangerous, rising power during the coming "Pacific Century," the PLAN's existing naval forces have been created by mixing and matching equipment from over a dozen countries.

The Chinese navy's greatest challenge during the first quarter of the twenty-first century will be how well it can integrate both the old and the new platforms into a fully interoperable fleet structure. To do this successfully will require not just better naval technology, but also better training and education for its officer corps. Proper training is essential if the PLAN hopes to use these indigenous and foreign-bought systems effectively. In this regard the Chinese navy has recently undertaken comprehensive reforms in strategy and tactics, equipment acquisition, and coordination of different fleets and other PLA forces. But it will probably be in the area of officer training and naval education where the true success or failure of China's maritime reforms will become clear.

China is easing the block obsolescence operational problem of ship types with recent serial production trends. The numerous old patrol and small missile boats are being replaced by the sophisticated forty newly constructed Houbei class. Large numbers of old frigates are being replaced by the predicted thirty-ship production run of modern, multimission 054A frigates. The old diesel submarines will be replaced by Kilos, new Yuan boats, and even newer SSN designs soon. The last modernization phase yet to be decided is which DDG design will replace the elderly Luda class. This will happen when the decision is made as to which follow-on Luyang- or Luzhou-class DDG is to go into serial production.

Western navies, especially the U.S. Navy, emphasize minimum manning and maximum technology, enabling them to put smaller crews in modern vessels. The assumption is that the PLAN is manpower intensive in its warships, but this may be a misconception, one deliberately left uncorrected by China, so the PLAN's technology advances will be underestimated. Some recent examples include China's 20,000-ton LPD 996, with a crew of only 120 according to GlobalSecurity.org, while the USS *San Antonio* has a crew of 396. The Houbei missile boat crew numbers 12, as opposed to the similar-size Huangfeng, with a crew of 26. The Luyang-class DDG's crew of 280 is smaller than the 348 personnel on an Aegis-type DDG, but it is comparable, since the Luyang's 6,500 tons is 3,000 tons less than the Aegis-type DDG. An anomaly is the very modern, automated 054A frigate's crew of 180, as compared to the French *La Fayette*–class frigate's crew of 143. However, the *La Fayette* has no ASW sonar or weapons and has short-range SSM and SAM launchers; the 054A has 8 long-range SSM cells and a 32-cell VLS.

The pattern and methodology is very clear. Even if the PLAN has fewer personnel during the next decade, it will be greatly more capable from littoral to distant waters, on and below the surface. The PLAN's sixtieth anniversary naval parade held in Qingdao on 23 April 2009 symbolizes how far it has come as an emerging world naval power. It showcased twenty-three surface warships, four submarines, including the first public appearance of two SSNs, and thirty-one PLAN aircraft. Fourteen nations sent twenty-one warships to participate in the parade and celebration.

China's four-dimensional naval battlespace—air, sea, underwater, and the time it takes to integrate the three—presents five future challenges to the PLAN. The first major challenge to the PLAN's abilities will be to determine how efficient China's new sensing systems are, and how integrated they are with the weapon systems. The second challenge will be the effectiveness of the PLAN's FC systems, especially its systems-of-systems ability to network-centric the entire fleet. A third challenge will be the PLAN's willingness to use its enhanced ship mobility, more rapid reaction times, and forward basing to respond to outside threats. The fourth challenge will be the PLAN commanders' strategic and operational leadership skills and their ability to adapt to rapidly changing circumstances. Finally, the fifth major challenge facing the PLAN will be the willingness of Beijing to accept a higher level of risk based on the government's faith in the as-yet untested abilities of the PLAN in battle. All of these factors will be discussed in greater detail below.

Interoperability of Sensing and Shooting

The maritime environment is completely nonlinear, and threats can come from any dimension, including from under the sea and from overhead. The senses, enhanced by technology, are crucial for locating the enemy. "Finding the other guy" is vital, but being able to escape detection while doing so is equally important. Because of the three-dimensional battlespace, naval warfare is not sequential as in land battles, and constant maneuver is a way of life. On the ocean it is usually pattern recognition that allows you to locate the enemy, and to identify patterns one must have top-of-the-line sensing equipment.

Chinese sensing systems have gone through enormous changes during the past forty years. Beginning in the 1960s and 1970s, China received all its naval equipment from the USSR. In the 1980s China began to import high-technology equipment to fill key sensor and weapon roles. In the 1990s new PLAN warships included complex radars and weapon systems that were manufactured in China. Since 2000 China has produced illegal copies of major imported aircraft, sensors, and weapons, often without the benefit of full documentation, logistical support, or training.

It is an open question whether these disparate components can be made to work together efficiently through CSI, or whether dis-integration will undermine the PLAN's military effectiveness. There are serious shortfalls with systems integration regarding maintenance and supply facilities. Even those surface ships and submarines produced wholly in China rely "heavily on foreign-designed/produced engineering, weapons, and sensor systems."[1]

Irrespective of how powerful the Russian-built Sovremennyy destroyers and Kilo submarines are, if they are forced to act alone, or protect numerous lower-quality Chinese-built platforms from destruction, they could offer limited resistance. China's much publicized modern imports cannot alter the fact that more than three-quarters of the PLAN's submarines, surface ships, and aircraft are almost totally obsolete for today's modern combat requirements.

According to many reports, China also does not have the facilities to fix these top-of-the-line foreign-built ships should the Sovremennyys or Kilos ever be damaged, and so they might have to be returned to Russia for repairs and refitting. While merely troublesome during times of peace, any similar delay during war could prove fatal. Therefore, even the most powerful-appearing foreign-bought equipment can prove to be a liability should supplies run short or essential platforms be damaged in times of war.

Likewise, availability of adequate Russian armaments remains a major problem. The Sunburn ship-to-ship missile, currently one of China's most lethal naval weapons, has been purchased from Russia. The first Sovremennyys to arrive in China reportedly included fifty-four Sunburn missiles, and China now probably has about a hundred in its arsenal. But the number of more advanced "Sizzlers" owned by China could be much smaller, and the arrival of new supplies is uncertain. Meanwhile, the Kazakh Shkval 195-knot torpedoes purchased by China could be virtually useless without the associated fire control systems.

While such weapons might be sufficiently deadly for a one-time attack or if used against a lone opponent, the lack of system interoperability could undermine the long-term effectiveness of China's naval equipment and its power-projection capabilities. Problems of buy versus build will soon begin to plague China's naval forces, if they have not begun already. Beijing appears to be repeating the troublesome nineteenth-century historical pattern whereby China would build its own support ships with foreign help, even while purchasing high-tech ships from abroad as a vanguard. This policy ended in failure during the First Sino-Japanese War.[2]

Integration of Fire Control Systems

Part of the PLAN's interoperability problem will be figuring out how to make many ships' fire control systems work with each other, which requires systems integration. As Admiral William F. Halsey stated after World War II, "A fleet is like a hand of cards at poker or bridge. You don't see it as aces and kings and deuces. You see it as a hand, a unit. You see a fleet as a unit, not carriers, battleships and destroyers. You don't play individual cards, you play the hand."[3] Individual cards won't win China's naval "game"; it will take the entire hand for it to succeed.

During the 1980s China tried, but failed, to add British and American combat direction systems to its Luda-class destroyers; the post-Tiananmen sanctions blocked these purchases. Soviet NTDS-like integrated communication systems were adopted instead, and the versatile Russian Mineral-ME (NATO name: Band Stand) missile FC radar with active, passive, and data link systems are on the Luyang DDGs. For the first time, the 250-kilometer-range active and 450-kilometer-range passive radars were linked to the 30-kilometer-range S-band target designator/data link system. Currently some of China's Ludas and all of its new Houbei catamarans, newest frigates, and Luyang DDGs have the Chinese HN-900 tactical data link system. However, this does not mean that one ship is fully integrated with others. Full fire control integration is undoubtedly weakened by the PLAN's lack of battlefield experience and real-world training.

Jointness has also been a constant problem, not just between services, but even among the various naval fleets. On this note, Beijing's decision to retain the traditional three fleets within the modern Chinese navy—instead of unifying all of these contiguous forces into one—suggests that the central government might be concerned about giving any one fleet, or naval leader, too much power. To this end Beijing leaders have been careful to keep power divided so that the navy will not be able to unify and challenge the government, which further undermines integration.[4]

While the PLAN leadership appears justifiably proud of its most recent Chinese-built Luhu-, Luhai-, Luyang-, and Luzhou-class DDGs, its most effective fighting strength resides in the Russian-built Sovremennyy-class destroyers, equipped with Sunburn and Sizzler missiles. How well these modern foreign fire control systems can work together with the obsolete majority of China's naval ships could be the key to its future success or failure.

Mobility, Command, and Forward Basing

Speed of systems communication and decision making is a third important element, since this supports mobility and maneuver. In battle, speed is relative, not fixed, and maintaining a higher reaction speed than one's enemy is all-important. If you can get inside your enemy's decision-making loop, and act faster than they can, then you can win. New equipment alone does not necessarily give greater mobility and maneuver, because officer education and crew training are crucial for making effective use of that equipment.

To maximize the use of its equipment, the PLAN's command structure must be willing to take risks and face up to uncertainty. After 1949 the

PLAN's organization was deeply impacted by its growth out of PLA infantry units, which meant that for a long time its command-and-control structure, its political hierarchy, and even its logistical system differed "considerably from their [naval] predecessors."[5] The political commissar system is particularly strong. This indicates that the Chinese navy will remain under tight government control for some time.

However, this PLA domination of the PLAN is gradually changing. During December 2005, for example, Chinese President Hu Jintao reshuffled the highest commanders of four of China's seven military regions. As reported in the Hong Kong press: "In this round of personnel reshuffle, several senior naval and air force generals have been promoted to important posts usually filled by army generals in the past. This suggests that in order to cope with changes in new military strategy, generals [flag officers, including admirals] with combat experience and technological background from the Navy and Air Force have [for the first time ever] been put in important positions."[6]

Meanwhile, during the past few decades the PLAN's actual battlefield experience has remained small, as has its focus on real-world training. This only changed in the 1990s with China's decision to move toward a "blue-water navy." When he was commander in chief of the PLAN, and on the Central Military Commission until 1997, Admiral Liu Huaqing provided direction on how the PLAN should purchase high-technology naval platforms, including Sovremennyys, Kilo-class diesel submarines, and Su-27 and Su-30 aircraft. China has also obtained four derelict aircraft carriers, including the Kuznetsov-class aircraft carrier *Varyag* from Ukraine, which suggests a major acceleration in China's long-quiescent aircraft carrier program. As far back as March 2007, one unidentified Chinese admiral even stated that China might have its own aircraft carrier as soon as 2011.[7]

By home-porting new vessels in southern Hainan, China appears to be carrying out a naval strategy in the South China Sea of exerting regional maritime control incrementally. Extrapolating from the rapid growth of its communications, intelligence gathering, and naval supply structure on Hainan and its island bases in the South China Sea, China appears to have linked these bases with a modern electronic communications network.[8] Many of the islands and reefs occupied in the SCS have a few buildings and a few antennas with a rudimentary pier. The only all-purpose base including aircraft shelters and support is located on Woody Island. Although crude, such outposts are being improved, if space is available, and could add to the PLAN's overall mobility and ability to outmaneuver any regional competitors.

Strategic and Operational Independence and Adaptability

With technical advances, greater interoperability, systems integration, and education and training come greater strategic and operational independence and adaptability. Navies that are flexible can adapt quickly to new circumstances. With the end of the Cold War, in particular, the Soviet navy was eliminated almost overnight as the world's second most powerful naval force, and Russia's Pacific Fleet is now so poorly supplied and equipped that it rarely leaves port. This unprecedented reversal of fortunes has created a maritime vacuum throughout East Asia that China hopes to fill, although the U.S. Pacific Fleet still has a powerful deterrent presence with its Asian allies.[9]

Regional concerns have been driving China's naval strategy. Taiwan is the PRC's most important regional opponent. In the past Beijing has described the Taiwan situation as "grim," and has criticized the U.S. government for increasing "quantitatively and qualitatively, its arms sales to Taiwan, sending a wrong signal to the Taiwan authorities. The US action does not serve a stable situation across the Taiwan Straits."[10] To Beijing the recent decisions by the United States to sell arms to Taiwan is "in violation of the principles established in the three Sino-U.S. joint communiqué, causing serious harm to Sino-U.S. relations as well as peace and stability across the Taiwan Straits."[11] One strategic objective, therefore, of the most recent PLAN acquisitions has been to attempt to keep the U.S. Navy at arm's length through sea denial, should tensions over Taiwan ever erupt into war.

The perceived threat of a rearmed Japan, meanwhile, plays an important role in the development of China's contemporary naval operations. In 2008 Chinese warships were observed in the Tsushima Strait, and in 2005 a Chinese submarine was discovered transiting submerged through Japanese waters, which resulted in a Japanese protest and a halfhearted Chinese apology. Meanwhile, the October 2005 intrusion in Japanese waters by a Chinese Tu-154 converted with various reconnaissance sensor pods, an event that followed almost a dozen intrusions by Y8 electronic-warfare units in 2004, also indicates preliminary operations toward Japan. The North Sea Fleet's addition of the highly capable 051C Luzhous, with superior command, control, and navalized S-300 area air defense system, also indicates increased Chinese concerns with Japan and contested sea claims.

Although Taiwan and Japan are undoubtedly China's most important political problems, the territorial dispute over the South China Sea comes in as a close third because of its economic importance. Beijing currently claims all of the Paracel and Spratly islands, plus much of the waters in the South China Sea, and its navy has clashed with forces from Vietnam and the

Philippines. According to John Pike, head of GlobalSecurity.org, "What is the next big problem the PLA navy could solve for the political leadership? The South China Sea. It has an incredible capability to grab everything down there. If I was in the PLA navy, that's a no-brainer."[12]

China's territorial and economic interests in this area arguably go hand in hand, since major shipping lanes, extensive fisheries, and a wide variety of energy sources are either located in these regions or transit the all-important SLOC that passes India and reaches China via the SCS. Counterbalancing India, exerting maritime control as far as the Malacca Strait, and ensuring the continued viability of this invaluable SLOC are high priorities.[13] Currently China has good relations with Pakistan and seeks to support port and ELINT works by Myanmar to help compensate for its lack of aircraft carriers, which are possessed by India and Thailand.

In particular, a high percentage of China's petroleum and natural gas reserves lie untapped in offshore waters. Chinese estimates for oil and gas reserves in the South China Sea are impressive, reaching 213 billion barrels for the first and 2,000 trillion cubic feet for the second. These figures contrast with more conservative U.S. Department of Energy predictions of 28 billion barrels of oil and widely varying gas reserve estimates. Although such forecasts may be inflated, China's belief in these estimates is arguably as much or perhaps even more important than their accuracy. China's desire to absorb greater energy sources under its direct control will undoubtedly strengthen its determination to protect its sovereignty claims in the East China Sea, as well as throughout the SCS generally. A Chinese trawler collided with two Japanese patrol boats near Diaoyu Islands in September 2010.

Viewed from this perspective, therefore, two of China's main strategic motivations behind building a strong navy are to be able to enforce its territorial claims and to secure energy import sea-lanes. These objectives are reflected in increased PLAN operations throughout the maritime regions along its border, including Taiwan, the Diaoyu Islands, the Paracel Islands, the Spratly Islands, the largely empty waters of the South China Sea, and China's maritime border with Vietnam. These operations suggest a greater degree of independence and risk taking by the PLAN.

Beijing's Willingness to Accept Risk

A hundred years ago imperial Japan was a rising Pacific Ocean power, and so was in much the same position as China is today. Then, the world's failure to introduce Japan peacefully into the international political order cost it dearly. Today, the amazingly short development time of the Luyang DDGs shows that the PRC is starting a world-class blue-water navy through foreign naval acquisitions, particularly of high-tech ships and armaments from Russia, and from a robust indigenous shipbuilding program.

Beijing appears willing to risk much to obtain its military ambitions. China might be looking not just to reclaim Asian territories, lost to it during the so-called century of humiliation from the 1840s onward, but also to move out into the Pacific to challenge the United States to protect its interests. In particular the PRC's decision to purchase four Russian-made Sovremennyy-class guided-missile destroyers and a total of twelve Kilo-class diesel submarines, both of which are based mainly in the East Sea Fleet, will add greatly to China's rapidly growing capability to threaten Taiwan, on the one hand, and to challenge Japan for East Asian naval supremacy, on the other. All of these vessels offer superb "sea-denial" capabilities, which will make it very difficult for foreign navies to intervene in China's littorals.

China's growing submarine fleet is especially important when assessing the PLAN's long-term threat. The number of active PLAN submarines is currently only thirty-two, compared to fifty-two active U.S. Navy submarines, but an additional thirty-one PLAN reserve submarines could be used in stationary barriers to keep enemy forces out of Chinese waters. China's new-construction trends point to a future imbalance, since it is outbuilding the U.S. in new submarines by four to one over the last ten years, and by eight to one over the last five years. The diminished U.S. Navy ASW forces will be hard put to handle the rapidly rising number of modern PLAN submarines. Should the most modern Yuan-class diesel submarine possess air-independent propulsion, as some sources suggest, this submarine could be even harder to detect. The next-generation SSN 093 and SSBN 094 are a new increased level of threat as well.

Geography makes these growing submarine numbers even more threatening from the U.S. perspective, since all of these PLAN submarines are located in their own waters, and so face minimal transit distances. By contrast, until recently half of the U.S. Navy submarines have been based in the Atlantic, and even those submarines based at Pearl Harbor are a long distance from China. Therefore, any American submarine sent to Chinese waters could easily be outnumbered ten to one. The PLAN diesel submarines are on average ten to twenty years younger than American submarines, and are much quieter than the older Chinese submarines.

Finally, China's large and growing mine-laying capabilities are a threat that could be used to interfere with free movement in the Taiwan Strait and elsewhere. Although such weapons are considered relatively low tech, especially when compared to China's modern destroyers and submarines, they could prove to be a viable deterrent to the U.S. Navy's coming to Taiwan's aid, and cut off the key commercial ports that are Taiwan's lifeline. As Ryan Henry, the former principal deputy undersecretary of defense for policy, warned: "It looks like they [the PRC] are preparing for something other than a political solution to the Taiwan problem. And we find that disconcerting."[14]

The PRC may hope, therefore, to adopt a maritime strategy beyond the familiar "offshore active defense" based on a robust navy that will allow it to claim the so-called First Island Chain by retaking Taiwan, and then move beyond this area deeper into the Pacific. PLAN exercises beyond the First Island Chain during March–April 2010 would tend to support this thesis. The PRC's military domination of Taiwan may not be an end stage, therefore, but merely the first step in this larger plan. New terms appeared from Beijing after the Somali deployments, such as "national interest frontier," that extend the PLAN's missions. Another is "greater periphery security" to support the building of PLAN aircraft carriers.[15] China's greater periphery includes the Persian Gulf and the Indian Ocean to the west, whereas the familiar Second and Third Island Chains were to the east. A third new term is "far sea defense," which lies outside the two-hundred-nautical-mile EEZ.[16]

Beijing has already spent large sums opening friendly diplomatic relations with a number of Pacific Island nations. China has also sought to establish warmer political and commercial relations with a number of Central and South American and African governments. Chinese companies have been contracted to control the Pacific and Atlantic entrances to the Panama Canal. In an eighteen-month period during 2005–6 Chinese president Hu Jintao visited five Latin American nations with anti-American foreign policies, and four of these countries have coastlines with seaports.

Assuming China continues to strengthen its Central and South American and African diplomatic relationships, this policy could indicate a major change in the PLAN's operations—from being just a western Pacific naval force to one that includes the central and eastern Pacific to protect vital oil sources. One immediate benefit of this new policy is that in 2005 Venezuela reportedly offered to send China one or more F-16 engines obtained from the United States that Chinese aircraft companies could reverse engineer for more advanced technology.[17] On the other hand, China has made efforts to improve dialogue and make international agreements regarding naval disputes. This is especially true in the South China Sea relations with ASEAN member nations, which suggests that China might be willing to utilize diplomatic means before adopting a military solution.

Assessing China's Future Intent

China has faced up to the five challenges confronting its hopes of creating a blue-water navy, including improving its sensing platforms, integrating its fire control systems, building more forward bases to support great mobility and maneuver, pushing PLAN commanders into assuming ever more independence in their day-to-day operations, and—finally—accepting greater risk to obtain its long-term strategic goals. These changes are largely in line with policies beginning in 1997, when China's president Jiang Zemin urged the Chinese navy to "build the nation's maritime great wall."[18]

But modern navies are technology dependent and resource intensive. Integration problems associated with purchasing foreign-made equipment, as opposed to producing it indigenously, will undoubtedly continue to plague China's navy for some time to come. To overcome these technical and financial shortcomings requires a coherent naval strategy. China has found such a strategy by adopting certain preconceptions from the former Soviet Union, including the view that the United States is the primary threat.

From a military standpoint China cannot currently challenge the U.S. Navy as a peer. It probably hopes instead to develop a maritime strategy that will allow it to overcome its shortcomings in doctrine, equipment, and training, and to target asymmetric American weaknesses, as demonstrated by the January 2007 ASAT kill. If done properly, such a strategy should allow China to retake Taiwan, achieve parity with Japan's naval technology, secure its territorial claims to the South China Sea, and protect its vital SLOC through the Malacca Strait. China's strategy may currently be based on sea denial in the littorals, but the PLAN is quickly building up its coastal defense capabilities so that it can extend its reach farther afield. In recent years the area to be defended has increased to more than two hundred miles from shore.

Based on Beijing's rhetoric, China's primary national goal would appear to be to regain Taiwan, through threats of force if possible, and by the use of actual force if absolutely necessary. To succeed, one might expect the PLAN to position its most modern offensive platforms in the East Sea Fleet facing the Taiwan Strait. Also, the East Sea Fleet should be the largest and have the newest warships. Somewhat surprisingly, as this text has shown, many of the newest DDGs, frigates, and submarines tend to be based in the South Sea Fleet. This configuration does not necessarily support a Taiwan conflict, but does match a future mission of escorting oil convoys to the Middle East, or asserting greater sovereignty over Chinese claims to the South China Sea. The Luyang DDGs 168 and 169 and the Luyang DDGs 170 and 171 form the core of two battle group formations based at Yulin for distant operations.

Beyond foreign country cruises to show the flag or exercises with area navies, the first extended military deployment opportunity was the Somalia pirate mission. Somali pirates captured the Chinese fishing vessel *Tian Yu 8* on 14 November 2008, attempted capture of the *Zhenhua* on 4 and 16 December 2008, and captured the cargo ship *De Xin Hai* on 19 October 2009. On 27 December 2009 the 052C *Haikou* (DDG 171) and the 052B *Wuhan* (DDG 169), along with the large replenishment ship *Weishanhu* (AO 887), departed Yulin to join Task Force 151 in antipiracy operations. They joined sixteen other navies in escort operations and gained the experience that only extended joint operations can provide. As of 20 March 2010, the four CNETs had escorted 1,768 ships in 179 groups and rescued 23 ships from pirates.[19] In September 2010 the new hospital ship 866 began an eighty-seven-day humanitarian Africa/Middle East cruise, similar to the annual cruises USNS *Mercy* has taken since 2004. Who can foresee the future missions by the impressive newest South Sea Fleet warships?

The location of the newest amphibious naval forces and marine units should also be facing Taiwan, assuming that island nation was their future landing and assault goal. In fact the South Sea Fleet is the home of the largest marine battalion and amphibious platforms. China has recently built a large hospital ship, which would normally be based in the area of planned assault casualties. This hospital ship is also located in Hainan, along with two earlier hospital conversions, as part of the South Sea Fleet, not in Fujian province across from Taiwan.

The recent emphasis on the south has been shown most graphically by the relocation of China's new attack SSNs and SSBNs from the traditional Qingdao area to Yulin, in Hainan province. The construction of a large underground tunnel for protection is a major undertaking and shows a long-term commitment to this move. This South China Sea bastion offers unimpeded exits to the open ocean, and so the SSN and SSBN operating areas are not as restricted by vulnerable geography as they would be farther to the north. If U.S. bases in the western Pacific, such as Guam or Okinawa, were the PLAN's potential targets, then the South Sea Fleet certainly offers the most favorable port.

During the next decade, the PLAN may be able to add even greater prestige by commissioning its first aircraft carrier. Admiral Hu Yanlin, former political commissar of the PLAN, said that the building of aircraft carriers is a symbol of an important nation and is very necessary for China's future.[20] An anticipated PLAN carrier keel-laying announcement during the sixtieth anniversary celebration of the PRC and the PLAN in mid-2009 failed to occur, but is still possible in the coming years. If the Soviet-era carrier *Varyag* were to be activated to full warship status, it could become an important training platform for naval aviation and key carrier systems. In the past Western experts have claimed that China would never build or buy carriers because it lacked the associated battle group platforms, similar to U.S. Navy carrier strike groups. However, the recent commissioning of modern multimission Luyang DDGs and Jiangkai frigates would qualify as indigenously produced carrier support ships. Meanwhile, Su-27/33MKK purchases from Russia would provide carrier air groups and naval air cover to support just such a deployment.

The most intriguing question would be where to base the home port of any future PLAN aircraft carrier. If a carrier were to face the U.S. Navy in protection of a Taiwan assault, then East Sea Fleet or North Sea Fleet basing would be logical. The current emphasis on southern basing for some of China's most modern ships and submarines, however, hints at SLOC convoy missions, which would be greatly reinforced if the future carrier was also to be based in the south. In particular the life expectancy and impact of a PLAN carrier on energy SLOC support would be far greater than the expected lifetime of a PLAN carrier facing a U.S. Navy battle group off Taiwan. The same logic could be applied to the two Aegis-like Luyang IIs or Fuzhou DDGs.

Asymmetric PLAN capabilities have created major risks and countermeasures that largely offset the minimal Chinese investment. Recent examples include the successful targeting of a satellite by one Chinese missile, jeopardizing U.S. reliance on space for C4I. Another are China's latest supersonic over-the-horizon missiles, which are unmatched by most Western offensive missiles. There are also several new-construction warships with unique capabilities, and their location hints at anticipated new missions. For example, the two new Luzhou DDGs, which are AAW mission ships with the navalized S-300 land-based area air defense radar and VLS, are both located in the North Sea Fleet. Although not necessarily representing a PLAN asset, the efforts to modify and enhance the DF-21/CSS-5 MRBM to an antiship ballistic missile (ASBM) is a threat of increasing impact to U.S. carriers and forces in the western Pacific in coming years.

China's Future Maritime Path

Although China has made enormous strides recently, particularly in merging foreign and indigenous naval combat systems, even a simple comparison between China's nineteenth-century imperial navy and the contemporary PLAN suggests that in times of war the current Chinese navy could face a crippling capabilities mismatch between its Chinese- and Russian-built ships, a limited supply of armaments, and a limited ability to maintain or adequately repair its high-tech combat systems in port and at sea.

The outcome of any future naval conflict will clearly depend on high levels of command and control, interoperability of equipment both on a single ship and among different ships within the same fleet, and jointness not only between different services but also more importantly within the three Chinese regional fleets, as well as on the quality of the training and education received by Chinese naval personnel.

Finally, China's reliance—some would argue overreliance—on Soviet-era naval equipment means that Beijing's good relations with Moscow would be absolutely essential during any actual naval conflict. This relationship has been harmed by events such as the multiyear discussions on Su-33 sales that ended in failure and by China's flagrant illegal copying of the Russian AL31FN turbofan engine as the Chinese WS10, the Su-27 SK as its J-11B, and the SU-33 as its J-15 carrier plane. The position of Russia in 2009 is that no Su-35 engines or radar will be permitted to go to China, although Vietnam and India are obtaining them. Therefore, this serious downturn in Sino-Russian relations will greatly restrict China's future naval air advances.

Although the PLAN is modernizing with new high-technology warships and rapidly gaining greater prestige within the region, there is growing concern as well. A number of Southeast Asian countries have begun to buy more naval equipment, in order to beef up their naval capabilities. Fears of a rising China could backfire, making it easier for the U.S. Navy to forge an anti-China coalition, should the need ever arise. Therefore, China must tread carefully if it hopes to use the PLAN to obtain its national objectives, while avoiding a naval arms race.

——— Appendix ———

Western and PLAN Combat System Designations

NATO NAME	PLAN DESIGNATION	FUNCTION
	ASR-3A	Optic FC
	BM/HZ 8610	ESM
	CSAN-2	SAM
	CY-1	ASW missile
	EAJ7	Jammer
	ECIC-1	CDS
Rice Lamp	EFR-1	CIWS radar
	EH-5	Sonar
	EH-5A	Sonar
	ERC-1	Decoy
	ESS-1	Sonar
	ESS-2	Sonar
	GDG-775	E-O FC
	HN-900	Data link
Crotale	HQ-7	SAM
	HQ-9	SAM VLS
	HQ-16	VLS
	HZ-100	ECM
	JM-83	Optic FC
Aspide	LN-60	SAM
	NJ-813	ECM (French copy)
	OFC-3	E-O gun director
	PJ-33A	100-mm gun
Jug Pair	RW 23-1	Jammer
	RWD8	ECM

continued

NATO NAME	PLAN DESIGNATION	FUNCTION
Rice Screen	Sea Eagle	3-D radar
	SJD3	HF sonar
	SJD-5	MF sonar
	SO7H	MF sonar
	SR-210	EW intercept
	Yu-1	Surface torpedo
	Yu-2	Air torpedo
	Yu-3	ASW torpedo
	Yu-4	Antiship torpedo
	Yu-6	Heavy ASW torpedo
	Yu-7	ASW torpedo
	2JD5	ASW system
	2JK3	CDS
	2JK5	ASW display
Knife Rest	17C	LR radar
	054	12.7-mm AA gun
	061	25-mm AA gun
	062	ASW mortar
BMB-2	064	Depth charge
	065	Surface search
	066	57-mm AA gun
AK-230	069	Twin 30-mm gun
FQF-2500	075	ASW mortar
	076A	37-mm gun
	079A	100-mm/56 gun
	081	ASW mortar
	085	FC radar
	087	ASW mortar
	88C	Weapon control system
	90	Rocket launcher
	341	100-mm gun FC
Wasp Head	343	Radar (Wok Wan director)
	344	SSM/gun FC
Castor	345	SAM FC
Aegis	346	Phased-array radar
Rice Bowl	347	Gun radar

continued

Western and PLAN Combat System Designations *continued*

NATO NAME	PLAN DESIGNATION	FUNCTION
Rice Lamp	347G	Gun radar
Pot Head	351	Surface radar
Square Tie	352	SSM FC
Eye Shield	354	Air search radar
Seagull	360, 364, SR-64	Target designate radar
ESR-1	362	Surface radar
Sea Tiger	363	Surface radar
Rice Screen	381	LR radar 3-D
Bean Sticks	515	LR air search radar
Knife Rest	517	Air search radar
Eye of God	518	REL-1 LR air search radar
	AK 630	Soviet CIWS
	651	IFF
PL-9	715	SAM
	730	Goalkeeper CIWS
Decca	756	Navigation radar
Fin Curve	765	Navigation radar
	825	ESM
Stop Light	921A	ESM
	923	ESM RWR
	928	ESM
	945	Chaff launcher
	946	Decoy
	947	Chaff launcher
	981	Jammer
	984	Jammer I-band
	985	Jammer E/F-band
Ball End		Surface search radar
Fog Lamp		SAM FC radar
Pea Sticks		LR radar
Post Lamp		FC radar
Round Ball		Gun FC radar
Skin Head		Surface search radar
Top Plate		3-D air search radar
Twin Eye		Optic FC director
Wok Wan		Gun direction radar

Notes

Chapter 1. Systems Integration and China's Naval Technology Growth, 1949–89

1. The names given for Russian weapon systems used by China are based on NATO designations. See Federation of American Scientists, "Russian Air Defense Radars," FAS Military Analysis Network, http://www.fas.org/man/dod-101/sys/missile/row/radar-rus.htm (accessed 10 November 2010).

2. V. Averyanov et al., *Sudovye Radiolokatsionnye Stantsii i ix Primenenie (Spravochnoe Rukovodstvo)* [Ship Radiolocation Station and Application (Reference Guidance)], vol. 3 (Leningrad: Sudostroenie, 1970), 10.

3. V. I. Kamanin, A. V. Lavrent'ev, and R. A. Skubko, *Shturman Flota* [Navy Navigation] (Moscow: Voennoe, 1986), 170.

4. Jim Bussert, "PRC Military Electronic Systems Evaluated," *Defense Electronics* (Palo Alto, Calif.: EW Communications) 12, no. 6 (June 1980): 70.

5. Tong Yuan, "Technical Advances in Shipbuilding Industry Reported," *Handelsblatt*, 31 March 1987.

6. China Shipbuilding Trading Company, "China Shipbuilding Trading Co., LTD.," http://www.chinaships.com /co/cssc.html (accessed 27 May 2009).

7. The MiG-21 follow-up prototype was not produced by the USSR.

8. Federation of American Scientists, "FROG-7A (3R-11, 9K21, 9M21, R-65), FROG-7B (9K52, 9M52, R-70), Luna-M," FAS Military Analysis Network, http://www.fas.org/man/dod-101/sys/missile/row/frog-7.htm (accessed 10 November 2010).

9. Nuclear Weapon Archive, "China's Nuclear Program," China's Nuclear Weapons, http://nuclearweaponarchive.org/China/ChinaTesting.html (accessed 10 November 2010).

10. Christopher Chyba, "U.S. Military-Support Equipment Sales to the People's Republic of China," *Asian Survey* 21, no. 4 (April 1981): 469–84.

11. SinoDefence.com, "Strategic Missile Force," http://www.sindofence.com/strategic/default.asp (accessed 16 November 2010).

12. Ding-Jong Tyan, "Taiwan Analysis of PLA Air Attack, Response," *Taiwan Defense Affairs* 4, no. 1 (1 October 2003), translation at Open Source Center (shortened hereafter to OSC) CPP20050830000264.

13. Society of British Aerospace Companies, "China Special: Opening Doors—China's Growing Market for Aircraft," 24 October 2006, http://www.sbac.co.uk.

14. Geoffrey Manners, "China's First Modernisation Expo," *Jane's Defence Weekly* 5, no. 6 (15 February 1986): 233.

15. Bob Furlong, "ASIANDEX Part 1—China Launches Defense Export Drive," *International Defense Review* 14, no. 1 (January 1987): 23–27.

16. The official Chinese defense budgets in 1980 and 1981 were particularly low, and from 1980 through 1988 only increased from 19.4 billion yuan to 21.8 billion yuan. See Wang Shaoguang, "Estimating China's Defence Expenditure: Some Evidence from Chinese Sources," *China Quarterly*, no. 147 (September 1996): 889–911.

17. Jikun Huang, Chunlai Chen, Scott Rozelle, and Francis Tuan, "Trade Liberalization and China's Food Economy in the 21st Century: Implications to China's National Food Security," paper presented at the meetings of the American Association for the Advancement of Science, Washington, D.C., February 2000, University of California Agricultural Issues Center, Economics of Agriculture in China, http://aic.ucdavis.edu/research1/rozelle.htm (accessed 10 November 2010).

18. Information Office of the State Council of the People's Republic of China, *China's National Defense in 2008*, special report, Beijing, January 2009, Federation of American Scientists, http://www.fas.org/programs/ssp/nukes/2008DefenseWhitePaper_Jan2009.pdf (accessed 10 November 2010), 66.

19. Wang Cho-chung, "PRC Generals Call for Reinforcing Actual Strength of Navy," *Taipei Chung-Kuo Shih-Pao*, 25 March 2001, translation at OSC CPP20010326000046.

Chapter 2. Earlier Chinese Destroyers

1. Stephen Chumbley, ed., *Conway's All the World's Fighting Ships, 1947–1995* (London: Conway Maritime Press, 1995), 58–67.

2. M. J. Whitley, *Cruisers of World War Two: An International Encyclopedia* (London: Cassell, 1995), 104.

3. Incorrectly identified as Silkworm by the press, so this more common name will be used.

4. Four basic models—A, B, C, and G—of the HY-2 were evidently produced, each with different characteristics. See Federation of American Scientists, "C-201/HY-2/SY-1/CSS-N-2/CSS-C-3/SEERSUCKER," FAS Military Analysis Network, http://www.fas.org/man/dod-101/sys/missile/row/c-201.htm (accessed 12 November 2010).

5. S. Balakin, *Legendarnye "Semerki"* [Legendary "Seven"] (Moscow: EKSMO, 2007).

6. Jim Bussert, "China Builds Destroyers around Imported Technology," *Signal* 58, no. 12 (August 2004): 68.

7. Srikanth Kondapalli, "China's Naval Equipment Acquisition," *Strategic Analysis* 23, no. 9 (December 1999), Columbia International Affairs Online Net, http://www.ciaonet.org/olj/sa/sa_99kos01.html.

8. For information on U.S. economic sanctions against China, see Dianne E. Rennack, "China: Economic Sanctions," Congressional Research Service, Library of Congress, updated 1 February 2006, Federation of American Scientists, http://www.fas.org/sgp/crs/row/RL31910.pdf (accessed 12 November 2010).

9. K. V. Chuprin, *Voennaya moshch' Podnebesnoy: Vooruzhennye sily* KNR (Minsk: Harvest, 2007), 420.

10. Norman Friedman, *The Naval Institute Guide to World Naval Weapons Systems, 1997–1998* (Annapolis, Md.: Naval Institute Press, 1997), 122.

11. "China Develops French-Type Sonar with U.S. Technology," *Jane's Defence Weekly* 30, no. 14 (7 October 1998): 6.

12. Friedman, *Naval Institute Guide to World Naval Weapons Systems*, 584.

13. Bob Furlong, "ASIANDEX Part 1—China Launches Defvvnse Export Drive," *International Defense Review* (January 1987): 27.

14. Chuprin, *Voennaya moshch' Podnebesnoy*, 420.

15. V. Averyanov et al., *Sudovye Radiolokatsionnye Stantsii i ix Primenenie (Spravochnoe Rukovodstvo)* [Ship Radiolocation Station and Application (Reference Guidance)], vol. 3 (Leningrad: Sudostroenie, 1970), 10.

16. I. P. Shirokie, *Remont Sudovie Radio-navigatsionnogo Priborov* [Repair Ship Radionavigation Equipment] (Moscow: Transport, 1985), 198.

17. Jim Bussert, "Chinese Destroyers Incorporate Western Technology, Designs," *Signal* 49, no. 7 (March 1995): 55.

18. *Korabli i Vooruzhenie Voenno-Morskogo Flota* [Warships and Weapons of the Military Naval Fleet], vol. 3 of *Oruzhie Rossii Katalog* [Russian Arms Catalog] (Moscow: Voennyy Parad, 1996), 501.

19. Chuprin, *Voennaya moshch' Podnebesnoy*, 496–98.

20. Friedman, *Naval Institute Guide to World Naval Weapons Systems*, 579.

21. "China Develops French-Type Sonar," 6.

22. Andrei Pinkov, "China Develops the New Radar Wave Absorbing Materials," Kanwa.com, http://www.kanwa.com/english/990307c.html (accessed 12 November 2010).

23. Jim Bussert, "New Missile Destroyers Deploy for Blue-Water Operations," *Signal* 54, no. 3 (November 1999): 31.

24. Ibid.

25. Stockholm International Peace Research Institute, "International Arms Transfers," http://www.sipri.org/contents/armstrad/REG_IMP_CHI-EU_89–05.pdf/download.

26. A. S. Pavlov, *Warships of the USSR and Russia, 1945–1995* (Annapolis, Md.: Naval Institute Press, 1997), 114, 125.

27. Christopher Bodeen, "China Ends 1st World Military Cruise," Associated Press, 24 September 2002.

Chapter 3. New-Generation Destroyers

1. "Maintenance of 956E DDGs," *Kanwa Asian Defence* 62 (December 2009): 17.

2. "First Lot of Moskit Missiles Shipped to Chona," ITAR-TASS News Agency, BBC Summary of World Broadcasts, 26 May 2000, cited by http://www.nti.org/eresearch/profiles/China/Missile/ (accessed 15 November 2010).

3. *Vooruzhenie i Voenno-Morskaya Tekhnika Rossii* [Russia's Naval Ships, Armament and Equipment] (Moscow: Voennyy Parad, 2005), 185.

4. Charles R. Smith, "China Is on the Move," Newsmax.com, 3 January 2006, http://www.archive.newsmax.com/archives/articles/2006/1/2/164456.shtml (accessed 16 November 2010).

5. *Vooruzhenie i Voenno-Morskaya*, 113.

6. John R. Benedict, "The Unraveling and Revitalization of U.S. Navy Antisubmarine Warfare," *Naval War College Review* 58, no. 2 (Spring 2005): 93–120.

7. *Vooruzhenie i Voenno-Morskaya*, 185.

8. K. V. Chuprin, *Voennaya moshch' Podnebesnoy: Vooruzhennye sily KNR* (Minsk: Harvest, 2007), 429.

9. "China Developing New Wireless Stations and Countermeasure Equipments," *Kanwa Defense Review* 2006, no. 9 (September 2006).

10. Norman Friedman, *The Naval Institute Guide to World Naval Weapons Systems, 1997–1998* (Annapolis, Md.: Naval Institute Press, 1997), 328.

11. Kerry Plowright, *The People's Liberation Army Navy (PLAN)*, China Files, People's Liberation Army Navy Ships, ADF V.2.1 Research Sheets, 2008, Scribd, http://www.scribd.com/doc/37524007/Plan-Ships (accessed 12 November 2010), 21.

12. Bill Gertz, "Four Arrests Linked to Chinese Spy Ring," *Washington Times*, 5 November 2005.

13. Jan Prokop, *Computers in the Navy* (Annapolis, Md.: Naval Institute Press, 1976), 131.

14. "Russian Data Link Systems in Chinese Military: Combat Prospect Analysis," *Kanwa Defense Review* (1 April 2005): 14, translation at OSC CPP20050407000122.

15. "054A FFG of PLA Navy East Sea Fleet Visits Hong Kong," *Kanwa Defense Review* 2010, no. 64 (February 2010).

16. Jim Bussert, "China Debuts Aegis Destroyers," *Signal* 59, no. 11 (July 2005): 60.

17. MissileThreat.com, "YJ-83," Cruise Missiles, http://www.missilethreat.com/cruise/id.67/cruise_detail.asp (accessed 12 November 2010).

18. "China's Military Facility Construction," *Kanwa Defense Review* 2006, no. 5 (May 2006): 69.

19. SinoDefence.com, "Type 052C (Luyang-II Class) Missile Destroyer," Naval Forces: Vessels, http://www.sinodefence.com/navy/surface/type052cluyang2.asp (accessed 12 November 2010).

20. "PRC C4I Activities 14 Sep–27 Oct 05," Beijing Xinhua Asia Service, 14 November 2005, *People's Daily*, http://www.english.people.com.cn/90001/90776/90786/index.html (accessed 14 November 2005).

21. Jim Bussert, "Chinese Destroyers Incorporate Western Technology, Designs," *Signal* 49, no. 7 (March 1995): 54.

22. Friedman, *Naval Institute Guide to World Naval Weapon Systems*, 396.

23. Ibid., 71.

24. Keiichi Nogi, "Weapon Systems of New Chinese Warships," *Tokyo Sekai no Kansen*, 1 February 2008, magazine.

25. "Fregate Type 54 Classe Ma'Anshan," 27 October 2005, forum discussion, Air-Defense.net, http://www.air-defense.net/forum/index.php/topic,3096.msg44901.html (accessed 25 January 2006).

26. "Monthly Features Photos of New Chinese Naval Vessels," *Tokyo Sekai no Kansen*, 1 September 2007.

Chapter 4. Chinese Frigates

1. A. S. Pavlov, *Warships of the USSR and Russia, 1945–1995* (Annapolis, Md.: Naval Institute Press, 1997), 138.

2. Jim Bussert, "China Frigates Evolve into Capable Competitors," *Signal* 49, no. 4 (December 1994): 23.

3. A. D. Baker III, *Combat Fleets of the World* (Annapolis, Md.: Naval Institute Press, 1997), 85.

4. GlobalSecurity.org, "Type 053 *Jianghu*-class Frigates," http://globalsecurity.org/military/world/china/jianghu.htm (accessed 17 November 2010).

5. "Chinese Navy Shows Its Defects," *Jane's Defence Weekly* 10, no. 7 (20 August 1988): 295.

6. Bussert, "China Frigates Evolve," 25.

7. "China Exercises RF-61 Surface-to-Air Missile," *Jane's Defence Weekly* 24, no. 19 (11 November 1995): 3.

8. A. D. Baker III, "Combat Fleets," *Proceedings* (Annapolis, Md.: U.S. Naval Institute) 124/2/1, 140 (February 1998): 93.

9. "Western Equipment for Frigate," *Jane's Defence Weekly* 19, no. 9 (27 February 1993): 9.

10. "SR64 Radar, Anti-Missile Capability of PRC's Next Generation Surface Battleship," *Kanwa Defense Review* 2006, no. 8 (August 2006): 62.

11. "Fregate Type 54 Classe Ma'Anshan," 27 October 2005, forum discussion, Air-Defense.net, http://www.air-defense.net/forum/index.php/topic,3096.msg44901.html (accessed 25 January 2006).

12. "Why the Building of Type 054 FFG Was Delayed," *Kanwa Defense Review* 2006, no. 4 (April 2006): 16.

13. "NATO-China Relations in Transformation," *Kanwa Asian Defence* 2007, no. 36 (July 2007): 17.

14. Office of the Secretary of Defense, *Annual Report to Congress: Military Power of the People's Republic of China 2009*, U.S. Department of Defense, 25 March 2009, http://www.defense.gov/pubs/pdfs/China_Military_Power_Report_2009.pdf (accessed 12 November 2010), 36.

15. Robert Karniol, "The RTN's Two-Ocean Ambition," *Jane's Defence Weekly* 22, no. 22 (3 December 1994): 17–22.

16. Prasun Sengupta, "Thailand Apace: Force Modernisation Continues in Thailand," *Military Technology* 19, no. 9 (1995): 26.

17. Robert Karniol, "Myanmar Boosts Naval Power with Frigates," *Jane's Defence Weekly* 22, no. 7 (20 August 1994): 1.

18. A. D. Baker III, "Combat Fleets," *Proceedings* (Annapolis, Md.: U.S. Naval Institute) 121/6/1, 108 (June 1995): 83.

Chapter 5. PLAN Submarines

1. Jim Bussert, "Chinese Submarines Quietly Amass Strength in Pacific," *Signal* 49, no. 10 (June 1995): 75.

2. Jurg Meister, *Soviet Warships of the Second World War* (New York: Arco, 1977), 204.

3. Ibid., 192.

4. A. S. Pavlov, *Warships of the USSR and Russia, 1945–1995* (Annapolis, Md.: Naval Institute Press, 1997), 76.

5. Ibid., 36.

6. Norman Polmar, *Cold War Submarines* (Dulles, Va.: Potomac Books, 2004), 109.

7. Kenneth Sewell, *Red Star Rogue* (New York: Simon & Schuster, 2005), 31.

8. Jim Bussert, "Chinese Submarines Pose a Double-Edged Challenge," *Signal* 58, no. 4 (December 2003): 61.

9. Robert Sae-Liu, "China 'Stretches' Latest Ming Submarine," *Jane's Defence Weekly* 35, no. 1 (3 January 2001): 15.

10. Robert Sae-Liu, "China Looks to Invest More in Undersea Rescue," *Jane's Defence Weekly* 36, no. 12 (19 September 2001): 20–21.

11. SinoDefence.com, "Type 039G/G1 (Song Class) Diesel-Electric Submarine," http://www.sinodefence.com/navy/sub/type039song.039.asp (accessed 25 November 2010).

12. GlobalSecurity.org, "Type 039 Song S20 Class," http://www.globalsecurity.org/military/world/china/song.htm (accessed 16 November 2010).

13. SinoDefence.com, "Chinese Submarine Threat," http://www.sinodefenceforum.com/navy/Chinese-submarines-thread-42-929.html (accessed 16 November 2010).

14. "Chinese Submarine to Test Missile Derivative," *Jane's Defence Weekly* 27, no. 15 (16 April 1997): 15.

15. SinoDefence.com, "Type 039A/B (Yuan Class) Diesel-Electric Submarine," http://www.sinodefence.com/navy/sub/yuan.asp (accessed 25 November 2010).

16. *Vooruzhenie i Voenno-Morskaya Tekhnika Rossii* [Russia's Naval Ships, Armament and Equipment] (Moscow: Voennyy Parad, 2005), 176.

17. Charles R. Smith, "Russian 'Rocket' Torpedo Arms Chinese Subs," Newsmax.com, 24 April 2001, http://www.newsmax.com/archives/articles/2001/4/23/220813.shtml.

18. SinoDefence.com, "Type 091 (Han Class) Nuclear-Powered Attack Submarine," http://www.sinodefence.com/navy/sub/type091han.asp (accessed 15 November 2010).

19. Federation of American Scientists, "Type 09-1," http://www.fas.org/nuke/guide/china/slbm/type_91.htm (accessed 12 November 2010).

20. Bussert, "Chinese Submarines Quietly Amass Strength in Pacific," 76.

21. "Chinese Xia SSBN in Underwater Launches," *Jane's Defence Weekly* 10, no. 24 (17 December 1988): 1538.

22. Damon Te-men Chen, "Assessment of the PLA Navy Modernization Based upon Its Development of Naval Strategy," *Taiwan Defense Affairs* (1 December 2001).

23. Bussert, "Chinese Submarines Pose a Double-Edged Challenge," 64.

24. Bill Gertz, "China Advances Missile Program," *Washington Times*, 22 June 2005.

25. Robert Karniol, "China to Buy Russian 'KILO' Submarines," *Jane's Defence Weekly* 22, no. 20 (19 November 1994): 1.

26. *Vooruzhenie i Voenno-Morskaya*, 30.

27. *Vooruzhenie Voenno-Morskogo Flota* [Naval Weapons], vol. 3 of *Oruzhie i Tekhnologii Rossii Entsiklopediya XXI Bek* [Russia's Arms and Technologies: Twenty-first Century Encyclopedia] (Moscow: Oruzhie i Tekhnologii, 2001), 471.

28. "China Should Receive Its Third 'KILO' by November," *Jane's Defense Weekly* 28, no. 4 (30 July 1997): 16.

29. "KILO Encounters Questions in China," *Kanwa Asian Defence* 2009, no. 62 (December 2009): 18.

30. Yuri Baskov and Andrei Chang, "Latest Round of Russia-China Military Technology Cooperation Conference Ends on a Sour Note," *Kanwa Asian Defence* 2010, no. 66 (April 2010): 22–24.

31. Rear Admiral Eric A. McVadon, USN (Ret.), testimony before the U.S.-China Economic and Security Review Commission, 15 September 2005, http://www.uscc.gov/hearings/2005hearings/written_testimonies/05_09_15wrts/mcvadon_eric_wwrt.htm (accessed 12 November 2010).

32. K. V. Chuprin, *Voennaya moshch' Podnebesnoy: Vooruzhennye sily KNR* (Minsk: Harvest, 2007), 413.

33. "China's First Submarine Rescue Vehicle Unveiled," *Jane's Defence Weekly* 11, no. 6 (11 February 1989): 204.

34. William M. Arkin and Richard W. Fieldhouse, *Nuclear Battlefields* (Cambridge, Mass.: Ballinger, 1985), 290–91.

35. SinoDefence.com, "Yulin (Sanya) Naval Base," http://www.sindofence.com/navy/facilities/yulin.asp (accessed on 16 November 2010).

36. This term is not Chinese, but was coined in a Booz Allen Hamilton study entitled "Energy Futures in Asia," cited in "China Builds Up Strategic Sea Lanes," by Bill Gertz, *Washington Times*, 18 January 2005.

37. Major Lawrence Spinetta, USAF, "Cutting China's 'String of Pearls,'" *Proceedings* (Annapolis, Md.: U.S. Naval Institute) 132/10/1, 244 (October 2006): 40–42.

38. Norman Friedman, *The Naval Institute Guide to World Naval Weapons Systems, 1997–1998* (Annapolis, Md.: Naval Institute Press, 1997), 670.

39. Chuprin, *Voennaya moshch' Podnebesnoy*, 518–20.

40. "China Has Yet to Fire Torpedoes," *Jane's Defence Weekly* 32, no. 8 (25 August 1999): 15.

41. "Chinese Unable to Operate Torpedo," *Jane's Defence Weekly* 32, no. 7 (18 August 1999): 15.

42. A. B. Shirokorad, *Oruzhie Otechestvennogo Flota, 1945–2000* [Armament of the Motherland Navy, 1945–2000] (Minsk: Harvest, 2001), 323.

43. "Ukraine Provides Naval Weapon Technologies to China," *Kanwa Defense Review* (July 2005): 64.

44. "Russia, China Have Widening Differences on Battleship, Submarine Maintenance," *Kanwa Asian Defence* 2009, no. 59 (September 2009): 2.

45. Bill Gertz, "China Sub Stalked U.S. Fleet," *Washington Times*, 13 November 2006.

46. STRATFOR Global Intelligence, "China: People's Liberation Army Navy," special series, pt. 2, March 2009, www.stratfor.com, 2.

47. "Chinese Navy 1st Nuclear Submarine Zhidui Base Has Underground Submarine Facilities," U.S. Army Asian Studies Detachment, Camp Zama, Japan, 16 July 2007.

48. "Underground Facilities of Chinese Nuclear Submarine," *Kanwa Defense Review* 2006, no. 5 (May 2006).

49. George Percivall, "GEOSS: Architecture Increases Availability of Atmospheric Data and Models: Demonstration in Beijing," *Imaging Notes* (Winter 2006), www.imagingnotes.com/go/article_free.php?mp_id=73 (accessed 12 November 2010).

50. John Wilson Lewis and Xue Litai, *China's Strategic Seapower* (Stanford, Calif.: Stanford University Press, 1994), 47.

51. Carl Boyd and Akihiko Yoshida, *The Japanese Submarine Force and World War II* (Annapolis, Md.: Naval Institute Press, 1995), 46.

52. "Underground Facilities of Chinese Nuclear Submarine," *Kanwa Intelligence Review*, 30 March 2006, translation at OSC CPP20060419905011.

53. Joseph Coleman, "Photos of Japanese Kidnapping Victim Intensify Outrage," Associated Press, 17 November 2004.

54. "China 'Sorry' over Mystery Sub," BBC News, 16 November 2004, http://cdnedge.bbc.co.uk/1/hi/world/asia-pacific/4015211.stm (accessed 16 November 2010).

55. Edward Chung, "MND Says Spratly Airport Strategic," *Taipei Taiwan News*, 6 January 2006, translation at OSC CPP20060106968041.

Chapter 6. Coastal Defense and PLAN Amphibious Capability

1. You Ji, "A New Era for Chinese Naval Expansion," *China Brief* 6, no. 5 (2006), Nautilus Institute for Security and Sustainability, Australian Policy Forum 06-06A, 9 March 2006, http://www.globalcollab.org/publications/essays/apsnet/policy-forum/2006/0606a-you-ji.html (accessed 21 November 2010).

2. "PLA Navy Destroyers Spotted Near Chunxiao Gas Fields in East China Sea," *Tokyo Sekai no Kansen*, 5 April 2005, 6–7, cited in "Growing Asymmetries in the China-Japan Naval Balance," by Richard Fisher Jr., International Assessment and Strategy Center, 22 November 2005, http://www.strategycenter.net/research/pubID.83/pub_detail.asp.

3. "China Defends Drills in East China Sea," *People's Daily*, April 23, 2010, http://www
   .english.people.com.cn/90001/90786/6960403.html (accessed 22 April 2010).

4. Norman Polmar, *Spyplane: The U-2 History Declassified* (Osceola, Wis.: MBI
   Publishing, 2001), 199.

5. Larry Tart and Robert Keefe, *The Price of Vigilance* (New York: Ballantine, 2001),
   xxix.

6. Jim Bussert, "China Taps Many Resources for Coastal Defense," *Signal* 57, no. 3
   (November 2002): 30.

7. Barbara Starr, "Sub Collides with Sonar Array Towed by U.S. Navy Ship," 12
   June 2009, CNN, http://www.cnn.com/2009/US/06/12/china.submarine/index
   .html?iref+allsearch (accessed 13 November 2010).

8. Carlo Kopp, "China's Air Defence Missile Systems," *Defence Today* 8, no. 20 (25
   October 2008): 23.

9. "Long-Range SAMs Deployed in Qingdao," *Kanwa Asian Defence* 2010, no. 67
   (May 2010): 12.

10. Philip Young, "Navy of the PLA," *Chinese Military Digest*, www.gsprint.com/cmd/
    airforce/uav.atm.

11. Philip J. Klass, "Avionics in China: CAAC Modernizes Its Air Traffic Control,"
    Aviation Week & Space Technology 118, no. 24 (13 June 1983): 79–84.

12. John Mulberry, "Offshore Patrol Vessels and Fast Attack Craft in the Asia Pacific,"
    Asian Military Review 21 (December 2009).

13. Office of the Secretary of Defense, *Annual Report to Congress: Military Power
    of the People's Republic of China 2009*, U.S. Department of Defense, 25 March
    2009, http://www.defense.gov/pubs/pdfs/China_Military_Power_Report_2009.pdf
    (accessed 12 November 2010), 49.

14. GlobalSecurity.org, "Houbei Class (Type 022) Fast Attack Craft, Missile," http://
    www.globalsecurity.org/militayr/world/china/houbei/htm?iframe=true&width=100
    %&heihei=100% (accessed 17 November 2010).

15. Bussert, "China Taps Many Resources," 32.

16. Office of the Secretary of Defense, *Annual Report to Congress: Military Power of
    the People's Republic of China 2009*, 49.

17. Bussert, "China Taps Many Resources," 32.

18. Jim Bussert, "China Builds a Modern Marine Corps Force," *Signal* 60, no. 8 (April
    2006): 51.

19. Chris Rahman, "Ballistic Missiles in China's Anti-Taiwan Blockade Strategy," in
    Naval Blockades and Seapower: Strategies and Counter-strategies, 1805–2005, ed.
    Bruce A. Elleman and S. C. M. Paine (London: Routledge, 2006), 215–24.

20. Wang An, "Just Like a Battlefield—Student's Group Training Exercise through the
    Eyes of a Research Fellow," *Beijing Jiefangjun Bao,* 21 November 2005, translation
    at OSC CPP20051123502002.

21. Jane's Information Group, "122 mm NORINCO artillery rockets (China), Artillery
    rockets," http://www.janes.com/articles/Janes-Ammunition-Handbook/122-mm
    NORINCO-artillery-rockets-China.html (accessed 17 November 2010).

22. Vu Duc Vuong, "Between a Sea and a Hard Rock," *AsianWeek*, 8 January 2008.

Chapter 7. The PLAN Air Force (PLANAF) and China's Future Aircraft Carrier

1. Information Office of the State Council of the People's Republic of China, *China's National Defense in 2004*, special report, Beijing, 27 December 2004, Federation of American Scientists, http://www.fas.org/nuke/guide/china/doctrine/natdef2004 .html (accessed 14 November 2010).

2. *China Today: Aviation Industry* (Beijing: China Aviation Industry Press, 1989), 15.

3. Ibid., 43.

4. Ibid., 63.

5. Ibid., 256.

6. "Shenyang J-8," Jane's All the World's Aircraft Supplement, published in *Air Force Magazine* 68, no. 4 (April 1985): 130–31.

7. *China Today: Aviation Industry*, 281.

8. Ibid., 264.

9. Ibid., 281.

10. Richard Halloran, "Guam a Focal Point for U.S. Military Plans," *Honolulu Advertiser*, 14 May 2006.

11. Jim Bussert, "PRC Avionics Catching Up to Aircraft Technology," *Defense Electronics* (Palo Alto, Calif.: EW Communications) 18, no. 5 (May 1986): 133.

12. Jim Bussert, "PLAAF Avionics Technology and Upgrades," *Defense Electronics* (Palo Alto, Calif.: EW Communications) 22, no. 6 (June 1990): 70.

13. Joseph S. Bermudez Jr., "China's Export Mission for Multi-Role Fighter," *Jane's Defence Weekly* 27, no. 16 (23 April 1997): 29.

14. Bill Gertz, "Beijing Readies China Sea Exercises," *Washington Times*, 17 May 2001.

15. Feilong, "Strength of PLA Naval Air Force," *Jianchuan Zhishi* [Naval & Merchant Ships], August 2006, translation at OSC CPP20060802476001.

16. Vitaliy Denisov, "Russian Minister of Defense Visits China, Military-Technical Cooperation Talks," *Krasnaya Zvezda*, 17 December 2008.

17. Piotr Butowski and Bernard Bombeau, "Modernized Sukhoi Su-33K for Beijing," *Air & Cosmos,* 8 December 2006, translation at OSC EUP20061211338001.

18. "Sukhoi Highly Satisfied with 5th Generation Fighter," *Kanwa Asian Defence* 66 (April 2010): 3.

19. "Flight Tests of J15 Shipborne Fighter Start," *Kanwa Asian Defence* 2010, no. 711 (September 2010): 2.

20. "Comparison of AWACS at Taiwan Strait," *Kanwa Defense Review* 2006, no. 6 (June 2006): 2.

21. Ling Chao, "Il-78s Fly to China—Also on Comparison Between US and Russian Large Active Duty Aerial Refueling Aircraft," *Xian Binggong Keji,* 1 October 2005, translation at OSC CPP20051123318001.

22. Andrei Chang, "'Wuhan Aircraft Carrier' Shocks Russian & Western Shipyard's Experts in Langkawi," *Kanwa Asian Defence* 2010, no. 66 (April 2010): 19.

23. Johnathan Weng, "A Simulation Aircraft Carrier Platform Being Built in Central China," China Military Power Mashup, 11 October 2009, http://www.China defense-mashup.com/?tag=veryag (accessed 12 November 2010).

24. Chang, "'Wuhan Aircraft Carrier,'" 19.

25. "Soviet Aircraft Carriers Find a New Home in China," *Jane's Intelligence Review* 14, no. 24 (April 2002): 38.

26. The island of Taiwan was taken by Qing naval forces in 1683. Strategy Page, "China Renames the Varyag," 9 January 2008, http://www.strategypage.com/htmw/htnavai/articles/20080109.aspx (accessed 13 November 2010).

27. The Federation of American Scientists has posted what appears to be a full description of this Chinese carrier at http://www.fas.org/nuke/guide/china/aircraft/proj ect9935.pdf (accessed 13 November 2010).

28. Most recently, it was reported that the Shanghai Jiangnan Shipyard is building China's first 78,000-ton-class steam turbine aircraft carrier, with a budget of 3 billion yuan. "Does China Need an Aircraft Carrier?" *Beijing Xinjing Bao*, 19 December 2006.

29. Information Office of the State Council of the People's Republic of China, *China's National Defense in 2006*, special report, Beijing, 29 December 2006, Federation of American Scientists, http://fas.org/nuke/guide/china/doctrine/wp2006.html (accessed 13 November 2010).

30. Kenji Minemura, "China to Start Construction of 1st Aircraft Carriers Next Year," Asahi Shimbun News Service, 31 December 2008.

31. Quoted in "PLA Navy to Guard China's Global Interests," by Andrei Chang, UPI Asia.com, 20 February 2009, www.upiasia.com/Security/2009/02/20/pla_navy_to_guard_chinas_interests/1570/ (accessed 27 November 2010).

32. Ben Blanchard, "China Fears Containment as Defense Spending Rises," Reuters, 20 January 2009, http://www.reuters.com/article/idUSTRE50J0DH2009 0120 (accessed 25 November 2010).

Chapter 8. Antiair-Warfare (AAW) Radar and Weapon Systems

1. Andrei Chang, "China to Receive Latest SAMS from Russia," *Kanwa Asian Defence Review* 2008 (2 May 2008).

2. Martin Streetly, *Jane's Radar and Electronic Warfare Systems, 1996–97*, 8th ed. (Coulsdon, Surrey, U.K.: Jane's Information Group, 1996), 13.

3. Ibid., 8.

4. Ibid., 10.

5. Ibid., 11.

6. John Wise, info@radars.org.uk, 17 March 2010.

7. Christopher F. Foss, "China Launches New SAM System," *Jane's Defence Weekly* 23, no. 26 (1 July 1995): 23.

8. "KS-1 SAM System Revealed," *Jane's Defence Weekly* 24, no. 22 (2 December 1995): 5.

9. *Vooruzhenie i Voenno-Morskaya Tekhnika Rossii* [Russia's Naval Ships, Armament and Equipment] (Moscow: Voennyy Parad, 2005), 113.

10. A. M. Petrov et al., *Oruzhie Rossiiskogo Flota* [Armament of the Russian Navy] (Saint Petersburg: Sudostroenie, 1996), 113.

11. K. V. Chuprin, *Voennaya moshch' Podnebesnoy: Vooruzhennye sily KNR* (Minsk: Harvest, 2007), 504.

12. Tomohiko Tada, "Chinese Naval Weapons Systems," *Tokyo Sekai no Kansen*, 1 September 2005, translation at OSC JPP20051109326004.

13. Nikolay Poroskov, "The 'Modern' Is Even More Modern," *Vremya Novostey* (Moscow), 3 October 2006, translation at OSC CEP20061005330001.

Chapter 9. Antisubmarine-Warfare (ASW) Sonar and Weapon Systems

1. Jim Bussert, "The Destruction of U.S. Anti-Submarine Warfare," *Defense Electronics* (Palo Alto, Calif.: EW Communications) 25, no. 5 (April 1993): 53–55.

2. Jim Bussert, "China Pursues Antisubmarine Warfare," *Signal* 59, no. 3 (November 2004): 59.

3. K. V. Chuprin, *Voennaya moshch' Podnebesnoy: Vooruzhennye sily KNR* (Minsk: Harvest, 2007), 433–42.

4. Ibid., 442.

5. Jim Bussert, "Chinese Naval Sonar Evolves from Foreign Influences," *Signal* 57, no. 4 (December 2002): 60.

6. Norman Friedman, *The Naval Institute Guide to World Naval Weapons Systems, 1997–1998* (Annapolis, Md.: Naval Institute Press, 1997), 584.

7. *Vooruzhenie Voenno-Morskogo Flota* [Naval Weapons], vol. 3 of *Oruzhie i Tekhnologii Rossii Entsiklopediya XXI Bek* [Russia's Arms and Technologies: Twenty-first Century Encyclopedia] (Moscow: Oruzhie i Tekhnologii, 2001), 303.

8. *Korabli i Vooruzhenie Voenno-Morskogo Flota* [Warships and Weapons of the Military Naval Fleet], vol. 3 of *Oruzhie Rossii Katalog* [Russian Arms Catalog] (Moscow: Voennyy Parad, 1996), 415.

9. A. M. Petrov et al., *Oruzhie Rossiiskogo Flota* [Armament of the Russian Navy] (Saint Petersburg: Sudostroenie, 1996), 239.

10. Bussert, "China Pursues Antisubmarine Warfare," 60.

11. *Vooruzhenie Voenno-Morskogo Flota*, 308.

12. Friedman, *Naval Institute Guide to World Naval Weapons Systems*, 670.

13. Ibid., 604.

14. Ibid., 606.

15. "China's PLA Navy Seeks Helicopter ASW System," *Jane's Defence Weekly* 9, no. 5 (6 February 1988): 202.

16. Greg Torode, "Troubled Waters," *South China Morning Post*, 11 October 2010.

Chapter 10. The South China Sea (SCS) and the Mine Threat

1. Le-wei Li, "High-Frequency Over-the-Horizon Radar and Ionospheric Backscatter Studies in China," *Radio Science* 33, no. 5 (1998): 1445–58.

2. Jim Bussert, "South China Sea Electronics," *Signal* 58, no. 2 (October 2003): 60.

3. Lockheed Martin, "Vessel Traffic Management Information Systems (VTMIS)," http://www.lockheedmartin.com/products/VesselTrafficMIS/index.html (accessed 16 November 2010).

4. "Underground Facilities of Chinese Nuclear Submarine," *Kanwa Defense Review* 2006, no. 5 (May 2006): 56.

5. Bradley Hahn, "Maritime Dangers in the South China Sea," *Pacific Defence Reporter* 11, no. 11 (May 1985): 15.

6. Ray Bonds, ed., *Chinese War Machine: A Technical Analysis of the Strategy and Weapons of the People's Repubic of China*, in consultation with James E. Dornan and Nigel de Lee (New York: Crescent, 1979), 158.

7. World Aero Data, "Woody Island," http://worldaerodata.com/wad.cgi?runway=PF9777523 (accessed 13 November 2010).

8. Bill Gertz, "Woody Island Missiles," *Washington Times*, 15 June 2001.

9. Federation of American Scientists, "Rocky Island (Shi-tao), Paracel Islands," FAS Intelligence Research Program, http://www.fas.org/irp/world/china/facilities/shi-tao.htm (accessed 14 November 2010).

10. Wolfgang Schippke, DC3MF, "Itu Aba Island," 425 DX News, www.425dxn.org/dc3mf/ituaba/html (accessed 14 November 2010).

11. Bussert, "South China Sea Electronics," 62.

12. Keith Jacobs, "China's Military Modernization and the South China Sea," *Jane's Intelligence Review* 4, no. 6 (June 1992): 278–81.

13. Frédéric Lasserre, "Once Forgotten Reefs . . . Historical Images in the Scramble for the South China Sea," Cybergeo, http://www.cybergeo.revues.org/index5782.html#texte (accessed 14 November 2010).

14. Ian Storey, "Manila Looks to USA for Help over Spratlys," *Jane's Intelligence Review* 11, no. 8 (August 1999): 46–50.

15. Bussert, "South China Sea Electronics," 62.

16. Zhang Xin, "China Charts Course toward Secure South China Sea," *China Daily*, 1 July 2009, http://www.chinadaily.com.cn/china/guangxisessions/2009-07/01/content_9394099.htm.

17. Jim Bussert, "Chinese Mines Pose Taiwan Blockade Threat," *Signal* 59, no. 10 (June 2005): 69.

18. A. S. Pavlov, *Warships of the USSR and Russia, 1945–1995* (Annapolis, Md.: Naval Institute Press, 1997), 192.

19. Ibid., 193.

20. Clifford Funnell, ed., *Jane's Underwater Warfare Systems, 2008–2009* (Coulsdon, Surrey, U.K.: Jane's Information Group, 2008), 363.

21. Military Training Department of the Navy, "Chronicle of Events of Military Training," *Guangzhou Zhanshi Bao*, 27 December 2005, 1, 3, translation at OSC CPP20060224318002.

22. K.V. Chuprin, *Voennaya moshch' Podnebesnoy: Vooruzhennye sily KNR* (Minsk: Harvest, 2007), 530.

23. Jim Bussert, "Foreign Navies Combat System Disintegration," *Signal* 57, no. 7 (March 2003): 50.

24. Bussert, "Chinese Mines Pose Taiwan Blockade Threat," 71.

25. A. B. Mahapatra, "Commanding the Ocean," *NewsInsight*, 16 May 2001, http://www.newsinsight.net/archivespecialreports/nat2.asp?recno=21&ctg=World.

Chapter 11. Combat System Integration, Electrical, and Training Issues

1. The 4 March 2002 battle of Takur Ghar (better known as Roberts Ridge) in Afghanistan is an example of how "technological over-reliance" led to operational setbacks. Malcolm MacPherson, *Roberts Ridge: A Story of Courage and Sacrifice on Takur Ghar Mountain, Afghanistan* (New York: Delacorte, 2005), 293.

2. Jim Bussert, "Foreign Navies Combat System Disintegration," *Signal* 57, no. 7 (March 2003): 50.

3. Ibid.

4. K. V. Chuprin, *Voennaya moshch' Podnebesnoy: Vooruzhennye sily KNR* (Minsk: Harvest, 2007), 501.

5. "China Strengthens Military Cooperation with Kazakhstan," Kanwa Information Center, 20 May 2001, http://www.kanwa.com/free/2002/03/e0319a.htm.

6. International Association of Marine Aids to Navigation and Lighthouse Authorities (IALA), "China Vessel Traffic System (VTS)," http://www.iala2006.info/inchina_album_2.asp (accessed 1 February 2003); China Education and Research Network (CERNET), "China to Open Marine High-Accuracy Positioning System," http://www.edu.cn/20011228/3015694.shtml (accessed [1 February] 2003).

7. SinoDefence.com, "Beidou 1 Experimental Satellite Navigation System," http://www.sinodefence.com/space/spacecraft/beidou1.asp (accessed 25 November 2010).

8. Zhao Huanxin, "China to Put 10 Satellites into Orbit in 2004," *China Daily*, 6 January 2004, http://www.chinadaily.com.cn/en/doc/2004-01/06/content_295900.htm (accessed 14 November 2010).

9. Indrani Bagchi, "China's Anti-satellite Test Worries India," *Times of India*, 5 February 2007.

10. Jim Bussert, "Chinese Warships Struggle to Meet New Command, Control and Communications Needs," *Signal* 63, no. 6 (February 2009).

11. *Korabli i Vooruzhenie Voenno-Morskogo Flota* [Warships and Weapons of the Military Naval Fleet], vol. 3 of *Oruzhie Rossii Katalog* [Russian Arms Catalog] (Moscow: Voennyy Parad, 1996), 510.

12. *Vooruzhenie Voenno-Morskogo Flota* [Naval Weapons], vol. 3 of *Oruzhie i Tekhnologii Rossii Entsiklopediya XXI Bek* [Russia's Arms and Technologies: Twenty-first Century Encyclopedia] (Moscow: Oruzhie i Tekhnologii, 2001), 586, 587.

13. MAN Diesel & Turbo, "V28/33D Four-Stroke Diesel Engine," http:mandiesel turbo.com/files/news/filesof11498/V28_33D.pdf (accessed 16 November 2010).

14. Chuprin, *Voennaya moshch' Podnebesnoy*, 422.

15. A. S. Pavlov, *Warships of the USSR and Russia, 1945–1995* (Annapolis, Md.: Naval Institute Press, 1997), 138.

16. Ibid., 125.

17. I. P. Shirokie, *Remont Sudovie Radio-navigatsionnogo Priborov* [Repair Ship Radionavigation Equipment] (Moscow: Transport, 1985), 51.

18. Srikanth Kondapalli, *China's Naval Power* (New Delhi: Knowledge World, 2001), 137–38.

19. Ding Jidong, "Excellent Staff Officer Appraisal System Implemented," *Beijing Jiefangjun Bao,* 7 December 2005, translation at OSC CPP20051213502022.

20. Kondapalli, *China's Naval Power*, 213.

21. Information Office of the State Council of the People's Republic of China, *China's National Defense in 2004*, special report, Beijing, 27 December 2004, Federation of American Scientists, http://fas.org/nuke/guide/china/doctrine/nat def2004.html (accessed 14 November 2010).

22. Gao Yi and Peng Jiu, "Why Does the 'Popular Commodity' Become the 'Hot Potato'? Investigation into the Job Adjustment of Middle- and Senior-Ranking Noncommissioned Officers of a South Sea Fleet Submarine Flotilla," *Beijing Renmin Haijun,* 26 October 2009, 2, translation at OSC CPP20091208478018.

23. "Pacific Exercises," *Jane's Defence Weekly* 15, no. 24 (15 June 1991): 1025.

24. Gurpreet S. Khurana, "China's 'String of Pearls' in the Indian Ocean and Its Security Implications," *Strategic Analysis* 32, no. 1 (January 2008), translation at OSC SAP20080730524001.

25. Jim Bussert, "China's Fleet Joins the World's Navies off Somalia," *Signal* 65, no. 2 (October 2010): 33–35.

26. Andrei Chang, "China's Aircraft Carrier and Greater Peripheral Security," *Kanwa Asian Defence* 63 (January 2010): 21.

Chapter 12.   The PLAN Fleet in the Twenty-first Century

1. Bernard D. Cole, *The Great Wall at Sea* (Annapolis, Md.: Naval Institute Press, 2001), 93.

2. Bruce A. Elleman, "Western Advisors and Chinese Sailors in the 1894–95 Sino-Japanese War," in *The Face of Naval Battle*, ed. John Reeve and David Stevens (Crows Nest, Aus.: Allen & Unwin, 2003), 55–69.

3. Roger W. Barnett, "Strategic Culture and Its Relationship to Naval Strategy," *Naval War College Review* 60, no. 1 (Winter 2007): 28, citing www.tinyurl.com/ydoxcm.

4. Christopher Bell and Bruce Elleman, eds., *Naval Mutinies of the Twentieth Century: An International Perspective* (London: Frank Cass, 2003), 232–45.

5. Srikanth Kondapalli, *China's Naval Power* (New Delhi: Knowledge World, 2001), xxiv.

6. Wen Han, "Navy and Air Force Generals Take Up Important Posts in Reshuffles in Four Military Regions," *Hong Kong Wen Wei Po,* 19 December 2005, translation at OSC CPP20051219510001.

7. "The Chinese Hope to Have an Aircraft Carrier Built within Four Years," *Hong Kong Wen Wei Po,* 7 March 2007, translation at OSC CPP20070307710005.

8. Bruce A. Elleman, "Maritime Territorial Disputes and Their Impact on Maritime Strategy: A Historical Perspective," in *Security and International Politics in the*

South China Sea: Towards a Cooperative Management Regime, ed. Sam Bateman and Ralf Emmers (London: Routledge, 2009), 42–58.

9. Robyn Lim, *The Geopolitics of East Asia: The Search for Equilibrium* (New York: Routledge, 2003), 140–63.

10. Information Office of the State Council of the People's Republic of China, *China's National Defense in 2004*, special report, Beijing, 27 December 2004, Federation of American Scientists, http://www.fas.org/nuke/guide/china/doctrine/natdef2004.html (accessed 14 November 2010).

11. Information Office of the State Council of the People's Republic of China, *China's National Defense in 2008*, special report, Beijing, January 2009, Federation of American Scientists, http://www.fas.org/programs/ssp/nukes/2008DefenseWhitePaper_Jan2009.pdf (accessed 10 November 2010), 10.

12. Chris O'Brien, "Beijing Hospital Ship Harbors Soft Power," *Washington Times*, 26 January 2009.

13. Interestingly, the December 2004–February 2005 humanitarian relief program Operation Unified Assistance in northern Sumatra showed China that, without any prior warning, U.S. naval forces could travel to the western entrance to the Malacca Strait in less than a week and begin humanitarian operations there. Bruce A. Elleman, *Waves of Hope: The U.S. Navy's Response to the Tsunami in Northern Indonesia*, U.S. Naval War College, *Newport Paper No. 28*, 2007.

14. "U.S. Worries about China's Intent with Taiwan," *USA Today*, 9 February 2006.

15. Chen Xiangyang, "Expert Calls for Greater Periphery Strategy to Cope with Security Threats," *Liaowang* (Beijing) 29 (17 July 2006): 64.

16. Office of the Secretary of Defense, *Annual Report to Congress: Military Power of the People's Republic of China 2009*, U.S. Department of Defense, 25 March 2009, http://www.defense.gov/pubs/pdfs/China_Military_Power_Report_2009.pdf (accessed 12 November 2010), 18.

17. Mikhail Krasnov, "Chavez Winked at America," *Moscow Gazeta*, 11 January 2006, translation at OSC CEP20060112018002.

18. Quoted in Chun-ming Cha, "Chinese Navy Heads Toward Modernization," *Ta Kung Pao* (Hong Kong), 11 April 1999, B6, in Foreign Broadcast Information Service-China 1999-0418, cited in Cole, *Great Wall at Sea*, 10, 11.

19. Xin Dingding, "Hijackings of Ships to Increase," *China Daily*, 20 March 2010.

20. Bao Daozu, "Build Aircraft Carriers Soon," *China Daily*, 6 March 2009.

Selected Bibliography

Arkin, William M., and Richard W. Fieldhouse. *Nuclear Battlefields*. Cambridge, Mass.: Ballinger, 1985.

Averyanov, V., et al. *Sudovye Radiolokatsionnye Stantsii i ix Primenenie (Spravochnoe Rukovodstvo)* [Ship Radiolocation Station and Application (Reference Guidance)]. Vol. 3. Leningrad: Sudostroenie, 1970.

Baker, A. D., III. *Combat Fleets of the World*. Annapolis, Md.: Naval Institute Press, 1997.

Balakin, S. *Legendarnye "Semerki"* [Legendary "Seven"]. Moscow: EKSMO, 2007.

Bell, Christopher, and Bruce Elleman, eds. *Naval Mutinies of the Twentieth Century: An International Perspective*. London: Frank Cass, 2003.

Blanchard, Ben. "China Fears Containment as Defense Spending Rises." Reuters, 20 January 2009, http://www.reuters.com/article/idUSTRE50J0DH2009 0120 (accessed 23 November 2010).

Blechman, Barry M., and Robert P. Berman. *Guide to Far Eastern Navies*. Annapolis, Md.: Naval Institute Press, 1978.

Bonds, Ray, ed. *Chinese War Machine: A Technical Analysis of the Strategy and Weapons of the People's Republic of China*. In consultation with James E. Dornan and Nigel de Lee. New York: Crescent, 1979.

Boyd, Carl, and Akihiko Yoshida. *The Japanese Submarine Force and World War II*. Annapolis, Md.: Naval Institute Press, 1995.

Bussert, Jim. "Catamarans Glide through Chinese Waters." *Signal* 62, no. 4 (December 2007): 37–40.

———. "China Adds Air Defense to Destroyer's Resume." *Signal* 62, no. 2 (October 2007): 33–36.

———. "China Builds Destroyers around Imported Technology." *Signal* 58, no. 12 (August 2004): 67–69.

———. "China Builds a Modern Marine Corps Force." *Signal* 60, no. 8 (April 2006): 49–52.

———. "China Debuts Aegis Destroyers." *Signal* 59, no. 11 (July 2005): 59–62.

————. "China Deploys New Littoral Ships." *Signal* 61, no. 9 (May 2007): 67–70.

————. "China Frigates Evolve into Capable Competitors," *Signal* 49, no. 4 (December 1994): 23–25.

————. "China Pursues Antisubmarine Warfare." *Signal* 59, no. 3 (November 2004): 59–62.

————. "China's Fleet Joins the World's Navies off Somalia." *Signal* 65, no. 2 (October 2010): 33–35.

————. "China's Naval Capabilities Are Increasing, but Slowly." *Defense Electronics* (Palo Alto, Calif.: EW Communications) 17, no. 3 (March 1985): 129–36.

————. "China Taps Many Resources for Coastal Defense." *Signal* 57, no. 3 (November 2002): 29–32.

————. "Chinese Destroyers Incorporate Western Technology, Designs." *Signal* 49, no. 7 (March 1995): 53–55.

————. "Chinese Mines Pose Taiwan Blockade Threat." *Signal* 59, no. 10 (June 2005): 69–71.

————. "Chinese Modernization Aids Air Defense Radar, Missiles." *Signal* 48, no. 11 (July 1994): 63–64.

————. "Chinese Naval Sonar Evolves from Foreign Influences." *Signal* 57, no. 4 (December 2002): 57–60.

————. "Chinese Submarines Pose a Double-Edged Challenge," *Signal* 58, no. 4 (December 2003): 61–64.

————. "Chinese Submarines Quietly Amass Strength in Pacific." *Signal* 49, no. 10 (June 1995): 75–77.

————. "Chinese Warships Struggle to Meet New Command, Control and Communications Needs." *Signal* 63, no. 6 (February 2009): 43–45.

————. "The Destruction of U.S. Anti-Submarine Warfare." *Defense Electronics* (Palo Alto, Calif.: EW Communications) 25, no. 5 (April 1993): 51–56.

————. "Foreign Navies Combat System Disintegration." *Signal* 57, no. 7 (March 2003): 49–51.

————. "Modernization of China's Military Electronics Promises to Be Slow." *Defense Electronics* (Palo Alto, Calif.: EW Communications) 13, no. 10 (October 1981): 73–82.

————. "New Missile Destroyers Deploy for Blue-Water Operations." *Signal* 54, no. 3 (November 1999): 29–31.

————. "PLAAF Avionics Technology and Upgrades." *Defense Electronics* (Palo Alto, Calif.: EW Communications) 22, no. 6 (June 1990).

————. "PRC Avionics." *Defense Electronics* (Palo Alto, Calif.: EW Communications) 18, no. 5 (May 1986): 124–35.

————. "PRC Avionics Catching Up to Aircraft Technology." *Defense Electronics* (Palo Alto, Calif.: EW Communications) 18, no. 5 (May 1986).

————. "PRC Avionics Industry." *Signal* 53, no. 6 (February 1999): 77–79.

————. "PRC Military Electronic Systems Evaluated." *Defense Electronics* (Pal Alto, Calif.: EW Communications) 12, no. 6 (June 1980): 69–77.

————. "South China Sea Electronics." *Signal* 58, no. 2 (October 2003): 59–62.

China Today: Aviation Industry. Beijing: China Aviation Industry Press, 1989.

The Chinese Armed Forces Today. Reproduced from Defense Intelligence Agency, *Handbook on the Chinese Armed Forces* (DDI-2680-32-76, Washington, D.C.). Englewood Cliffs, N.J.: Prentice-Hall, 1979.

Chumbley, Stephen, ed. *Conway's All the World's Fighting Ships, 1947–1995.* London: Conway Maritime Press, 1995.

Chung, Edward. "MND Says Spratly Airport Strategic." *Taipei Taiwan News*, 6 January 2006, "Politics" page. Translation at Open Source Center (shortened hereafter to OSC) CPP20060106968041.

Chuprin, K. V. *Voennaya moshch' Podnebesnoy: Vooruzhennye sily KNR.* Minsk: Harvest, 2007.

Cole, Bernard D. *The Great Wall at Sea.* Annapolis, Md.: Naval Institute Press, 2001.

Coleman, Joseph. "Photos of Japanese Kidnapping Victim Intensify Outrage." Associated Press, 17 November 2004.

Ding, Jidong. "Excellent Staff Officer Appraisal System Implemented." *Beijing Jiefangjun Bao,* 7 December 2005. Translation at OSC CPP20051213502022.

Elleman, Bruce A. "Maritime Territorial Disputes and Their Impact on Maritime Strategy: A Historical Perspective." In *Security and International Politics in the South China Sea: Towards a Cooperative Management Regime,* edited by Sam Bateman and Ralf Emmers. London: Routledge, 2009.

————. *Waves of Hope: The U.S. Navy's Response to the Tsunami in Northern Indonesia.* U.S. Naval War College, *Newport Paper No. 28,* 2007.

————. "Western Advisors and Chinese Sailors in the 1894–95 Sino-Japanese War." In *The Face of Naval Battle,* edited by John Reeve and David Stevens. Crows Nest, Aus.: Allen and Unwin, 2003.

Elleman, Bruce A., and S. C. M. Paine, eds. *Naval Blockades and Seapower: Strategies and Counter-strategies, 1805–2005.* London: Routledge, 2006.

Friedman, Norman. *The Naval Institute Guide to World Naval Weapons Systems, 1997–1998.* Annapolis, Md.: Naval Institute Press, 1997.

Funnell, Clifford, ed. *Jane's Underwater Warfare Systems, 2008–2009.* Coulsdon, Surrey, U.K.: Jane's Information Group, 2008.

Furlong, Bob. "ASIANDEX Part 1—China Launches Defense Export Drive." *International Defense Review* 14, no. 1 (January 1987): 23–27.

Gao Yi and Peng Jiu. "Why Does the 'Popular Commodity' Become the 'Hot Potato'? Investigation into the Job Adjustment of Middle- and Senior-

Ranking Noncommissioned Officers of a South Sea Fleet Submarine Flotilla." *Beijing Renmin Haijun*, 26 October 2009, 2. Translation at OSC CPP20091208478018.

Gertz, Bill. "Beijing Readies China Sea Exercises." *Washington Times*, 17 May 2001.

———. "China Advances Missile Program." *Washington Times*, 22 June 2005.

———. "China Builds Up Strategic Sea Lanes." *Washington Times*, 18 January 2005.

———. "China Sub Stalked U.S. Fleet." *Washington Times*, 13 November 2006.

———. "Four Arrests Linked to Chinese Spy Ring." *Washington Times*, 5 November 2005.

———. "Woody Island Missiles." *Washington Times*, 15 June 2001.

Goldstein, Lyle, and William Murray. "Undersea Dragons: China's Maturing Submarine Force." *International Security* 28, no. 4 (Spring 2004): 161–96.

Hahn, Bradley. "The Chinese Marine Corps." *Proceedings* (Annapolis, Md.: U.S. Naval Institute) 110/3/973 (March 1984): 121–27.

———. "Fast Attack Craft Predominate in Chinese Navy." *Combat Craft* 1, no. 4 (July 1983): 130–31.

———. "Maritime Dangers in the South China Sea." *Pacific Defence Reporter*, May 1985.

———. "PRC Naval Weapon System Developments." *Combat Craft* 3, no. 5 (September–October 1985): 163–69.

Hakim, Peter. "Is Washington Losing Latin America?" *Foreign Affairs* 85, no. 1 (January–February 2006): 39–53.

Information Office of the State Council of the People's Republic of China. *China's National Defense in 2004*. Special report, Beijing, 27 December 2004. Federation of American Scientists. http://www.fas.org/nuke/guide/china/doctrine/natdef2004.html (accessed 14 November 2010).

———. *China's National Defense in 2006*. Special report, Beijing, 29 December 2006. http://fas.org/nuke/guide/china/doctrine/wp2006.html (accessed 13 November 2010).

———. *China's National Defense in 2008*. Special report, Beijing, January 2009. Federation of American Scientists. http://www.fas.org/programs/ssp/nukes/2008DefenseWhitePaper_Jan2009.PDF (accessed 10 November 2010).

Jacobs, G. "China's Amphibious Navy." *Asian Defence Journal* (June 1985): 34–43.

Jacobs, G., and R. Cheung. "China's 'Jianghu' Frigate Programme." *Jane's Defence Weekly* (21 March 1987): 507–9.

Kamanin, V. I., A. V. Lavrent'ev, and R. A. Skubko. *Shturman Flota* [Navy Navigation]. Moscow: Voennoe, 1986.

Kaplan, Brad. "China's Navy Today: Storm Clouds on the Horizon . . . or Paper Tiger?" *Sea Power* 42, no. 12 (December 1999): 28–33.

Klass, Philip J. "Avionics in China: CAAC Modernizes Its Air Traffic Control." *Aviation Week & Space Technology* 118, no. 24 (13 June 1983): 79–89.

Kondapalli, Srikanth. "China's Naval Equipment Acquisition." *Strategic Analysis* 23, no. 9 (December 1999). Columbia International Affairs Online Net. http://ciaonet.org/olj/sa/sa_99kos01.html (accessed 23 November 2010).

———. *China's Naval Power.* New Delhi: Knowledge World, 2001.

———. "China's Naval Structure and Dynamics." *Strategic Analysis* 23, no. 7 (October 1999): 1095–1116.

Kopp, Carlo. "China's Air Defence Missile Systems," *Defence Today* 8, no. 20 (25 October 2008).

Korabli i Vooruzhenie Voenno-Morskogo Flota [Warships and Weapons of the Military Naval Fleet]. Vol. 3 of *Oruzhie Rossii Katalog* [Russian Arms Catalog]. Moscow: Voennyy Parad, 1996.

Krasnov, Mikhail. "Chavez Winked at America." *Moscow Gazeta*, 11 January 2006. Translation at OSC CEP20060112018002.

Lague, David. "Aircraft Carrier for China." *International Herald Tribune*, 31 January 2006.

Lewis, John Wilson, and Xue Litai. *China's Strategic Seapower.* Stanford, Calif.: Stanford University Press, 1994.

Li, Andrew. "The Luta Fleet." *Proceedings* (Annapolis, Md.: U.S. Naval Institute) 108, no. 3 (March 1982): 131–32.

Lim, Robyn. *The Geopolitics of East Asia: The Search for Equilibrium.* New York: Routledge, 2003.

Ling Chao. "Il-78s Fly to China—Also on Comparison between US and Russian Large Active Duty Aerial Refueling Aircraft." Xian Binggong Keji, 1 October 2005. Translation at OSC CPP20051123318001.

Lockheed Martin. "Vessel Traffic Management Information Systems (VTMIS)." http://lockheedmartin.com/products/VesselTrafficMIS/index.html (accessed 16 November 2010).

MacPherson, Malcolm. *Roberts Ridge: A Story of Courage and Sacrifice on Takur Ghar Mountain, Afghanistan.* New York: Delacorte, 2005.

Meister, Jurg. *Soviet Warships of the Second World War.* New York: Arco, 1977.

Military Training Department of the Navy. "Chronicle of Events of Military Training." *Guangzhou Zhanshi Bao*, 27 December 2005, 1, 3. Translation at OSC CPP20060224318002.

Office of the Secretary of Defense, *Annual Report to Congress: Military Power of the People's Republic of China 2009.* U.S. Department of Defense, 25 March 2009. http://www.defense.gov/pubs/pdfs/China_Military_Power_Report_2009.pdf (accessed 12 November 2010).

Pavlov, A. S. *Warships of the USSR and Russia, 1945–1995*. Annapolis, Md.: Naval Institute Press, 1997.

Petrov, A. M., et al. *Oruzhie Rossiiskogo Flota* [Armament of the Russian Navy]. Saint Petersburg: Sudostroenie, 1996.

"PLA Navy Destroyers Spotted near Chunxiao Gas Fields in East China Sea." *Tokyo Sekai no Kansen*, 5 April 2005. Cited in "Growing Asymmetries in the China-Japan Naval Balance," by Richard Fisher Jr. International Assessment and Strategy Center, 22 November 2005. http://www.strategy center.net/research/pubID.83/pub_detail.asp.

Plowright, Kerry. *The People's Liberation Army Navy (PLAN)*. China Files, People's Liberation Army Navy Ships, ADF V.2.1 Research Sheets, 2008. Scribd. http://www.scribd.com/doc/37524007/Plan-Ships (accessed 12 November 2010).

Polmar, Norman. *Cold War Submarines*. Dulles, Va.: Potomac Books, 2004.

———. *Spyplane: The U-2 History Declassified*. Osceola, Wis.: MBI Press, 2001.

"PRC C4I Activities 14 Sep–27 Oct 05." Beijing Xinhua Asia Service, 14 November 2005. *People's Daily*. http://english.people.com.cn/90001/90776/90786/index.hmtl (accessed 14 November 2005).

Prokop, Jan. *Computers in the Navy*. Annapolis, Md.: Naval Institute Press, 1976.

Sewell, Kenneth. *Red Star Rogue*. New York: Simon & Schuster, 2005.

Shirokie, I. P. *Remont Sudovie Radio-navigatsionnogo Priborov* [Repair Ship Radionavigation Equipment]. Moscow: Transport, 1985.

Shirokorad, A. B. *Oruzhie Otechestvennogo Flota, 1945–2000* [Armament of the Motherland Navy, 1945–2000]. Minsk: Harvest, 2001.

Spencer, Richard. "£9m Aircraft Carrier for Sale at Theme Park." *London Daily Telegraph*, 18 February 2006.

Storey, Ian. "Manila Looks to USA for Help over Spratlys." *Jane's Intelligence Review* 11, no. 8 (August 1999): 46–50.

Storey, Ian, and You Ji. "Chinese Aspirations to Acquire Aircraft Carrier Capability Stall." *Jane's Intelligence Review* 14, no. 4 (April 2002): 36–39.

Streetly, Martin. *Jane's Radar and Electronic Warfare Systems, 1996–97*. 8th ed. Coulsdon, Surrey, U.K.: Jane's Information Group, 1996.

Sviatov, George. "Kursk Loss Offers Lessons." *Proceedings* (Annapolis, Md.: U.S. Naval Institute) 129, no. 6 (June 2003): 71–74.

Tart, Larry, and Robert Keefe. *The Price of Vigilance*. New York: Ballantine, 2001.

"Troops of China's Three Armed Services Are Being Assembled in Shantou." *Hong Kong Wen Wei Po*, 27 August 2001. Translation at OSC CPP20010827000051.

"U.S. Worries about China's Intent with Taiwan." *USA Today*, 9 February 2006.

Vooruzhenie i Voenno-Morskaya Tekhnika Rossii [Russia's Naval Ships, Armament and Equipment]. Moscow: Voennyy Parad, 2005.

Vooruzhenie Voenno-Morskogo Flota [Naval Weapons]. Vol. 3 of *Oruzhie i Tekhnologii Rossii Entsiklopediya XXI Bek* [Russia's Arms and Technologies: Twenty-first Century Encyclopedia]. Moscow: Oruzhie i Texnologii, 2001.

Wang An. "Just Like a Battlefield—Student's Group Training Exercise through the Eyes of a Research Fellow." *Beijing Jiefangjun Bao,* 21 November 2005. Translation at OSC CPP20051123502002.

Wang Cho-chung. "PRC Generals Call for Reinforcing Actual Strength of Navy." *Taipei Chung-Kuo Shih-Pao,* 25 March 2001. Translation at OSC CPP20010326000046.

Wen Han. "Navy and Air Force Generals Take Up Important Posts in Reshuffles in Four Military Regions." *Hong Kong Wen Wei Po,* 19 December 2005. Translation at OSC CPP20051219510001.

Whitley, M. J. *Cruisers of World War Two: An International Encyclopedia.* London: Cassell, 1995.

You Ji. "A New Era for Chinese Naval Expansion." *China Brief* 6, no. 5 (2006), Nautilus Institute for Security and Sustainability, Australian Policy Forum 60-60A, 9 March 2006, http://www.globalcollab.org/publications/essays/apsnet/policy-forum/2006/0606a-you-ji.html.

Young, Philip. "Navy of the PLA." *Chinese Military Digest,* www.gsprint.com/cmd/airforce/uav.atm.

Yuan, Tong. "Technical Advances in Shipbuilding Industry Reported." *Handelsblatt,* 31 March 1987.

Zhou Yougao. "Life on a Chinese Destroyer." Proceedings (Annapolis, Md.: U.S. Naval Institute) 116, no. 3 (March 1990): 47–48.

Index

Page numbers followed by a *t* or an *f* indicate tables and figures. All platforms are PLAN unless otherwise indicated.

About the Authors

JAMES C. BUSSERT has worked in antisubmarine warfare (ASW) for fifty-six years since enlisting in the U.S. Navy in 1954. He served twenty-five years on active duty on destroyers, retiring as a master chief sonarman. Following his retirement in 1979, he has continued working in ASW for the government, and is currently employed at the Naval Surface Warfare Center (NSWC), Dahlgren, Virginia. His hobby is freelance writing on foreign military technology. After winning the USNI Enlisted Essay Contest in 1972 and 1973, Mr. Bussert published nearly two hundred military/technical articles in various professional journals. Mr. Bussert obtained a BA degree from National University in 1981 and has taken postgraduate classes in the Russian language. His writing focus shifted from the USSR to mainland China after 1990, with an emphasis on PLAN combat systems technology. The opinions expressed in this book do not necessarily reflect the views of the Department of Defense or the U.S. Navy.

BRUCE A. ELLEMAN is a research professor in the Maritime History Department, Center for Naval Warfare Studies, at the U.S. Naval War College in Newport, Rhode Island. Mr. Elleman received his BA (1982) from the University of California, Berkeley, and his MA (1984) and PhD (1993) from Columbia University. He is the author of fifteen books, including *Diplomacy and Deception: The Secret History of Sino-Soviet Diplomatic Relations, 1917–1927* (Armonk, N.Y.: M. E. Sharpe, 1997); *Modern Chinese Warfare, 1795–1989* (London: Routledge, 2001; translated into Chinese); *Wilson and China: A Revised History of the Shandong Question* (Armonk, N.Y.: M. E. Sharpe, 2002); *Japanese-American Civilian Prisoner Exchanges and Detention Camps, 1941–45* (London: Routledge, 2006); and *Moscow and the Emergence of Communist Power in China, 1925–30: The Nanchang Uprising and the Birth of the Red Army* (London: Routledge, 2009).